Teaching Methods in Science Subjects Promoting Sustainability

Special Issue Editor
Eila Jeronen

MDPI • Basel • Beijing • Wuhan • Barcelona • Belgrade

Special Issue Editor
Eila Jeronen
University of Oulu
Finland

Editorial Office
MDPI AG
St. Alban-Anlage 66
Basel, Switzerland

This edition is a reprint of the Special Issue published online in the open access journal *Education Sciences* (ISSN 2227-7102) from 2016–2017 (available at: http://www.mdpi.com/journal/education/special_issues/ promoting _sustainability).

For citation purposes, cite each article independently as indicated on the article page online and as indicated below:

Author 1; Author 2. Article title. *Journal Name* **Year**, *Article number*, page range.

First Edition 2017

ISBN 978-3-03842-650-9 (Pbk)
ISBN 978-3-03842-651-6 (PDF)

Table of Contents

About the Special Issue Editor

Eila Jeronen is a Doctor in Philosophy, Docent (comparable with Adjunct Professor) in Education at the University of Oulu and University of Lapland, and Docent (comparable with Adjunct Professor) in Sustainable Development at the University of Helsinki, Finland. She is also a Master and Licentiate in Philosophy, and has a teaching certificate in Biology and Geography. Her main research interests are in the field of Subject Didactics, Environmental Education, Sustainability Education, and Sustainable Development Education. She has been educating student teachers in Biology and Geography Education for nearly 40 years. Currently, she is a University Lecturer (Emerita) in Biology and Geography Education at University of Oulu. Eila.Jeronen@oulu.fi, University of Oulu, Faculty of Education, P.O.Box 2000, FI-90014 University of Oulu.

Preface to "Teaching Methods in Science Subjects Promoting Sustainability"

Education was mentioned as a key to sustainable development in the United Nations document "Agenda 21" as early as 1992, and nowadays sustainability is internationally emphasized as an essential aim of education. Both of the concepts are problematic, in that there is no consensus on their definitions. Furthermore, many teachers and teacher educators do not know these concepts at all, or do not want to use them in their teaching. Teacher education offers the basis to discuss, plan and carry out teaching and learning processes. However, students are the epicenters of a teacher's action, and she/he should support them to understand life and its phenomena. Therefore, knowledge of sustainability is important as an origin point of teaching and learning processes.

In designing their teaching, teachers continuously discuss how subject content knowledge should be arranged so that students feel motivated to study and learn. What kind of understanding do the teaching and learning processes support, and what is the relationship between everyday life, and the teaching and studying processes? They also discuss what kinds of teaching methods are best for the personal development of a student. One aim of the planning process is to find out methods that help students understand, and if possible, solve problems they undergo during their life.

Understanding environmental issues demands sustainability knowledge. During teaching, studying and learning processes, teachers and students therefore discuss what the meaning of knowledge and skills is for the students' life now and in the future. Preservation of life requires concern about the environment, and a way of living that takes care of the environment. The basis for this is created at schools.

Sustainability education is a multi-sided and challenging task. It demands that the teachers and teacher educators develop their knowledge and skills continuously. Teachers' professional development is a long-lasting process. Student teachers need continuous support from teachers and teacher educators.

This book offers ideas of pedagogical content knowledge and subject content knowledge, especially for mathematics and science teachers and teacher educators. Curriculums and subject content knowledge change from time to time. The methodological and other pedagogical ideas presented in this book offer valuable support for teaching, studying and learning processes concerning sustainability and sustainable development in higher education and in schools.

I would like to extend my thanks to the authors of the articles contained in this book, which include a multi-sided view of sustainability and sustainable development, and many useful teaching methods for promoting them in mathematics and science, at different educational levels.

Eila Jeronen
Special Issue Editor

Article

High Performance Education Fails in Sustainability? —A Reflection on Finnish Primary Teacher Education

Lili-Ann Wolff [1,*], Pia Sjöblom [2], Maria Hofman-Bergholm [2] and Irmeli Palmberg [2]

1 Faculty of Educational Sciences, University of Helsinki, Helsinki 00014, Finland
2 Faculty of Education and Welfare Studies, Åbo Akademi University, Vaasa 65100, Finland;
   psjoblom@abo.fi (P.S.); mhofman@abo.fi (M.H.B.); ipalmber@abo.fi (I.P.)
* Correspondence: lili-ann.wolff@helsinki.fi; Tel.: +358-50-4487-088

Academic Editor: Eila Jeronen
Received: 31 October 2016; Accepted: 17 February 2017; Published: 1 March 2017

Abstract: Sustainability is internationally often emphasized as an essential aim of higher education, but more as a principle than on the practical level. This is also obvious in the academic education of primary teachers in Finland. Therefore, it is a great challenge for Finnish teachers to include sustainability in their teaching and everyday life in schools. The aim of this article is to critically analyze why the implementation of sustainability in teacher education is so intricate and to discuss possible solutions with Finland—a country highly valued for its education—as an example. The article reports outcomes from educational policy documents and research on educational, philosophical, scientific and social aspects of sustainability, including evaluation of how sustainability has been implemented in schools and at universities, especially among teacher educators. In addition, the article builds on analyses of comprehensive university strategies and primary school teacher education programs. We found these reasons for the ignoring of sustainability in the Finnish teacher education: sustainability is in conflict with overall trends in society and politics, teacher education takes place at universities and is based on separate academic disciplines. Sustainability is also intricate because it is strongly connected to ecological literacy and it is value dependent. Universities need to overcome these obstacles and become forerunners in the sustainability process.

Keywords: higher education; university education; teacher education; primary school teachers; sustainable development; sustainability; implementation of sustainability; sustainability education; education for sustainability; Finland

---

1. Introduction

"We are faced with a paradox: Is education the problem or the solution in working toward a sustainable future? At current levels of unsustainable practice and over consumption it could be concluded that education is part of the problem. If education is the solution then it requires a deeper critique and a broader vision for the future" [1] (p. 59).

The words above are from a UNESCO publication from 2005 and much has taken place after that since "education for sustainable development" has frequently been on the agenda for the last decade. Many international education policy documents from this decade contain terms related to sustainability. One clear reason is that UNESCO declared the decade 2005–2014 as the "UN decade of education for sustainable development" with a mission to promote sustainable development at all levels of education in the member states. However, education was mentioned as a key to sustainable development in the United Nation's document "Agenda 21" as early as 1992 [2], so thus we step back to the 1990s.

The concept of *sustainable development* has been much used in politics since the UN Conference on Environment and Development in Rio de Janeiro in 1992 [2] and it is since then interpreted in various ways. In short, the complex concept denotes a social and economic development where the utilization of natural resources takes place with future generations' analogous life opportunities in mind. In the so called Brundtland report that preceded the UNCED conference, the concept is interpreted as follows: "[S]ustainable development is a process of change in which the exploitation of resources, the direction of investments, the orientation of technological development, and institutional change are all in harmony and enhance both current and future potential to meet human needs and aspirations [3] (p. 46)."

The principle of sustainable development focuses actually at the same time on humans living today and in the future. According to Sachs [4] sustainable development is both a worldview and a method of solving worldwide problems. Besides emphasizing the three commonly defined dimensions of sustainable development, economic, social and environmental (the environmental dimension is also called the ecological, and the social dimension is often split into two: social and cultural, see Section 3.3 below), he, therefore, also distinguishes two approaches: an analytic and an ethical. "Sustainable development is both a way of looking at the world, with a focus on the interlinkages of economic, social, and environmental change, and a way of describing our shared aspirations for a decent life, combining economic development, social inclusion, and environmental sustainability. It is in short both an analytic theory and a 'normative' or ethical framework [4] (p. XIII)."

The three (or four) dimensions of sustainable development include several different aspects. For example, cultural aspects and health aspects are parts of the social dimension; political aspects are mainly parts of the economic dimension, but also of the other two dimensions. This means that the different aspects as well as the dimensions are complexly interrelated. Sustainability is, thus, not only an environmental issue to be controlled by scientists, it is a multifaceted and interdisciplinary matter related to both local and global circumstances and past events as well as future prospects.

Yet, the concept sustainable development is also problematic. Many scholars and others are critical against using the word 'development' to denote indisputable belief in a steady economic and technological progress. Like numerous other authors we, therefore, will use the single concept of *sustainability* and the two word concept *sustainability education* in this article, with exception of situations where the authors we refer use the concept of sustainable development or education for sustainable development. By sustainability we mean *creating and living a human life on Earth in a way that does not damage life but that preserves its various life forms for the future*—not only future human life. We thus recognize challenges on ethical, cognitive as well as practical levels.

After the Rio conference, the concept 'education for sustainable development' (ESD) gradually became common in educational policy documents and included the three dimensions of sustainable development as educational goals. There is, however, no consensus regarding the educational content of ESD [5]. Already in the 1970s, the political goal of 'environmental education' was to change learners' attitudes [6], and the UN goal for ESD in 2014 still focused on influencing learners' values and attitudes [7]. Many educational researchers have claimed that the whole concept limits education to merely a tool for reaching sustained economic growth [8,9]. Researchers have also criticized the idea behind the concept for neglecting teachers as reflective agents [10].

Vare and Scott [11], on the other hand, point out that ESD needs to be seen as two approaches that complement each other, like the Chinese concept of yin and yang. The authors define the term ESD 1 as promoting changes in what people do, promoting behaviors and ways of thinking through a learning *for* sustainable development, while the complementary term ESD 2 promotes learning *as* sustainable development through the capacity to build critical thinking and the exploration of inherent contradictions. Some researchers have reacted negatively to the preposition 'for' in the concept of ESD and consider it normative [12,13]. To avoid the preposition 'for', the concept 'sustainability education' has become an alternative [14,15].

When, in this article, we follow many forerunners and adopt the concept of *sustainability education*, we thus move the focus from the question of what teachers are supposed to teach to the question: what is an education focusing on sustainability supposed to achieve? When first and foremost reflecting on what to achieve, the main focus is on action competence, critical thinking, deliberation and understanding of how one's choices affect local and global societies and the entire biosphere. Vare and Scott [11], on the other hand, emphasize that ESD is a learning process that should build the learners' capacity to analyze, negotiate, question alternatives and develop their ability to make sound choices. Furthermore, the role of sustainability education is to deal with inequality and power issues and encourage critique of the systems of which the students' and educators' daily life and education is a part [12].

What we are asking for, as researchers, is an interdisciplinary, even transdisciplinary, learning in a context of diversity [16]. Transdisciplinary processes encourage collaboration between science and society, and thus emphasize joint undertakings and learning [17], and diversity means that various views are appreciated. There is a growing interest in transdisciplinary approaches to the sustainability challenge, approaches that can handle complex authentic problems and create practice-oriented learning situations [17].

Sustainability education is characterized by a holistic approach when it comes to content and a pluralistic approach when it comes to teaching [18]. Holism implies in this sense that all the dimensions and perspectives of sustainability are integrated in the instruction. Pluralistic teaching, on the other hand, is teaching so that different views and perspectives concerning sustainability are acknowledged, reflected on and discussed, and the aim is to improve the student's democratic action competence [19].

The role of educators subsequently becomes to improve the students' joint involvement and participation in authentic environmental activities and critical discourses [20–22]. In Denmark 'action competence' has been a favored approach and key concept in environmental education and health education research since the 1980s [23]. According to action competence, the role of education is not to serve political goals or promote strongly normative purposes. The approach is based on the idea that environmental problems involve social conflicts of interests and has to be handled by problem-oriented and cross-curricular methods. Therefore, the role of education is to encourage students and provide learning conditions that transform them into critical, political agents [23]. Action competence relates to the German *Bildung* concept based on the central idea that human beings have intrinsic possibilities for self-development, but also for the joint development of society [24]. In higher education this means that sustainability becomes "a dynamic and flexible synergy issue for different sciences and subjects so that science, education, art and practices are combined, transformed and developed" [24] (p. 62).

When *Bildung* is an educational ideal, elementary critical questions are: where is education heading and what is the ultimate goal of education? The sustainability education ideal is an education where the transformation of oneself and society is a dual task [12]. Education has to promote a planetary consciousness and a visioning of a different world in a cosmic perspective, according to Gadotti [25], but also a vision of a better self through self-reflection and authenticity, according to Wolff [12]. However, it is fruitless to teach people about sustainability and at the same time ignore the unsustainability problems in a neoliberal society, applying aims that are in contradiction with the whole idea of sustainability [8,26,27], and blaming others for not acting appropriately [28]. The history and the culture of societies (both local and global) transform people every day, and with that in mind the mission is to create new models of mutual living in more sustainable ways [29], which demands braveness and political action competence.

In many countries environmental and sustainability issues have increased in education on all levels from nursery schools to universities over the last decade [7,30]. Still, it has been argued that the development is too slow [8,12]. In the evaluation of the impact of the Decade of Education for Sustainable development, UNESCO found that in most UN member states ESD was increasing, but few states could report full implementation across education systems, as well as across policies and planning [7]. More and more commentators have actually argued that the educational efforts have not been radical enough to address the most urgent problems of our time [27,31,32]. There is obviously still much to do and many challenges to face [33].

Even if there are tasks enough for many players, teachers have for decades been cited as key agents in the sustainability process [3,34]. To prepare teachers for this important task, analysts have asked for a stronger emphasis on teacher education [34,35]. Yet, teacher education in many countries has failed in this respect [36–41]. According to Martin and Carter [42], education settings need to become "proactive in sustainability" and to make that happen, ESD needs to be a *core concept* in teacher education. Since there are risks of both normatively steering and narrowing of the scope, we would rather say that "sustainability" has to be the core and its implementation obvious in policy, campus practice, and last but not least, in research, teaching and learning.

In this article, Finland has been used as an example in identifying how and why teacher education, especially primary teacher education, has failed in sustainability and what need to be changed in teacher education to improve the situation. Even if we focus on primary school teachers, some of the studies we use in our analysis include secondary schools. We begin with an overview of Finnish teacher education, including both international and national policy documents concerning the implementation of sustainability in teacher education.

2. Finnish Teacher Education

Finnish teacher education has a worldwide reputation, since Finnish students have performed very well in international comparisons, such as PISA (The Programme for International Student Assessment of OECD). As one of the contributory factors behind these successful achievements, reference has been made to the high quality of Finnish teacher education [43,44]. Finnish teacher education has a fairly long academic tradition by international standards, entering Finnish universities in the 1970s [45,46]. Of the sixteen Finnish universities and six regional university centers running today, eight main universities and two centers provide teacher education.

Apart from Finnish teacher education's international reputation, it is also very popular nationally and many would-be teachers apply every year. Both primary and secondary school teacher education leads to a higher academic degree (300 ECTS), and primary school teachers have education as their major subject. Together with multidisciplinary school subject studies this qualifies graduates to teach in grades 1–6. Primary school teachers are also qualified to teach in grades 7–9 if they take further studies in one or more school subjects. However, most of the teaching in grades 7–9 and in upper secondary school is carried out by "subject teachers", who have a major in one of the teaching subjects and a minor in one or two other school subjects, and who also have studied education (60 ECTS), including teacher training [43]. Table 1 shows what qualifications are needed for teachers in Finland at different school levels.

Table 1. Type of school and teachers' qualifications in Finland (modified from Jakku-Sihvonen and Niemi [45] (p. 11)).

Age	Type of school	Teachers' qualification
0–6	Kindergarten	Kindergarten teachers (BA) 180 ECTS
6	Pre-school	Kindergarten teachers (BA) or primary school teacher (MA)
7–12	Comprehensive school, 1–6	Primary school teachers (MA) 300 ECTS
13–15	Comprehensive school, 7–9	Subject teachers (MA)
16–	Upper secondary school	Subject teachers (MA)
16–	Vocational school	Subject teachers (BA or MA)[i]
19–	Higher education	Teachers with higher academic degree (Ph. D)

Notes: [i] If it is not organized in higher education courses in the subject they teach or if they have received competence in other ways, they can get exemption from this rule.

Research-based teaching and learning is one of the major aims of Finnish teacher education. By integrating theory and practice in a dialogic process, the aim is to produce reflective teachers who will become life-long learners with a readiness for professional development throughout their vocations [47]. The writing of a Master's thesis, together with studies in educational research methodology, is an important part of this process. Integration of research when dealing with various challenges in teachers' work is also considered a prerequisite for their future career [45,46,48]. Teachers are trained to develop their teaching analytically and systematically and create good learning environments [48]. However, this does not guarantee that they are trained in interdisciplinary procedures and in how to teach about complex global dilemmas.

Teaching practice is a crucial part of Finnish teacher education, but it does not necessarily give any training in how to teach about sustainability. Much of the teaching practice takes place in particular training schools belonging to the teacher education departments of the universities. The integration of teaching practice with educational theory, as well as with subject studies and subject teaching, is essential. This is accomplished through a three-part practice supervision in cooperation between a university lecturer, a teacher at the training school and the student teacher. Students also complete teaching practice in actual schools. As this section shows, Finnish teachers are well educated in general. Yet, even if many Finnish educational policy documents and action plans include sustainability education and training of students at many levels [49–51], sustainability undeniably plays a minor role in the education of Finnish teachers.

3. Sustainability in Finnish School Systems and Teacher Education

Even if policy documents and strategies on many levels request sustainability at all levels of education, the Finnish universities are autonomous and can therefore make their own decisions regarding the scope of sustainability in education and practice. Therefore, there are no common models of how to integrate sustainability into university courses and teacher education. There is also great variation in teacher educators' knowledge of and skills in integrating and teaching sustainable issues in higher education. The same problem is obvious in schools; graduated teachers do not know how to teach about sustainability.

3.1. Sustainability in Policy Documents

Numerous ambitious international and national policy documents and action plans describe goals and ideas on how to implement sustainability at all levels of education [37,52,53]. The Brundtland Report [3] and Agenda 21 in Finland [54] clearly emphasized the link between the environment and development, as well as the importance of the human dimension in all decisions concerning environmentally sound development. According to these documents, citizens have to learn to maintain social, cultural, and economic well-being without depleting natural resources or overloading nature's delicate balance. The faintly behavioristic goals suggest that it is the role of education and training to ensure that citizens of all ages have the knowledge, skills, readiness and vision that will enable them to build a sustainable and equitable future and commit to a sustainable way of life [55]. From 2001 sustainable development is included in Finnish basic education according to the decree on national goals of education and the Basic Education Act: "Students are educated to take responsibility and work together and to promote tolerance and trust between human groups, peoples and cultures. The teaching should also support the development of pupils into active members of society, and they are given skills to function in a democratic and equal society and *promote sustainable development*" [56] (translation and italics by the authors).

Already in the core curriculum for basic education 1985 [57] "the environment and nature protection" is one of the main aims, and in the curriculum of 1994 [58] human rights, equality, democracy, biodiversity and cultural diversity build the main values. The following Finnish national core curriculum for basic education from 2004 [59] and the current version from 2014 [60] emphasize sustainability to be implemented in several ways in education but also in the everyday life in schools. In the core curriculum from 2004, the goal of one of the cross-curricular themes is "to raise environmentally conscious citizens who are committed to a sustainable way of life" [59] (p. 39), and who will "learn to examine the challenges to sustainable development from several points of views" [59] (p. 29). Even if these goals were set more than ten years ago, the impact has not been particularly significant.

It is quite obvious that sustainability is even more important in the current curriculum for basic education from 2014 [60]. A sustainable future is mentioned in the curriculum in the very first paragraph, where the aim of the revision of the governance system of basic education is described. According to this, the aim is to improve the possibilities for basic education to take into account the changes in the world, and also to strengthen the role of education in the process of building a sustainable future. Overall, the concept of a sustainable future is mentioned 42 times, a sustainable lifestyle 45 times, sustainable development 40 times, and sustainability nine times in the 2014 core curriculum.

When the undertaking of basic education is described, the current curriculum states that education shall promote participation and a sustainable lifestyle, and also support the students' development as members of a democratic society. The "need for a sustainable lifestyle" is one of the four headlines defining the basic values of the core curriculum [60] (pp. 15–16, the authors' translation). The other headlines are "all pupils are unique and have a right to a good education"; "humanity, education, equality and democracy"; and "cultural diversity is richness" [60] (p. 16), which all relate to the social and cultural dimensions of sustainability. Hence, sustainability can clearly be regarded as a core component in the values of contemporary basic education in Finland.

The current core curriculum from 2014 also strives to develop a comprehensive competence among students. Comprehensive competence involves a unity of knowledge and skills, values, attitudes and also both the will and the ability to use the knowledge and skills in practice. The intention is that by applying its methods and contents every school subject contributes in its own way to comprehensive competence. Seven sectors build up the comprehensive competence, one of them being "an ability to participate, affect and contribute to a sustainable future" [60] (p. 24). Other sectors including issues of sustainability are everyday competence, digital competence, and cultural and communicative competence.

According to the current curriculum, sustainability is also an integral part of the working culture of the school. "Responsibility for the environment and a sustainable future" [60] (p. 39) is one of the important integrated themes. Sustainable development is emphasized as an example of an area within democracy education to increase the pupils' active participation (cf. action competence in the Introduction). Furthermore, the curriculum also underlines that learning organizations have to consider the environment and a sustainable future throughout their work, concerning for example the importance of the sustainable use of raw material and energy and the protection of biodiversity to the health of our planet and its ecosystems.

However, many other policy documents also influence the content of the basic education besides the school curriculum. The education system is expected to supply the labor market, at the same time as schools are expected to fulfill curriculum requirements [61]. Success in international comparisons is viewed as a consequence of good politics, though unfortunately an important goal of local educational politics is to decrease costs [62]. A similar problem of mixed signals is obvious in teacher education. Student teachers are trained by teacher educators in the university context for many years. If that context does not enhance sustainability, why should the graduated teachers be ready to take such steps when they start working in schools? In their study of teacher educators, Goodwin et al. [63] found that teacher educators realized that their work relates to the larger contexts in which it is situated. A quarter of the respondents saw it as challenging to navigate among agendas and policies at the universities, since these agendas are often in conflict with their own view of their work. In addition, these policies may be in conflict with the demands of the school curricula.

The official profile of the universities is stated in their strategies, and, consequently, these strategies are relevant when considering sustainability in teacher education. According to Hofman's [5] study, one can discern some rhetorical attempts by Finnish universities to live up to the Ministry of Education and Culture's agreement item "promotion of sustainable development." In 2010—2012 this agreement item was part of performance agreements with the universities that the Ministry makes every four years [64]. Hofman's [5] analysis of how the three dimensions of sustainable development are acknowledged in the policy documents, study plans and strategies of three universities revealed that none of these universities mentioned sustainable development more than twice in their strategies for 2012.

When examining the role of sustainability in the strategies of the eight Finnish universities offering teacher education programs in 2016 in comparison with earlier versions [5], it is obvious that the emphasis on sustainability has become stronger since the previous strategies, but the variation is still remarkable. In the strategies, which vary in length and depth, seven mention sustainability, six of them as a vision or basic focus area, and one as an objective in societal interaction. One university has omitted sustainability from this strategy version, and the extent to which universities mention sustainability varies from none to eleven times. Two universities talk about all the dimensions of sustainable development, but only one seems to have a strong sustainable profile, namely the University of Lapland. In most of the other Finnish universities other interests are much stronger. An international profile, for example, is very noticeable in seven universities. Other apparent ambitions are collaboration, efficiency and high-quality, whereas social equality and cultural diversity is nearly absent in all but one strategy. Three of the universities are eager to become top-ranking. The concept of sustainability is also mentioned as merely an economic attribute, and it is remarkable that no university mentions campus greening in its strategy. In conclusion, the strategic goals are diverse and sustainability might be difficult to fulfill at the universities offering teacher education, since interests are aimed in so many conflicting directions.

3.2. Sustainability in Schools

Currently, the aspect of sustainability is integrated into Finnish schools' practices in many different ways, and more or less frequently. An external evaluation carried out on behalf of the Ministry of Education and Ministry of the Environment in 2012 revealed that only 35% of the 917 primary and secondary schools participating in the questionnaire had programs for sustainable development [65]. This despite the political request for sustainable development programs in every school. The situation on the management stage is equally diverse. Susiluoma [66] investigated the situation regarding sustainable development management at the school level in Finnish basic education and general upper secondary education. Of the participating schools ($n = 597$), 16% had an environmental education program or plan, 20% had an environmental plan, 12% had a teacher who was responsible for environmental education, 23% had a person responsible for environmental issues, and 19% had an environmental group. Based on this investigation a conclusion could be that environmental issues are not generally prioritized on a management level in Finnish schools. Nevertheless, plans and responsible staff do not obviously guarantee sustainability education in the teacher's practice either. One of the reasons might be that primary school teachers do not have enough education in how to deal with sustainability issues to start such programs.

In a Finnish study including 442 lower secondary subject teachers from 49 schools, Uitto and Saloranta [67] found that the teachers did not consider sustainability issues very frequently in their teaching. Well-being and social sustainability were the most common aspects, while ecological, economic, and cultural aspects were less common. There were large differences in how teachers teaching different major subjects used different aspects of sustainability. The results indicate that teachers in biology, geography and history were generally more active teaching the three dimensions of sustainability in a holistic way, while teachers in the mother tongue, religion, visual arts, crafts, music, physical and health education considered two or three dimensions of sustainability, but were not teaching holistically. Teachers in mathematics, physics, chemistry and languages commonly used only one dimension of sustainable development. These results strengthen the view that sustainability issues are not seen as a common aspiration among teachers.

Since there is not much research from Finland about the implementation of sustainability in the school system it is also relevant to take into consideration how sustainability has been implemented in other countries. Sweden is culturally most similar to Finland, and there are Swedish studies that have investigated the implementation of ESD in schools. Borg et al. [68] have collected data from Swedish upper secondary school teachers (n = 3229) to identify barriers to implementing ESD. For the teachers in their study it seems to be a lack of inspiring examples and the absence of necessary expertise that are the most common obstacles for integrating sustainability into teaching. According to Borg et al. [68], more than half of the upper secondary school teachers in their study felt underprepared to integrate sustainability. The study also shows that the subject-based curricula in upper secondary schools set barriers for interdisciplinary work. This highlights the problem with subject-based curricula and the academic disciplines in teacher education as well.

Berglund et al. [69] studied the effect of the implementation of ESD in grade 12 in regular schools and in grade 12 in schools with an ESD profile (n = 638). They measured the students' sustainability consciousness, a concept built of knowledge, attitudes and behaviors in all the three dimensions of sustainability. Significant but small differences were found in sustainability consciousness between students in regular schools and students in schools with an ESD profile. Furthermore, when sustainability consciousness was analyzed dimension by dimension, it was only in the economic dimension where students in the ESD schools had significantly higher values.

Olsson et al. [70] conducted similar research, where they compared the effectiveness of ESD in regular and in ESD schools, but in grades 6 and 9 (n = 1773), and the results are in line with the findings of Berglund et al. [69]. The effect of implementation of ESD was relatively limited. In grade 6, there were significant differences in sustainability consciousness. Students in ESD schools scored higher on knowledge, attitudes and behavior in all dimensions of sustainability, than the students in regular schools. In grade 9 there were small differences between the regular schools and the schools with an ESD profile, but the results indicate a negative effect of the ESD profile on the students' sustainability consciousness. The social dimension was the one which contributed most to this difference. The authors discuss that the possible reason for this could be that the schools with an ESD profile have not been directed toward an ESD approach in teaching, characterized by holism and pluralism. The support might have only been aimed at the implementation of sustainability activities.

A study of Boeve-de Pauw et al. [18] showed that neither the holistic nor the pluralistic approach were commonplace in Swedish schools. The holistic approach was more common than the pluralistic, and these approaches were more frequent in higher grades than in lower. The results indicate that a more holistic approach in sustainability teaching increases the sustainability knowledge, while a more pluralistic approach generates more sustainable conduct. They conclude that ESD based on holism and pluralism effectively improves students' sustainability consciousness. However, pluralism is not commonplace in schools, the researchers suggesting that this might be the result of the "normativity paradox" [71], which means that pluralistic teaching in a sense is in conflict with the predefined aims of sustainable development. Boeve-de Pauw et al. [18] also point out that the strong rhetoric in steering documents does not seem to have affected the actual practice of teaching. Borg et al. [68] also regarded leadership as crucial when implementing sustainability education in schools. This reconnects to the situation in higher education and in particular to teacher education.

3.3. Sustainability in Teacher Education

No clear directions exist on how to teach future teachers about sustainability. Neither is there any strong commitment among the teacher educators. The respondents in a study including seven universities and ten polytechnics offering preservice training for various categories of teachers (including vocational teachers) had no answer about how higher education could guarantee that student teachers are prepared to teach sustainability [65]. The investigation was a part of a study organized by the educational division of the Finnish Commission on Sustainable Development and aimed at the educational organizations appointed as responsible for the implementation of sustainable development, such as higher education institutions offering teacher training, regional governmental agencies, and NGOs [65]. The results show that the promotion of sustainability in higher education is still very much dependent on enthusiastic key persons. Many of the respondents (administrators and governmental staff, $n = 45$) also hoped for stronger steering by the Ministry of Education and Culture. However, Pathan et al. [65] highlight that Finnish universities and higher education institutions play an important role in ensuring that teachers are provided with the necessary skills and competencies for teaching about sustainable development. They also conclude that the role of sustainable development should be increased in teacher education, and consider the lack of commitment to be basically a problem of leadership.

Since Finnish primary teacher education has to prepare future teachers to teach primary school subjects, most of the educational studies consist of compulsory courses. In addition, students mostly choose their minors among the subjects that are part of the school curricula. Sustainability as a theme to be implemented in all subjects has been a challenge for a long time and it has mainly been up to the teachers to actualize it. This has not only been a problem in schools, but also in teacher education.

In universities it is up to the lecturers how to implement the topic of sustainability in various courses in the teacher education programs. None of the universities offering teacher education have compulsory courses on sustainability for all at basic levels, according to a study from 2010 [65]. Our website analyze in 2016 showed that the number of courses on sustainability still differs between higher education institutions in Finland, and sustainability is seldom compulsory in teacher education programs.

Optional courses of different lengths might well be offered. It is unusual with extensive courses, but since 2015 it has been possible for student teachers at the University of Lapland to complete a master in environment and nature studies, and at Åbo Akademi University a master focusing on environmental education can be completed, but only if external funding is granted for the courses. Other universities offer basic courses providing different views on sustainability, which are open to students from all faculties, but they may be difficult to combine with the teacher education program for practical reasons. In addition, the topic of the various courses might be very different from what the trainee teacher needs.

As Goodwin et al. have pointed out, "Quality teacher education relies on quality teacher educators" [63] (p. 284). Therefore it is important to investigate teacher educators' views on sustainability and the implementation of sustainability in their work. However, only a few investigations have been carried out concerning this aspect of teacher educators' competence, though several have been concerned with other aspects. According to a study by Hökkä and Eteläpelto [48], rather than sustainability, the most important aspects for teacher educators in general were their professional learning and identity. However, for science teacher educators the main goals were "to promote meaningful learning of science concepts and to inspire students' interest in learning about science" [72] (p. 121). Buchanan [73] investigated sustainability education in Australian primary teacher education in a focus group study with teacher educators representing all the subjects in the curriculum of primary education. The analysis of the discussions in focus groups revealed that it was not easy to come to a common and unambiguous understanding of the concept of sustainability education. Social science and science were the subjects where sustainability issues were most frequently addressed, while these issues were only sporadically touched upon in other subjects, except for some cross-curricular subjects. However, the cross-curricular nature of sustainability education is a richness, but also a problem, as few take the responsibility for implementing it. Limited time resources were mentioned as the major obstacle for including sustainability issues in an already crowded curriculum. The implementation of sustainability in teacher education was scanty and sporadic, and sidestepped because of a lack of time both for teaching and preparing. Another obstacle according to the respondents was the presence of many other urgent teaching issues.

A nationwide questionnaire by Borg et al. [74] among Swedish upper secondary school teachers ($n = 3229$) revealed similar problems with adapting a holistic view as in Buchanan's study.

The conceptual understanding of sustainable development varied dependent on which subjects the teachers were teaching. Social science teachers emphasize the social dimension of sustainability, while science teachers concentrate on the ecological dimension. Even though the teachers were generally aware of the three dimensions, they did not have a holistic understanding of the concept of sustainable development, and consequently did not have the competence to teach sustainability issues holistically either. Borg et al. [74] suggest that the lack of holism in the conceptual understanding could be explained by a lack of sustainability education related to their subjects in their teacher education program. Compared with Hofman's [5] study that we present below this conclusion sounds accurate.

Hofman's [5] study of Finnish teacher education is to our knowledge the only Finnish study that focuses on teacher educators' view of how sustainable development has been implemented in their own teaching at the course level. It indicates that the whole undertaking has largely failed. The implementation of sustainability in teacher education is more a question of political rhetoric than a reality at the course level. Despite elective courses in environmental education or sustainable development, the aims of sustainability have not been reached.

We shall now take a closer look at Hofman's [5] material, summarizing the results concerning teacher educators' views on sustainability. When the respondents (154 teacher educators) were asked to describe how they personally understand the concept of sustainable development only 10 percent mentioned all the four integrated dimensions of sustainable development, i.e., ecological, economic, cultural and social dimensions (the cultural and social dimensions are often also counted as one, see Introduction). A slightly greater part (11%) touched upon three of the four dimensions, and did not include a cultural or social dimension.

The ecological (called "environmental" by several of the respondents) dimension was sometimes combined with some other aspects, like human well-being, which was stressed by nearly half of the teacher educators (49%). The rest of the teacher educators (30%) understood the concept in very different ways without naming any of the four (three) main dimensions. For example, they explained that sustainability was an ethical or moral question or simply the recirculation of waste products or continued growth in general. As many as 70% of the teacher educators in Hofman's study mentioned the ecological or environmental dimension, including those who represented subjects other than the natural sciences. Therefore, the teacher educators stated that sustainability does not concern them and they do not include it in their teaching (18%) (since the sustainability issue belongs to the natural science educators, according to them). More than half of the respondents said that they did not know if their department had defined the concept of sustainable development in their strategies or other policy documents. In conclusion, Hofman's study indicates that policy documents and recommendations have not had a major effect on teacher educators.

Nevertheless, up to 75% of Hofman's respondents considered that sustainability is extremely important for all student teachers [5]. They also mentioned education and awareness raising as the best ways for society to promote sustainable development, but they did not see their own work as an important contributor. The great majority of the teacher educators (87%) had not received any training or education in how to integrate sustainability into all subjects, although several policy documents maintain that universities and teacher training departments have to incorporate basic sustainability knowledge and that pedagogical skills should be highlighted as an important educational policy issue in in-service training of teachers and supervisors [34,55]. Sustainability is merely rhetoric if teacher educators training future teachers have not received any education in sustainability themselves. In the section below we will present our interpretation of why this topic has been addressed in such a piecemeal fashion until now.

4. Why is an "Excellent" Education Failing in Sustainability?

When we were searching for answers about why Finnish teacher education fails in the implementation of sustainability, we found many fundamental components that hindered the process. We identified five strong elements that prevent purposeful implementation. Three of them are connected to characteristics of Finnish teacher education, which *reflects a combination of overall trends in society and politics* that are contradictive to sustainability (1); *takes place at universities*, which means that it struggles with the same obstacles regarding sustainability as Finnish university education in general (2); and *is based on separate academic disciplines* and fragmented school curricula (3); Two other obstacles for a successful implementation are that sustainability demands a *profound ecologic literacy* (4); and *is strongly value dependent* (5). Below we explore these five obstacles in more detail. Our argumentation below is based on a critical analysis of actual literature on sustainability topics (research on sustainability in higher education; reports from the Worldwatch Institute, UN, and the Finnish government), educational research (policy documents, educational policy studies and empirical research), and social philosophy. Besides our analyses on current university strategies and comparisons of university courses on sustainability, results from our earlier empirical and theoretical studies have also been crucial complements to the literature.

4.1. Sustainability is in Conflict with Trends in Society

Finland is one of the richest countries in the world [75]. During the last century, domestic consumption has grown eleven times [76]. After World War II, in the 1950s and 60s, mass consumption became a part of the Finnish life style [76]. However, from a planetary perspective, this is not necessarily a favorable development. Since the Club of Rome published *Limits to Growth* in 1972, arguing that the limits of planet Earth had been reached, the sustainability issue has been continuously under consideration. Planet Earth suffers from air pollution, deforestation, decreased biodiversity and many other problems. Overpopulation, unequal distribution of food and access to water and sanitation are alarming global human issues. One of the major environmental threats is climate change. This is a complex problem that influences many levels of life, both human and non-human, including water availability, food production, biodiversity, health, equality, human rights and employment. According to the *Worldwatch Institute* [77] and the *Intergovernmental Panel on Climate Change* [78], climate scenarios are dominated by orthodox economic views with unrestricted growth as the hidden goal.

The speedily growing world population is predicted to be as large as between 9.4 and 10 billion by 2050 [79]. Therefore, future forecasts concerning material and resource usage are all but bright, and yet economists still recommend continued consumerism. In this situation people may well feel insecure about whether they should consume more to support the current economy or less to help ensure a sustainable future [26].

Consumerism has become a dominant paradigm throughout the world [80,81], and Finland is no exception. The average consumption of goods of the world population in 2008 was 10 tons per year. However, the variety was vast, from a few tons to nearly 30 tons [80]. The reason for such high consumption is not only to be found on the individual level or to prevalent choices, but is primarily due to policies, economies and structures that facilitate environmentally destructive behavior [82]. Over the decades many joint efforts have been made to create a growing demand for goods. This has taken place with the help of policymakers, marketers, media experts, business leaders, and many others [82]. Talented "consumerism architects" have succeeded in shaping norms, values and narratives that attract buyers to choose a lifestyle where they express themselves through consumption. Thus, individuals are not the only ones to blame; it might even be unfair to make single individuals responsible for consumerism [26]. This can absolve the state from responsibility.

However, great obstacles hinder change, since consumerism has become part of human identity [83]. It is a sign of what Foucault [84,85] calls *governmentality*, which means that individuals are governed so skillfully that they can no longer separate their own will and actions from the system. People always make choices in a context [26] and, thus, structural problems become personal moral issues [83]. Nonetheless, education cannot escape the dilemma between politics and ethics [31] and the formation of identities [85]. Studies show that economic growth has reached the point in industrialized countries where it no longer has a positive impact on people's subjective experience of well-being and happiness [86].

Undoubtedly, education has also become a consumer good and a remarkable vehicle for competition. This is also the case in Finland, where education is seen as a tool in Finland's economic success on the world market. The excellent results in the PISA comparison is seen as proof of a successful educational system [62]. Consequently, Finnish education has become a goal and is market oriented. This is especially the case with higher education, and teacher education is no exception. Teacher educators are subject to accountability in the same way as all other university lecturers.

4.2. Finnish Teacher Education is A Reflection of University Education in General

Finland signed the *Bologna Declaration of 19 June 1999* together with twenty-eight other European countries [87]. The aim of the declaration was to homogenize European higher education, but also to make students more competitive in the world educational market [88]. Since the 1990s, Finnish university evaluation has been institutionalized, and in 2004 the development of quality assurance and evaluation started [61]. Finnish universities have adopted the same values as the business sector and are steered by quality standards and top-down management [89]. When business ideologies became a part of the university strategies, the rhetoric also changed; learning became a form of market competition, and education developed into a sales product to be delivered to the market [90].

This has had a remarkable effect on both staff and students. According to Kallio and Kallio [91], university lecturers lack motivation for creative, knowledge-intensive work, because of the "management-by-results" atmosphere at their workplaces. Time efficiency decreases academic discussions and obstructs deeper understanding among teachers and students [89], elements that are crucial when dealing with challenging issues like sustainability. The idea of educating future teachers about sustainability is in conflict with a strong market-oriented agenda, but also with traditional practices. Although teacher education in Finland is research-based, it is not particularly critical [92] nor especially focused on development and adjustment [93]. Hökkä and Eteläpelto [48] have pointed to a lack of research on why the development of teacher education is so slow both on the individual and the collective level. Most educational research has applied a positivist approach and followed a normative agenda committed to the official values, according to Simola [92]. Sustainability, however, does not come about without open discussions about the issue of unsustainability.

Despite conflicting interests, international organizations, governments, industry and universities throughout the world have addressed the universities' urgent role in promoting the idea of a sustainable future among their students [53]. Yet, to promote sustainability, it is not enough that universities train students in sustainability; they need to *act* sustainably and focus on long-term goals [94].

Even if there have been major developments in higher education, there is still much to improve, according to Ramos et al. [95], who have studied implementation processes, participation, change management, assessment, and the popularity of sustainable development at the higher education level by reading of 33 academic papers from various countries. Higher education institutions can actually implement sustainability in three ways. One of these ways is called 'campus greening' and takes place through innovative planning, development of practical solutions and activities that promote sustainability in the daily life at the campuses. Examples of campus greening activities are often related to consumption; saving energy and water, reducing waste, etc. The other way of implementing sustainability is through teaching, and the third way is through research.

Sustainability is not only knowledge, among other things it is also an "open-minded and participative process" that has a connection to the students' own reality [96]. That means that universities are also life worlds for students. Innovative research and creative education build on academic freedom that together shape an ethical framework and prepare for the unpredictable [94]. Thus, universities should be seen as trustworthy institutions that train both scientists and citizens and conduct research that decreases uncertainty and ignorance. This is a field that needs a lot of development.

4.3. Separate Disciplines and Split Curricula Complicates the Implementation of Sustainability Education

Universities have three main tasks to fulfill: education, research and social engagement, and they are the leading producers of knowledge. At the same time, they are conservative institutions with a strong subject orientation. Research shows that there is a lack of interdisciplinary scientific understanding with an increasing numbers of specialists even though sustainability issues are widely connected [97]. For example, the environmental and the financial crisis is a mixture of finance and economy as well as of climate, resources and the environment. Sustainability education has to deal with ideology, social change, and political power relations, and could gain much from political science [98].

Declarations and documents about sustainability in higher education stress that sustainability has to include all students regardless of subject, and has to be a part of the study programs and teaching [53]. The reason for the slow implementation of sustainability in higher education is, according to Christie et al., both the complexity of the sustainability problematic and the epistemological differences between different disciplines, and Dillon [99] asks for interdisciplinary meta-knowledge when solving sustainability problems. Weber [33] also emphasizes the complexity and distinguishes between two interlinked dimensions, a natural one (focusing on planet Earth) and a social one (focusing on human societies). One apparent obstacle for implementing sustainability in higher education teaching is its interdisciplinary nature. Interdisciplinary research is still seen as challenging, a form of research that is not supplied by academic practice [65].

Arts, humanities and social sciences introduce other crucial views of the sustainability dilemma. Because of its complexity [53] it is easier to implement sustainability issues in creative disciplines rather than science subjects. Likewise, sustainability might require an innovative and student-centered pedagogy [52]. Students need to develop an ability to judge, criticize, argue and predict, as well as to fight ignorance and understand various perspectives when dealing with sustainability [33]. In a study among university students in the USA ($n = 552$), Fisher and McAdams [15] found that the way college professors approached the issue of sustainability, was also the way in which students framed the issue. This means that if the view the students receive is mainly one-sided or monodisciplinary, they will miss the complex picture. To deal with this problem, university teachers as individuals need to have both a complex understanding and a multidisciplinary approach in their teaching [15].

Teacher education is still based on separate academic disciplines and serves a fragmented school curriculum. Yet, according to Katehi [100], the multidisciplinary nature of universities provides grounds for jointly promoting new ideas and new practices. Since sustainability is more a matter of process than content, it turns the traditional curricula upside down in a quest for reorganization.

In Finnish schools, environmental and sustainability topics have often been passed to science lessons and delegated to science teachers (mostly biology and geography) [101]. Sustainability, however, cannot be handled only by natural sciences, even if these sciences are fundamental. Nevertheless, the core curriculum for basic education from 2014 emphasizes interdisciplinary teaching and learning to a much greater extent than earlier curricula [60]. Integrating teaching and multidisciplinary learning themes in the curriculum is a promising way forward from the view of sustainability education. The intention is that this educational approach will influence both content and teaching methods. The need for encouraging cross-curricular themes has also been underlined in earlier curricula, but the practical impact has not always been evident. Finnish teachers of grades 1–6 generally teach most subjects in the school class they are responsible for, which facilitates working interdisciplinary. However, sustainability is also emphasized within the curriculum contents and also in the aims of different subjects. Nevertheless, subjects like languages, mathematics, music, and history do not include sustainability issues in their aims and contents.

The new curriculum states that basic education in every school is obliged to arrange at least one cross-curricular learning theme during the school year, guaranteeing that each student has the opportunity to participate in this work. Furthermore, these themes are included in the assessment of the students, for example when assessing the subjects included in a particular learning theme. This clear statement in the curriculum might improve the conditions for working interdisciplinary, and this bodes well for dealing with the sustainability issue and the development work which has already started. Therefore, the conditions for the interdisciplinary perspective in general, and regarding sustainability education in particular, can possibly also improve teacher education at the university level.

4.4. Sustainability is Complicated without A Profound Ecological Literacy

For over thirty years environmental issues and sustainability has been discussed as something that should be faced comprehensively and should influence all education, but still very often these issues have been treated as "add-on topics". The complex concept of sustainability hides many components, among them nature. Nature is the basis of all life. Without nature there is, moreover, no social life and no economics or culture. That is why the idea of sustainability originally rose from biologists and the field of nature protection. Today, the climate change dilemma more obviously than ever before shows how dependent humans are on well-functioning ecosystems, but also how all kinds of human undertakings and social engagements are dependent upon careful observation of nature.

Nevertheless, nature and the ecological dimension of sustainability still seem to be increasingly ignored in the sustainability debate. Environmental education as a new educational approach in the 1960s included a basic ecological approach to environmental problems [102,103]. Later, when it was pointed out that environmental education does not only concern the natural sciences [3], other aspects of sustainability were paid more attention. The more recent concept, ESD [2], clearly pronounced the importance of the human dimension in all decisions concerning environmentally sound development [54] (see also the Introduction).

Environmental aspects do not, however, inevitably include basic ecological aspects. Therefore, ecological literacy and ecological understanding as a more positive approach than environmental problems form the bases of ecological sustainability. Ecological literacy means "understanding the key ecological systems using sound ecological thinking, and also understanding the nature of ecological science and its interface with society" [104] (p. 230). Ecological aspects of sustainability include both knowledge- and value-based issues of the sustainable use of natural resources, conserving bio- and genetic diversity and maintaining nature's ecological systems [105]. Therefore, an insight into natural resources, the fragility of the physical environment, and the effect of human activities on them, are environmental concern issues which should be considered in all social and economic policy development [34]. The fundamentals for sustainable development are the maintenance of biological diversity, the viability of ecosystems and the long-term reconciliation of economics and other human activity with the environment's carrying capacity [106]. Learning to care for all life on earth as early in life as possible is important as a basis for sustainability education [107].

However, the majority of student teachers and graduates in many universities are unable to explain the meaning of key integrating ecological concepts at even a minimum level of maturity, alluding to a possible systemic problem [108–110]. To achieve ecological literacy a greater understanding of ecological topics is needed. The ecologically literate person is, moreover, significantly more likely to engage in a set of pro-environment activities than someone who is not educated in ecology [111].

Future teachers ought to be profoundly trained, on the one hand, to understand ecologic components and ecological relationships and, on the other hand, to realize how nature and natural phenomena relate to social structures. Teachers unquestionably need a profound ecological knowledge to really understand, for example, the complex climate change dilemma. An ecologically literate teacher can also understand the complex relationships between human and ecological systems more easily [109]. Basic knowledge on many levels is a foundation for teachers, who have the task of integrating sustainability into all school subjects, but to do this they also need to be trained in ethical reasoning.

4.5. Sustainability Education is Complicated because of Its Value Dependence

The global sustainability challenges need to be tackled by knowledge and facts (to know how the world and the situations actually are) and tackled under real life conditions. Yet, the problems also need to be faced by normative questions, such as what ought we to do about it, and what is just to do [12,112–114]. As Moore and Nelson have said, "It is from the partnership between science and ethics that policies are born" [112] (p. 226), and education has to be designed so it triggers the students' own thinking and judgment [114,115]. However, ethics in education can be both a method and an aim. As a method in teacher education, ethics activates students morally and encourages even unpredictable transformations; but if regarded as a narrow aim, educators can only transmit a particular ethical view [12]. Without any determined aim, the outcome becomes undecided and makes room for future teachers to formulate visions and jointly shape temporal aims and even to disbelieve the entire "sustainable development" aspiration [12,116] and shape new projects and visions.

Humans' relation to nature and the idea of a sustainable future is wedded to many social dilemmas. Individual choices and fulfillment of personal desires do not necessarily promote socially valuable goals. Worldwide justice as well as intergenerational justice requires an equitable distribution of benefits as well as of burdens [112]. This calls for society-wide changes that involve the implementation of new policies, new infrastructures, new technologies and new laws [82]. To create a more sustainable course, there is a need for wider structural changes. Unsustainability is a global problem that is often in conflict with the individual quest for freedom of choices that has become a privilege in the wealthy countries. When considering the basic provision of the Universal Declaration of Human Rights, Article 3: "Everyone has the right to life, liberty and security of person" [117] it becomes obvious that interpreting the word "liberty" widely as "freedom of choice" easily turns the provision into a paradox. According to Moore and Nelson [112], these notions signal that the rich nations of today are carrying out the most severe violation of human rights.

The role of education is then also to train one's practical reason to consider the ethical conditions for mutual human undertakings and to identify the limits and terms nature sets for human life. Viewed this way, education has to offer both theoretical knowledge and provide possibilities for ethical deliberation, thus "provoking" students to form personal judgments and to participate in responsible actions based on both knowledge and reflection.

This ethical deliberation starts from an ethically conscious teacher education. A teacher education with sustainability as an important aim takes this mission seriously. In a qualitative study among upper secondary teachers, Sund [118] became convinced of the difficulty of teaching about ethical sustainability issues like global equity, fairness and responsibility to distant others. Emotions and passions were common elements when dealing with these kinds of issues, and she underscored that sustainability/unsustainability, justice/injustice and wealth/poverty are complex and demanding teaching topics which require talented teachers. A quick fix kind of training is definitely not enough.

5. Pedagogical Implications and Conclusions

A non-sustainable life has not come about suddenly and will not be overcome without joint efforts and fertile learning conditions. The concrete process towards sustainability needs to become a canon in teacher education in Finland and elsewhere. Words in policy documents are not enough; without training in sustainability education student teachers will hardly be able to teach this topic. If universities and other institutions offering teacher education do not regard sustainability as an important topic, there is a great risk that future teachers as well as teacher educators will enter the labor market without enough knowledge and skills to teach sustainability. The main actors to solve this issue are the leaders of universities, especially in Finland where the universities are autonomous. When leaders have embedded sustainability in the visions and goals of strategy documents they are responsible for the implementation of the issue in the university as a whole, including educational programs and research. However, somebody needs to take responsibility for a broad application, otherwise only those who have an economic interest in the topic will act.

Both strategies and national curricula are a good beginning, but without a purposeful interdisciplinary and transdisciplinary implementation that involves university leaders, teachers and students from different disciplines, and also other stakeholders, the policies will remain merely words. Universities have autonomy in terms of educational content, so to find a consensus between teacher educators about which subjects are most essential and have to be included in teacher education is challenging [65]. One teacher educator can seldom teach an interdisciplinary topic alone [65]. Another problem with the implementation of sustainability is the competition among so many compulsory subjects that must all be covered by the teacher education curriculum [65].

Pathan et al. [65] found that the strategies around sustainable development are most realized in the Finnish vocational institutions and in polytechnics when compared to other educational sectors in Finland. They argue that this is the case because vocational training has a closer relationship to workplaces and employers than higher education and especially university education has. Sustainability has, moreover, become a must in many workplaces. A Finnish study from 2001 shows that teachers in vocational education were more committed to teaching sustainability than teachers in primary and secondary schools [101]. One reason was that the leaders encouraged the teachers in vocational education to participate in sustainability in-service training. To rely too much on in-service training is though hazardous, since all schools might not have resources for that [65] or might prioritize other kinds of training courses. The teachers' preservice training at the university is without doubt the most important.

Universities in Finland and elsewhere are top knowledge institutions in a key educational position. Therefore, the sustainability process could create excellent opportunities for them to produce new ways of thinking as forerunners in a sustainable process. Then they become important participants in a dynamic and flexible synergy issue of different sciences and subjects where science, education, art and practices are combined, transformed and developed [119]. Universities already have both a research infrastructure, and staff with knowledge to train students in sustainability issues, according to Weber [33], so they even have a responsibility to jointly take the lead in the sustainability process as models and living laboratories [100]. As we have discussed the situation is sometimes less promising. The shortcomings of universities in general are obvious in the *2nd Glion declaration* of the *Glion Colloquium* (a forum that gathers university leaders and leaders from business and governments every second year in Glion, Switzerland to jointly consider what role the world's leading universities should play in addressing the great challenges and opportunities of our times.). The Glion Colloquium is still hopeful in their vision about the universities' role in the sustainability process: "Universities exist to liberate the unlimited creativity of the human species and to celebrate the unbounded resilience of the human spirit" [120].

A redesign of the universities and teacher education requires visionary leadership, social networking, and new forms of research and high levels of participation [7]. The sustainability trajectory becomes a joint commitment where visioning, planning, activities, daily conducts and evaluation continually follow each other in a steadily transforming process that engages both teachers and students in democratic processes and joint work that enables profound learning and the understanding of multiple views. There is a need for teacher education where future teachers learn to relate to sustainability issues as reflective practitioners and learning facilitators.

Because of the interdisciplinary nature of sustainability and the fact that universities are autonomous, the implementation of sustainability in teacher education is challenging. To prepare teachers for teaching about sustainability, this topic needs to be seen as important not only at the course level, but significant already in strategies, curricula and plans. Managers, administrators, teacher educators, researchers and students from various fields need to work together in this crucial development process. Student teachers have to be involved in campus greening, experiencing how sustainability is included in various school subjects both in theory and practice, but also treated as a subject in its own right. Another necessity is purposeful high quality sustainability in-service training for both teachers in general education and teacher educators at universities.

In 2013–2018 the new Finnish Education Evaluation Centre perform assessments of learning outcomes in sustainability in upper secondary vocational education [121]. No results of these assessments have been published yet. The same interest will hopefully soon be shown in general education, and why not in teacher education as well, even if the economic benefit of the sustainability knowledge of those graduated from general education might not be directly observable. Negligence on this level will be disastrous in the long run. Features like the learning outcomes of sustainability education, action competence or interdisciplinary skills have hitherto not been measured in PISA tests. Yet, according to a recent plan [122], 'global competency' will be a target for measurement in 2018. This will hopefully raise the sustainability issues to the agenda both in teacher education and schools in the countries involved, not least in Finland.

Author Contributions: Lili-Ann Wolff has been responsible for the writing project and is the main writer of Sections 1 and 5, and of Sections 4.1–4.3 and 4.5. Wolff has also analyzed the strategy documents of the eight Finnish universities offering teacher education and compared their teaching programs. Pia Sjöblom is the main author of Section 2 and of the Sections 3.1 and 3.2. She has also analyzed the Finnish core curricula. Maria Hofman-Bergholm has especially contributed to Section 1, and is the main author of Section 3.3. We are also many times referring to her empirical studies on Finnish teacher education and sustainability. Irmeli Palmberg is the main author of Section 4.4, and she has also taken much responsibility for the information searching, problematization and the logic of the entire article. However, the writing process has been a joint work. All authors have, therefore, planned the article and contributed to the discussion and conclusions in collaboration.

Conflicts of Interest: The authors declare no conflict of interest.

References

1. UNESCO (United Nations Educational, Scientific and Cultural Organization). *UN Decade of Education for Sustainable Development 2004–2005*; UNESCO: Paris, France, 2005.
2. UNCED (United Nations Conference on Environment and Development). *Agenda 21: Programme of action for Sustainable Development: Rio Declaration on Environment and Development; Statement of Forest Principles: The Final Text of Agreements Negotiated by Governments at United Nations Conference on Environment and Development (UNCED), 3–14 June 1992, Rio de Janeiro, Brazil*; United Nations Department of Public Information: New York, NY, USA, 1993.
3. WCED (World Commission on Environment and Development). *Our Common Future*; University Press: Oxford, UK, 1987.
4. Sachs, J.D. *The Age of Sustainable Development*; Colombia University Press: New York, NY, USA, 2015.
5. Hofman, M. *Hållbar utveckling i den finländska lärarutbildningen—politisk retorik eller verklighet? [Sustainable development in the Finnish Teacher Education—Political rhetoric or reality?]*; Research report 34; Faculty of Education, Åbo Akademi University: Vaasa, Finland, 2012. (In Swedish)
6. UNESCO. First Intergovernmental Conference on Environmental Education. Final Report. Tbilisi. Available online: http://www.gdrc.org/uem/ee/EE-Tbilisi_1977.pdf (accessed on 5 February 2017).
7. UNESCO. *Shaping the Future We Want. UN Decade of Education for Sustainable Development (2005–2014)*; Final Report; UNESCO: Paris, France, 2014.
8. Huckle, J.; Wals, A. The UN Decade of Education for Sustainable Development: Business as usual in the end. *Environ. Educ. Res.* **2015**, *21*, 491–505. [CrossRef]
9. Sauvé, L. Environmental education: Possibilities and constrains. *Connect* **2002**, *21*, 1–4.
10. Jickling, B.; Wals, A.E.J. Globalization and environmental education: looking beyond sustainable development. *J. Curric. Stud.* **2008**, *40*, 1–21. [CrossRef]
11. Vare, P.; Scott, W. Learning for a change: Exploring the relationship between education and sustainable development. *J. Educ. Sustain. Dev.* **2007**, *1*, 191–198. [CrossRef]
12. Wolff, L.-A. *Nature and Sustainability: An Educational Study with Rousseau and Foucault*; Lambert Academic Publishing: Saarbrücken, Germany, 2011.
13. Tani, S.; Cantell, H.; Koskinen, S.; Nordström, H.; Wolff, L.-A. Kokonaisvaltaisuuden haaste: Näkökulmia ympäristökasvatuksen kulttuuriseen ja sosiaaliseen ulottuvuuteen [The challenge of comprehensiveness: Views of the cultural and social dimensions of environmental education]. *Kasvatus* **2007**, *38*, 199–210. (In Finnish)
14. Jones, P.; Selby, D.; Sterling, S. *Sustainability Education: Perspectives and Practice across Higher Education*; Earthscan: London, UK, 2010.
15. Fisher, P.B.; McAdams, E. Gaps in sustainability education: The impact of higher education coursework on perceptions of sustainability. *Int. J. Sustain. High. Educ.* **2015**, *16*, 407–423. [CrossRef]
16. Hofman, M. What is an education for sustainable development supposed to achieve–a question about what, how and why. *J. Educ. Sustain. Dev.* **2015**, *9*, 213–228. [CrossRef]
17. Biberhofer, P.; Rammel, C. Transdisciplinary learning and teaching as answers to urban sustainability challenges. *Int. J. Sustainability High. Educ.* **2017**, *18*, 63–83. [CrossRef]
18. Boeve-de Pauw, J.; Gericke, N.; Olsson, D.; Berglund, T. The effectiveness of education for sustainable development. *Sustainability* **2015**, *7*, 15693–15717. [CrossRef]

19. Rudsberg, K.; Öhman, J. Pluralism in practice–experience from Swedish evaluation, school development and research. *Environ. Educ. Res.* **2010**, *16*, 96–111. [CrossRef]
20. Koskinen, S.; Paloniemi, R. Social learning processes of environmental policy. In *Handbook of Environmental Policy*; Meijer, J., der Berg, A., Eds.; Nova Science: New York, NY, USA, 2009; pp. 293–308.
21. Lange, E.; Chubb, A. Critical environmental adult education in Canada: Student environmental activism. *New Directions Adult Contin. Edu.* **2009**, *124*, 61–72. [CrossRef]
22. Wals, A.E.J. The end of ESD ... the beginning of transformative learning: Emphasizing the E in ESD. In *Kestävää kehitystä edistävä koulutus-seminaari 15.2.2006*; Cantell, H., Ed.; Finnish National Commission for UNESCO: Helsinki, Finland, 2006; pp. 41–59.
23. Mogensen, F.; Schnack, K. The action competence approach and the 'new' discourses of education for sustainable development, competence and quality criteria. *Environ. Educ. Res.* **2010**, *16*, 59–74. [CrossRef]
24. Wolff, L.-A. Drömmar i pedagogikens kraftfält [Dreams on the educational arena]. In *Det händer i pedagogiken: Röster om bildning i det senmoderna*; Uljens, M., Ed.; Faculty of Education, Åbo Akademi University: Vaasa, Finland, 2008; pp. 35–64. (In Swedish)
25. Gadotti, M. Education for sustainability: A critical contribution to the Decade of Education for Sustainable Development, green theory and praxis. *J. Ecopedagogy* **2008**, *4*, 15–64.
26. Dimick, A.S. Supporting youth develop environmental citizenship within/against a neoliberal context. *Environ. Educ. Res.* **2015**, *21*, 390–402. [CrossRef]
27. Bessant, S.E.F.; Robinson, Z.P.; Ormerod, R.M. Neoliberalism, new public management and the sustainable development agenda of higher education: History, contradictions and synergies. *Environ. Educ. Res.* **2015**, *21*, 417–432. [CrossRef]
28. Wolff, L.-A. Adult education in an unsustainable era. In *Adult Education and the Planetary Condition*; Harju, A., Heikkinen, A., Eds.; Finnish Adult Education Association: Helsinki, Finland, 2016; pp. 194–209.
29. De Lissovoy, N. *Education and Emancipation in the Neoliberal Era: Being, Teaching and Power*; Palgrave Macmillan: New York, NY, USA, 2015.
30. Wals, A. *Shaping the Education of Tomorrow: Full length Report on the UN Decade of Education for Sustainable Development*; UNESCO Education Sector: Paris, France, 2012.
31. Hursch, D.; Henderson, J.; Greenwood, D. Environmental education in a neoliberal climate. *Environ. Educ. Res.* **2015**, *21*, 299–318. [CrossRef]
32. Kopnina, H. Future scenarios and environmental education. *J. Environ. Educ.* **2014**, *45*, 217–231. [CrossRef]
33. Weber, L. Universities, hard and soft sciences: All key pillars of global sustainability. In *Global sustainability and the responsibilities of universities*; Weber, L.E., Duderstadt, J.J., Eds.; Economica: London, UK, 2012; pp. 3–14.
34. UNESCO. *Guidelines and Recommendations for Reorienting Teacher Education to Address Sustainability. Education for Sustainable Development in Action*; Technical Paper No. 2; UNESCO, Section for Education for Sustainable Development: Paris, France, 2005.
35. Lindberg, C. Vad gör lärarutbildningen för att främja hållbar utveckling? [How Does Teacher Education Promote Sustainable Development?]. Available online: http://www.skolaochsamhalle.se/flode/lararutbildning/carl-lindberg-vad-gor-lararutbildningen-for-att-framja-hallbarutveckling/ (accessed on 11 March 2015). (In Swedish)
36. Angelotti, M.; Perrazzone, A.; Tonon, M.D.; Bertolino, F. Educating the educators: Primary teacher education. In *Science, Society and Sustainability: Education and Empowerment for an Uncertain World*; Gray, D., Colucci-Gray, L., Camino, E., Eds.; Routledge: London, UK, 2009; pp. 154–187.
37. Birdsall, S. Measuring student teachers' understanding and self-awareness of sustainability. *Environ. Educ. Res.* **2014**, *20*, 814–835. [CrossRef]
38. Falkenberg, T.; Babiuk, G. The status of education for sustainability in initial teacher education programmes: A Canadian case study. *Int. J. Sustain. High. Educ.* **2014**, *15*, 418–430. [CrossRef]
39. Higgins, P.; Kirk, G. Sustainability education in Scotland: The impact of national and international initiatives on teacher education and outdoor education. In *Education for Sustainable Development. Papers in Honour of the United Nations Decade of Education for Sustainable Development (2005–2014)*; Chalkley, B., Haigh, M., Higgitt, D., Eds.; Routledge: London, UK, 2009; pp. 161–174.
40. Lozano, R. Diffusion of sustainable development in universities' curricula: An empirical example from Cardiff University. *J. Clean. Prod.* **2010**, *18*, 637–644. [CrossRef]

41. Muños-Pedreros, A. Environmental education in Chile: A pending task. *Ambiente Sociedade* **2014**, *17*, 175–194.

42. Martin, J.; Carter, L. Preservice teacher agency concerning education for sustainability (Efs): A discursive psychological approach. *J. Res. Sci. Teach.* **2015**, *52*, 560–573. [CrossRef]

43. Sahlberg, P. *Finnish Lessons. What Can the World Learn from Educational Change in Finland?* Teachers college press: New York, NY, USA, 2011.

44. Välijärvi, J.; Linnakylä, P.; Kupari, P.; Reinikainen, P.; Arffman, I. *The Finnish Success in PISA—and Some Reasons behind It;* Institute for Educational Research, University of Jyväskylä: Jyväskylä, Finland, 2002.

45. Jakku-Sihvonen, R.; Niemi, H. Introduction to the Finnish education system and teachers' work. In *Research-based Teacher Education in Finland. Reflections of Finnish Teacher Educators;* Jakku-Sihvonen, R., Niemi, H., Eds.; Finnish Educational Research Association: Research in Educational Sciences: Turku, Finland, 2006; pp. 7–13.

46. Simola, H. The Finnish miracle of PISA. Historical and sociological remarks on teaching and teacher education. *Comp. Educ.* **2005**, *41*, 455–470. [CrossRef]

47. Silander, T.; Välijärvi, J. The theory and practice of building pedagogical skill in Finnish teacher education. In *PISA, power, and policy: The Emergence of Global Educational Governance;* Meyer, H.-D., Benavot, A., Eds.; Symposium Books: London, UK, 2013; pp. 77–97.

48. Hökkä, P.; Eteläpelto, A. Seeking new perspectives on the development of teacher education: A study of the Finnish context. *J. Teach. Educ.* **2014**, *65*, 39–52. [CrossRef]

49. Ministry of Education. *Education for Sustainable Development / the Baltic 21E programme. A proposal by the ESD Committee for a Starting-up Plan for the Programme;* Committee Report 36; Ministry of Education: Helsinki, Finland, 2002.

50. Ministry of Education. *Sustainable Development in Education; Implementation of Baltic 21E Programme and Finnish strategy for the Decade of Education for Sustainable Development (2005–2014);* Reports of the Ministry of Education, Report 2006:6; Ministry of Education: Helsinki, Finland, 2006.

51. Ministry of the Environment. *Saving Nature for People: National Strategy and Action Plan for the Conservation and Sustainable use of Biodiversity in Finland 2006–2016;* Ministry of the Environment: Helsinki, Finland, 2007.

52. Christie, B.A.; Miller, K.K.; Cooke, R.; White, J.G. Environmental sustainability in higher education: What do academics teach? *Environ. Educ. Res.* **2013**, *19*, 385–414. [CrossRef]

53. Christie, B.A.; Miller, K.K.; Cooke, R.; White, J.G. Environmental sustainability in higher education: What do academics think? *Environ. Educ. Res.* **2015**, *21*, 655–686. [CrossRef]

54. Ministry of the Environment. *Implementation of Agenda 21 in Finland;* Ministry of the Environment, Finnish National Commission on Sustainable Development: Helsinki, Finland, 1992.

55. Finnish National Commission on Sustainable Development. *Strategy for Education and Training for Sustainable Development and Implementation Plan 2006–2014;* Finnish National Commission of Sustainable Development: Helsinki, Finland, 2006.

56. Finlex. Valtioneuvoston asetus perusopetuslaissa tarkoitetun opetuksen valtakunnallisista tavoitteista ja perusopetuksen tuntijaosta [Government Decree of the Basic Education Act]. Available online: http://www.finlex.fi/fi/laki/alkup/2001/20011435 (accessed on 15 May 2016). (In Finnish)

57. Finnish National Board of Education. *Grunderna för grundskolans läroplan [National Core Curriculum for Basic Education];* National Board of Education: Helsinki, Finland, 1985.

58. Finnish National Board of Education. *Grunderna för grundskolans läroplan [National Core Currriculum for Basic Education];* National Board of Education: Helsinki, Finland, 1994. (In Swedish)

59. Finnish National Board of Education. *National Core Curriculum for Basic Education;* National Board of Education: Helsinki, Finland, 2004.

60. Finnish National Board of Education. *National Core Curriculum for Basic Education;* National Board of Education: Helsinki, Finland, 2014.

61. Uljens, M.; Wolff, L.-A.; Frontini, S. Finland: NPM resistance or towards European neo-welfarism in education? In *New Public Management and the Reform of Education: European Lessons for Policy and Practice;* Gunter, H.M., Grimaldi, E., Hall, D., Serpieri, R., Eds.; Routledge: London, UK, 2016.

62. Kiilakoski, T.; Oravakangas, A. Koulutus tuotantokoneistona? Tulostavoitteinen koulutuspolitiikka kriittisen teorian valossa [Education as production machinery? Profit oriented educational politics in a critical light]. *Kasvatus Aika* **2010**, *4*, 7–25. (In Finnish)

63. Goodwin, A.L.; Smith, L.; Souto-Manning, M.; Cheruvu, R.; Tan, M.Y.; Reed, R.; Taveras, L. What should teacher educators know and be able to do? Perspectives from practicing teacher educators. *J. Teach. Educ.* **2014**, *65*, 284–302. [CrossRef]

64. Ministry of Education and Culture. *Högskolorna 2011: Universiteten och yrkeshögskolorna [Higher education 2011: Universities and polytechnics]*; Undervisnings- och kulturministeriets publikationer 2011:11; Ministry of Education and Culture: Helsinki, Finland, 2011. (In Swedish)

65. Pathan, A.; Bröckl, M.; Oja, L.; Ahvenharju, S.; Raivio, T. *Kansallisten kestävää kehitystä edistävien kasvatuksen ja koulutuksen strategioiden toimeenpanon arviointi* [Evaluation of the Implementation of the Strategies on Education for Sustainable Development]. Available online: http://www.ym.fi/download/noname/%7B7A0AC771-670C-48B8-B7F8-8FB0B173236F%7D/78365 (accessed on 20 February 2017). (In Finnish)

66. Susiluoma, S. *Kestävän kehityksen ohjelmat peruskouluissa ja lukioissa* [Programs for Sustainable Development in Basic Education and General upper Secondary Education]. Master's thesis, University of Jyväskylä, Jyväskylä, Finland, 2009. (In Finnish)

67. Uitto, A.; Saloranta, S. Subject teachers as educators for sustainability: A survey study. *Educ. Sci.* **2017**, *7*. [CrossRef]

68. Borg, C.; Gericke, N.; Höglund, H.-O.; Bergman, E. The barriers encountered by teachers implementing education for sustainable development: discipline bound differences and teaching traditions. *Res. Sci. Technol. Educ.* **2012**, *30*, 185–207. [CrossRef]

69. Berglund, T.; Gericke, N.; Chang Rundgren, S.-N. The implementation of education for sustainable development in Sweden: Investigating the sustainability consciousness among upper secondary students. *Res. Sci. Technol. Educ.* **2014**, *32*, 318–339. [CrossRef]

70. Olsson, D.; Gericke, N.; Chang Rundgren, S.-N. The effect of implementation of education for sustainable development in Swedish compulsory schools—assessing pupils' sustainability consciousness. *Environ. Educ. Res.* **2016**, *22*, 176–202. [CrossRef]

71. Wals, A.E.J. Between knowing what is right and knowing that is it wrong to tell others what is right: On relativism, uncertainty and democracy in environmental and sustainability education. *Environ. Educ. Res.* **2010**, *16*, 143–151. [CrossRef]

72. Berry, A.; van Driel, D.H. Teaching about teaching science: Aims, strategies, and backgrounds of science teacher educators. *J. Teach. Educ.* **2013**, *64*, 117–128. [CrossRef]

73. Buchanan, J. Sustainability education and teacher education: Finding a natural habitat? *Aust. J. Environ. Educ.* **2012**, *28*, 108–124. [CrossRef]

74. Borg, C.; Gericke, N.; Höglund, H.-O.; Bergman, E. Subject- and experience-based differences in teachers' conceptual understanding of sustainable development. *Environ. Educ. Res.* **2014**, *20*, 526–551. [CrossRef]

75. Digital Finance. The Richest Countries in the World. 2015. Available online: https://www.gfmag.com/global-data/economic-data/richest-countries-in-the-world (accessed on 1 June 2016).

76. Statistikcentralen. Finländarnas konsumtion elvadubblats på hundra år [The Finnish Consumption Has Grown Eleven Times in Hundred Years]. 2007. Available online: http://www.stat.fi/tup/suomi90/heinakuu_sv.html (accessed on 27 august 2015). (In Swedish)

77. Worldwatch Institute. *State of the World 2014: Governing for Sustainability*; Island Press: Washington, DC, USA, 2014.

78. IPCC. *Climate change 2014: Mitigation of Climate Change. Contribution of Working Group III to the Fifth Assessment Report of the Intergovernmental Panel on Climate Change*; Cambridge University Press: Cambridge, UK, 2014.

79. United Nations; Department of Economic and Social Affairs; Population Division. *World Population Prospects: The 2015 Revision, Key Findings and Advance Tables*; Working Paper No. ESA/P/WP.241; UN: New York, NY, USA, 2015.

80. Assadourian, E. Re-engineering cultures to create a sustainable civilization. In *State of the World 2013: Is Sustainability Still Possible? Worldwatch Institute*; Island Press: Washington, DC, USA, 2013; pp. 113–125.

81. Bauman, Z. *Consuming Life*; Polity Press: Cambridge, UK, 2007.

82. Leonard, A. Moving from individual change to societal change. In *State of the World 2013: Is Sustainability Possible? Worldwatch institute*, Island Press: Washington, DC, USA, 2013; pp. 244–254.

83. Hamilton, C. Consumerism, self-creation and prospect for a new ecological consciousness. *J. Clean. Prod.* **2010**, *18*, 571–575. [CrossRef]

84. Foucault, M. *The History of Sexuality: Vol 1, An introduction*; Hurley, R., Translator; Random House: New York, NY, USA, 1978.

85. Foucault, M. Governmentality. In *Essential works of Foucault 1954–1984: Vol. 3, Power*; Hurley, L., Translator; Faubion, J.D., Ed.; The New Press: New York, NY, USA, 2000; pp. 201–222.

86. Speth, J.G. *The Bridge at the Edge of the World. Capitalism, the Environment, and crossing from Crisis to Sustainability*; Yale University Press: London, UK, 2008.

87. Ministry of Education and Culture. (n.y.). The Bologna Process. Available online: http://www.minedu.fi/OPM/Koulutus/artikkelit/bologna/?lang=en (accessed on 17 December 2014).

88. The European Higher Education Area. The Bologna Declaration of 19 June 1999. Available online: http://www.magna-charta.org/resources/files/BOLOGNA_DECLARATION.pdf (accessed on 14 December 2014).

89. Filander, K. Orwell täällä tänään? [Orwell here today?]. *Kasvatus* **2012**, *43*, 526–533. (In Finnish)

90. Rinne, R. Ovatko kyyt kuolleet? Näkemyksiä uuden yliopiston ymmärtämiseksi [Are the vipers dead? Views to understand the new university]. *Kasvatus* **2012**, *43*, 540–546. (In Finnish)

91. Kallio, K.-M.; Kallio, T.J. Management-by-results and performance measurement in universities: Implications for work motivation. *Stud. High. Educ.* **2014**, *39*, 574–589. [CrossRef]

92. Simola, H. *The Finnish Education Mystery: Historical and Sociological Essays on Schooling in Finland*; Routledge: London, UK, 2015.

93. Sahlberg, P. Kuka ostaisi suomalaista koulutusosaamista? [Who would buy the Finnish school expertise?]. *Ammattikasvatuksen aikakauskirja* **2012**, *14*, 17–27. (In Finnish)

94. Beretz, A. Preparing the university and its graduates for the unpredictable and unknowable. In *Global Sustainability and the Responsibilities of Universities*; Weber, L.E., Duderstadt, J.J., Eds.; Economica: London, UK, 2012; pp. 143–151.

95. Ramos, T.; Caeiro, S.; van Hoof, B.; Lozano, R.; Huisingh, D.; Ceulemans, K. Experiences from the implementation of sustainable development in higher education institutions: Environmental management for sustainable universities. *J. Clean. Prod.* **2015**, *106*, 3–10. [CrossRef]

96. Barth, M.; Godemann, J.; Rieckmann, M.; Stoltenberg, U. Developing key competencies for sustainable development in higher education. *Int. J. Sustain. Educ.* **2007**, *8*, 416–430. [CrossRef]

97. Wijkman, A.; Rockström, J. *Bankrupting Nature: Denying Our Planetary Boundaries*, 2nd ed.; Routledge: New York, NY, USA, 2012.

98. Atkinson, H.; Wade, R. Education for sustainable development and political science: Making change happen. *Policy Pract. A Dev. Educ. Rev.* **2013**, *17*, 46–69.

99. Dillon, P. A pedagogy of connection and education for sustainability. In *Human Perspectives on Sustainable Future*; Rauma, A.-L., Pöllänen, S., Seitamaa-Hakkarinen, P., Eds.; Research Report 99; University of Joensuu, Faculty of Education: Joensuu, Finland, 2006; pp. 261–276.

100. Katehi, L.P.B. A university culture of sustainability: Principle, practice and economic driver. In *Global Sustainability and the Responsibilities of Universities*; Weber, L.E., Duderstadt, J.J., Eds.; Economica: London, UK, 2012; pp. 117–127.

101. Rajakorpi, A.; Salmio, K. (Eds.) *Toteutuuko kestävä kehitys kouluissa ja oppilaitoksissa? [Is Sustainable Development Implemented in Schools and Colleges?]*, National Board of Education: Helsinki, Finland, 2001.

102. Brody, M. Learning in nature. *Environ. Educ. Res.* **2005**, *11*, 603–621. (In Finnish) [CrossRef]

103. Stapp, W.; Bennett, D.; Bryan, W.; Fulton, J.; MacGregor, J.; Nowak, P.; Swan, J.; Wall, R.; Havlick, S. The concept of environmental education. *J. Environ. Educ.* **1969**, *1*, 30–31.

104. Berkowitz, A.R.; Ford, M.F.; Brewer, C.A. A framework for integrating ecological literacy, civics literacy, and environmental citizenship in environmental education. In *Environmental Education and Advocacy. Changing Perspectives of Ecology and Education*; Johnson, E.A., Mappin, M.J., Eds.; Cambridge University Press: New York, NY, USA, 2005; pp. 227–266.

105. Virtanen, A.; Salonen, A.-M. Sustainable development in natural resources and environment studies. In *Towards Sustainable Development in Higher Education: Reflections*; Kaivola, T., Rohweder, L., Eds.; Publications of Ministry of Education 6; Ministry of Education: Helsinki, Finland, 2007; pp. 86–95.

106. Ministry of the Environment. *Finnish Government Programme for Sustainable Development*; Council of State Decision-in-Principle on the Promotion of Ecological Sustainability, Ministry of the Environment: Helsinki, Finland, 1998.

107. Duhn, I. Making 'place' for ecological sustainability in early childhood education. *Environ. Educ. Res.* **2012**, *18*, 19–29. [CrossRef]
108. Palmberg, I.; Jonsson, G.; Jeronen, E.; Yli-Panula, E. Blivande lärares uppfattningar och förståelse av baskunskap i ekologi i Danmark, Finland och Sverige [Student teachers' conceptions and understanding of basic knowledge in ecology in Denmark, Finland and Sweden]. *Nord. Stud. Sci. Educ.* **2016**, *12*, 197–215. (In Swedish)
109. Puk, T.G.; Stibbards, A. Systemic ecological illiteracy? Shedding light on meaning as an act of thought in higher learning. *Environ. Educ. Res.* **2012**, *18*, 353–373. [CrossRef]
110. Yavetz, B.; Goldman, D.; Pe'er, S. How do preservice teachers perceive 'environment' and its relevance to their area of teaching? *Environ. Educ. Res.* **2014**, *20*, 354–371. [CrossRef]
111. Robelia, B.; Murphy, T. What do people know about key environmental issues? A review of environmental knowledge surveys. *Environ. Educ. Res.* **2012**, *18*, 299–321. [CrossRef]
112. Moore, K.D.; Nelson, M.P. Moving toward a global moral consensus on environmental action. In *State of the World 2013: Is Sustainability still Possible?* Worldwatch Institute, Island Press: Washington, DC, USA, 2013; pp. 225–234.
113. Jickling, B. Environmental thought, the language of sustainability, and digital watches. *Environ. Educ. Res.* **2001**, *7*, 167–180. [CrossRef]
114. Wolff, L.-A. Education for sustainable development needs a critical approach. In *Sustainable development through Education. International Conference on Environmental Education in Helsinki, Finland, 13th–15th June 2005. Proceedings of the Research Seminar*; Tani, S., Ed.; Department of Applied Science of Education, University of Helsinki: Helsinki, Finland, 2006; pp. 29–46.
115. Wals, A.E.J.; Alblas, A.H.; Margadant-van Arcken, M. Environmental education for human development. In *Environmental Education and Biodiversity*; Wals, A.E.J, Ed.; National Reference Centre for Nature Management: Wageningen, NL, USA, 1999; pp. 15–33.
116. Newton, A.C.; Cantarello, E. *An introduction to the green economy: Science systems and sustainability*; Routledge: London, UK, 2014.
117. United Nations. United Nations Universal Declaration of Human Rights 1948. Available online: http://www.un.org/en/udhrbook/index.shtml (accessed on 21 February 2017).
118. Sund, L. Facing global sustainability issues: teachers' experiences of their own practices in environmental and sustainability education. *Environ. Educ. Res.* **2016**, *22*, 788–805. [CrossRef]
119. Wolff, L.-A. The quest for a route to sustainable development in higher education. In *Towards Sustainable Development in Higher Education: Reflections*; Kaivola, T., Rohweder, L., Eds.; Finnish Ministry of Education: Helsinki, Finland, 2007; pp. 58–62.
120. Glion Colloquium. The 2nd Glion Declaration. Available online: http://www.glion.org/?p=736 (accessed on 5 February 2017).
121. Karvi (Finnish Education Evaluation Centre). National Plan for Education Evaluations 2016–2019. Available online: https://karvi.fi/en/publication/national-plan-for-education-evaluations-2016--2019--3/ (accessed on 9 February 2017).
122. OECD. Global Competence for an Inclusive World. Available online: http://www.oecd.org/pisa/aboutpisa/Global-competency-for-an-inclusive-world.pdf (accessed on 5 February 2017).

Article

Subject Teachers as Educators for Sustainability: A Survey Study

Anna Uitto * and Seppo Saloranta

Department of Teacher Education, University of Helsinki, Helsinki 00014, Finland; seppo.saloranta@helsinki.fi
* Correspondence: anna.uitto@helsinki.fi; Tel.: +358-9050-4482-511

Academic Editor: Eila Jeronen
Received: 30 October 2016; Accepted: 21 December 2016; Published: 4 January 2017

Abstract: Sustainability education (SE) is included in school curricula to integrate the principles, values, and practices of sustainable development (SD) into all education. This study investigates lower secondary school subject teachers as educators for sustainability. A survey was used to study the perceptions of 442 subject teachers from 49 schools in Finland. There were significant differences between the subject teachers' perceptions of their SE competence, and the frequency with which they used different dimensions of SE (ecological, economic, social, well-being, cultural) in their teaching varied. Teachers' age had a small effect, but gender, school, and its residential location were nonsignificant factors. Teachers could be roughly classified into three different subgroups according to their perceptions of the role of SE in their teaching; those who considered three SE dimensions rather often and used holistic sustainability approaches in their teaching (biology, geography, history); those who considered two or three dimensions often but were not active in holistic teaching (mother tongue, religion, visual arts, crafts, music, physical and health education, and home economics) and those who used one SE dimension or consider only one holistic approach in their teaching (mathematics, physics, chemistry and language). Subject teachers' awareness of their SE competence is important to encourage them to plan and implement discipline-based and interdisciplinary SE in their teaching. The specific SE expertise of subject teachers should be taken into account in teacher training and education.

Keywords: sustainability education; subject teachers; secondary school; survey; teaching

---

1. Introduction

1.1. Curricular Goals of Sustainability Education

The aim of education for sustainable development (ESD), or sustainability education (SE), is to integrate the principles, values, and practices of sustainable development (SD) into all aspects of education. This challenge was also underlined by the United Nations (UN) as the Decade for Education for Sustainable Development (DESD 2005–2014). During the decade, SE has been increasingly taken into account in the formal education of comprehensive schools around the world [1]. SE emphasizes the consideration of multiple aspects of sustainability including ecological, economic, social, and cultural aspects of SD. The consideration of all aspects of sustainability is crucial in sustainability teaching (ST), although aspects involving the ecological dimension have traditionally been emphasized in schools [2–4]. The Finnish National Core Curriculum for Basic Education [5] was in use in the schools during the DESD. According to the curriculum, natural diversity and the preservation of environmental viability is included in the underlying values of basic education. The curriculum also included "Responsibility for the environment, well-being and a sustainable future" as a cross-curricular theme and, according to the curriculum [5] (p. 39), schools should teach "future-oriented thinking and the building of the future upon ecologically, economically, socially and culturally sustainable premises". The curriculum highlights a holistic view, by which the students should, for instance "come to understand prerequisites for human well-being, the necessity of environmental protection, and the relationship between the two" [5] (p. 39). In the learning objectives and core contents of different school subjects, goals linked to SE have also been mentioned. The national curriculum was renewed in 2014 [6], with seven main areas of students' transversal competences emphasized in all subjects. One of these main competence areas is "Participation, agency and the building of a sustainable future". Thus, as sustainability aspects have been highlighted in the past and present curricula [5,6], it is important to study how the goals have been reached in the school.

1.2. Effectiveness of SE in School Education

Currently, SE is widely included in school curricula around the world [1], and research on the effects of SE is gradually increasing. However, very little is known about the effectiveness of SE. In general, the goals of SE are to influence the values, interests, and attitudes of students. In Finland, ninth-grade students' pro-environmental and pro-social values and attitudes, as well as their interest in environmental and human issues, have been found to be interconnected [7]. In a Finnish study [8], it was also found that ninth-grade students' interest, values, and attitudes pertaining to environmental issues correlated with each other. An important finding is that students' sustainability school experiences make a difference, as the Finnish ninth-grade students' ecologically sustainable behaviors outside the school could be influenced by their personal factors, like sustainability-related attitudes, values, and self-efficacy beliefs, which in turn were influenced by sustainability experiences in the school [9]. Sustainability-related social and agency experiences, in particular, have been found to be important in predicting these behaviors [9]. In Sweden, similar results were found [10], indicating that SE can impact student outcomes in terms of their sustainability consciousness. Thus, to study the educational effectiveness of SE in secondary school, it is also very important to more closely study the competence of the teachers in SE.

1.3. Teachers as Sustainability Educators

SE is a complex and controversial approach, and it may be a challenge for subject teachers. In their review on environmental education research, Hart and Nolan emphasized that teachers' knowledge, attitudes, and competence to consider versatile and complex phenomena in environmental education vary [11]. In general, teachers' pedagogical competence can be described as content knowledge, pedagogical knowledge, and pedagogical content knowledge [12]. Subject teachers' SE competence may be linked to their expertise areas, as well as to the tradition, methods, and practices of different subjects' teaching [13–17]. However, there are not many detailed studies on teachers' knowledge of SD and their pedagogical content knowledge related to SE. In general, understanding the different dimensions of sustainability has proven to be a challenge for teachers [13,15,16]. In general, many teachers may not feel very competent at including sustainability issues in their teaching [16]. Therefore, examining in-service subject teachers' knowledge and skills to implement SE is an important topic to research.

In general, secondary school subject teachers specialize in two or three academic disciplines in Finland. The qualification required for subject teachers is a master's degree from a university. For their master's degree, subject teachers need to have completed advanced studies in their major subject, and intermediate studies in their minor subjects, one of which is pedagogical studies in teacher education. For instance, a biology teacher has often studied biology as the major subject, and geography/earth sciences, chemistry, or health education as a minor subject, but these studies do include specific courses on SE.

The aim of this study is to determine to what extent subject teachers take different aspects and holistic approaches of SE into account in their teaching, as well as how competent they feel in teaching different SE dimensions. In this study, teachers' perceptions of all aspects of sustainability, namely ecological, economic, social, and cultural, as defined by [5], were investigated. The study questions for our research are:

How often do subject teachers implement different dimensions and holistic views of SE in their teaching?

How do subject teachers perceive their competence to teach different dimensions of SE?

Do subject teachers' perceptions differ from each other in terms of the following:

- teaching frequency of ecological, economic, social, and cultural sustainability;
- teaching a holistic view of SE;
- their competence to teach different dimensions of SE?

What is the relative importance of subject, gender, age, school, and the school's residential area in explaining the results?

2. Materials and Methods

2.1. Questionnaire and Data Sampling

A large-scale survey was carried out to study the implementation and effects of ESD in 2010 in Finland, see, e.g., [7,9,17]. A specific questionnaire was developed for the research. The background of the questionnaire is in the general recommendations given by UN on the dimensions of SD and SE (e.g., [18]). The items measuring teaching on different aspects of SE were developed using the main areas of sustainability commonly considered in SE [19,20] and the Finnish cross-curricular theme "Responsibility for the environment, well-being, and a sustainable future" [5], especially the ecological, economic, and social dimensions. Items for cultural and economic dimensions were developed using the FNBE recommendations that deepen the understanding of cross-curricula themes [21]. The recommendations of the OKKA Foundation [22] for sustainability schools were also used. OKKA is a foundation for teaching, education, and personal development supporting the educational sector. Its founding organizations are the Trade Union of Education in Finland (OAJ) and several teachers' associations in the vocational sector. The OKKA Foundation has the right to grant sustainable development certification of educational establishments in Finland.

The original questionnaire is composed of several pages with questions that consider teachers' sustainability-related teaching in the school. Only sections to elicit responses from teachers on items concerning their general schools practices and teaching on ecological, economic, social, and cultural sustainability at school were included in this study. The teachers were asked how often they considered different dimensions of sustainability (ecological, economic, social, and cultural) in their teaching: "Evaluate how often you consider the issues mentioned below in your own teaching. The teaching method is free depending on the subject and its nature. Choose the alternative that best fits with your own opinion". The frequency of different activities was rated on a five-point Likert-type scale: 5 = very often, 4 = rather often, 3 = sometimes, 2 = rather seldom, 1 = very seldom.

Teachers' perceptions of their competence in SE were assessed using five items with which the teachers could rate their responses on a five-point Likert scale: 1 = very poorly, 2 = rather poorly, 3 = satisfactory, 4 = rather well, 5 = very well. Teachers' perceptions of their knowledge of the cross-curricular theme "Responsibility for the environment, wellbeing and sustainable future" [5] were assessed similarly.

A stratified sampling procedure was used to select the lower secondary school for the study, so that different residential areas (urban, densely populated, and rural) were represented in the sample collected from the whole country. Fourteen teacher questionnaires were sent to each of the selected 54 lower secondary schools, of which five were Swedish-speaking schools. Altogether, 49 schools were included in the study.

The teachers were also asked to indicate their major and minor subject during their pre-service studies. There were 25 different disciplines in the questionnaire:

- Mother tongue and literature;
- Second national language Swedish;
- Second national language Finnish;
- English;
- German;
- French;
- Russian;
- Other language;
- Mathematics;
- Biology;
- Geography;
- hysics;
- Chemistry;

- Health education;
- Lutheranism religion;
- Lutheranism religion;
- Other religions;
- Ethics;
- History;
- Social studies;
- Music;
- Visual arts;
- Crafts;
- Physical education;
- Home economics

The groupings were carried out according to the two disciplines the subject teachers taught at their schools. The same teacher usually teaches two different subjects according to his/her pre-service major and minor studies, such as mother tongue and literature, history and social studies, physical and health education, or religion and ethics. The grouping was carried out according to the major subject of the teacher. Some disciplines occurred only as minor subjects, such as health education, orthodox religion or other religions, ethics, and social studies. For instance, only four teachers indicated that their major subject was health education, and thus these teachers were combined with the teachers of physical education.

Finnish as the mother tongue and Swedish as a second national language were the most common subjects of the language teachers. The third most common language was English. Because there were not many language teachers who had Finnish as a second national language or French, German, Russian, or other language as their major subject, they were combined to form a group of "other language teachers" in this study. Altogether 16 subject teacher categories were formed.

2.2. Statistical Analyses

An explorative factor analysis (EFA) was used to reduce the data and identify the latent variables of the data with IBM software, PASW 23. Maximum likelihood was used as the extraction method based on Eigenvalues larger than 1. Promax rotation was used, as is likely that the factors measuring different aspects of sustainability correlate with each other. Factor score coefficients were estimated using the regression method and the factor scores were used in statistical analyses. Average scales describing the variables were calculated, with the items' means representing the Likert scale from 1 to 5 according to the EFA pattern matrix. ANOVA was used to analyze the contribution of gender, age, teachers' subject, and schools' location in urban, densely populated, or rural areas.

The original questionnaire was composed of 53 items to find the most suitable solution to study the ecological, economic, social, and cultural aspects of SE. However, only 27 items were accepted into the final best fit factor solution of EFA. In this case, initial communalities varied between 0.441 and 0.774 and the Kaiser-Meyer-Olkin Measure of Sampling Adequacy was 0.91 indicating that the data were adequate to carry out the EFA. The five-factor solution explained 69.4% of the variance in initial Eigenvalues. The number of items per factor varied between three and eight, and the internal consistency (Cronbach's alpha) from 0.87 to 0.91.

3. Results

3.1. Subject Teachers

The data from 49 schools representing different parts of Finland were used in the study. The response rate for the schools was 92%, and for the teachers' questionnaires, 60%. A total of

442 teachers participated in the study, but 14 teachers did not indicate their subject. The teachers were grouped into four different age groups: 21–30 years (13%), 31–40 years (25%), 41–50 years (31%), and >50 years (30%) by age. Forty-nine percent of the schools were located in urban areas, while the contribution of densely populated areas was 21% and rural areas 30%.

The teachers were grouped according to the major subject they taught at school, which is commonly the same discipline they studied during their pre-service studies. In general there were more female teachers (53%–97%), with the exception of history, in which 65% of the teacher were male (Table 1).

Table 1. Teachers categorized according to major subject and gender.

Teachers	Women	Men	Total
Mother tongue	34	1	35
Swedish	22	1	23
Other languages	14	2	16
English	31	3	34
Biology	22	8	30
Geography	7	3	10
Physics	7	9	16
Chemistry	14	5	19
Mathematics	22	12	34
History	13	24	37
Religion	19	7	26
Home economics	35	3	38
Physical & health education	18	16	34
Music	14	8	22
Visual arts	17	4	21
Crafts	22	11	33
Missing	8	6	14
Total	319	123	442

3.2. Formation of SE Dimensions in Teaching

Five different sustainability dimensions were found by EFA, so that the number of items varied between three and eight in different ST factors (Table 2). For social sustainability, two different types of dimensions were found, namely the general social dimension at the school and society levels, and well-being at the individual level. The cultural dimension was also a factor. Cronbach's alpha of the different variables varied between 0.87 and 0.91, showing that the internal consistency of the variables was very high. Factor loadings were rather high in all variables. Items' means indicate that sustainability issues were not considered very frequently ($M = 2.7$–3.5) by the teachers. The item and variable averages indicate that well-being and social sustainability were the most frequently considered aspects, while ecological, economic, and cultural aspects were considered least frequently.

Table 2. Cronbach alfa, factor loadings, means, and standard deviations of different ST factors and their items.

ST Variables Found in EFA	Factor Loading	M	SD
Factor 1. Ecological sustainability (Alpha 0.91)		2.72	0.87
Environmental influences of industry, traffic, and power production.	0.92	2.79	1.13
Environmental influences of the use of natural resources.	0.88	2.98	1.12
Prerequisites of the well-being of living nature (e.g., sufficiency and good quality of habitat).	0.86	2.70	1.13
Nearby nature and its function (e.g., elements' cycling, energy flow).	0.79	2.71	1.18
Environmental influences of agriculture.	0.76	2.14	1.10
Built environment and its function (e.g., population, mills, traffic lanes).	0.68	2.58	1.10
Environmentally responsible ways to travel.	0.54	2.55	1.06
Recycling of goods.	0.39	3.35	1.09
Factor 2. Cultural sustainability (Alpha 0.91)		2.86	0.98
Scandinavian cultural heritage.	0.95	2.72	1.16
European cultural heritage.	0.95	2.84	1.22
Finnish cultural heritage.	0.85	3.19	1.21
Cultural identity and its formation.	0.73	2.98	1.22
Multiculturalism in Finland.	0.62	2.89	1.08
The cultural heritage of the school neighborhood.	0.62	2.57	1.11
Factors 3. Social sustainability (Alpha 0.87)		3.28	0.81
Democratic school community.	0.84	2.95	1.10
Preventing alienation.	0.73	3.15	1.06
Democratic society.	0.67	2.70	1.11
Preventing and intervening in bullying.	0.61	3.81	0.93
Human rights and equality.	0.57	3.27	1.07
Tolerance.	0.53	3.78	0.96
Factor 4. Well-being (Alpha 0.89)		3.46	1.03
Physical wellbeing (e.g., health).	0.85	3.53	1.14
Mental wellbeing (e.g., mental health).	0.85	3.29	1.19
Social wellbeing (e.g., social issues, relationships between people).	0.82	3.55	1.07
Factors 5. Economic sustainability (Alpha 0.87)		2.65	0.97
Consumption habits and their importance for one's own finances.	1.05	2.64	1.18
Personal economy (e.g., planning and care of one's own budget).	0.73	2.53	1.26
Consumption habits and their importance for sustainable development.	0.64	2.52	1.12
Lifestyles and consumption habits.	0.53	2.92	1.05

3.3. Sustainability Dimensions in Teaching

The frequency of the teachers' use of different sustainability dimensions (ecological, economic, social, wellbeing, and cultural) in their teaching was measured. Science teachers, especially biology and geography teachers, considered the ecological sustainability aspect rather often (Table 3). This aspect was least considered by language, religion, and music teachers. Other subject teachers considered ecological dimensions "rather seldom" (2 on the Likert scale) or "sometimes" (3 on the Likert scale). Economic aspects were considered most often by home economics, history, and biology teachers, but in this case the frequency was "sometimes" or "rather often" (4 on the Likert scale). Teaching on economic issues followed a similar pattern to the ecologic dimension, so that language and music teachers considered the dimension rather seldom, which was also common among other subject teachers.

Social aspects and well-being were the themes most commonly considered by the teachers. Social sustainability issues were considered rather often, especially by religion, history, and music teachers, and well-being by the teachers of physical and health education, home economics, biology, and geography. This aspect was least frequently considered by chemistry, mathematics, and physics teachers, and by the group of other language teachers. Cultural sustainability was considered especially by mother tongue, history, music, visual arts, and religion teachers. As in social sustainability, cultural issues were least frequently considered by chemistry, mathematics, and physics teachers (Table 3).

Table 3. Means (*M*) and standard deviations (*SD*) of teachers' ST, when calculated as an average of the items in each SE factor.

Teacher/ST	Ecological		Economic		Social		Well-Being		Cultural	
	M	*SD*	*M*	*SD*	*M*	*SD*	*M*	*SD*	*M*	*SD*
Mother tongue	2.15	0.61	2.40	0.77	**3.34**	0.74	**3.28**	0.86	**3.37**	0.75
Swedish	2.19	0.69	2.14	0.67	3.04	0.69	**3.20**	0.76	3.13	0.78
English	2.19	0.74	2.18	1.11	3.18	0.93	3.11	0.88	2.69	0.91
Other languages	2.06	0.68	1.94	0.77	2.68	1.02	3.02	1.01	2.70	0.64
Biology	**4.04**	0.45	3.08	0.74	**3.29**	0.61	**4.22**	0.63	2.93	0.76
Geography	**4.00**	0.56	2.65	1.10	3.13	0.67	**4.03**	0.87	2.67	0.67
Physics	**3.22**	0.73	2.38	1.10	2.85	0.78	2.57	0.98	1.80	0.85
Chemistry	3.09	0.68	2.21	0.85	2.58	0.65	2.23	0.63	1.47	0.47
Mathematics	2.90	0.67	2.42	0.81	2.82	0.79	2.66	0.81	1.83	0.77
History	2.71	0.92	**3.30**	0.93	**3.71**	0.76	3.18	0.94	**3.34**	0.85
Religion	2.50	0.58	2.83	0.87	**3.81**	0.74	**3.83**	0.97	**3.55**	0.65
Home economics	2.85	0.63	**3.50**	0.67	**3.39**	0.81	**4.23**	0.68	2.95	0.88
Physical & health education	2.59	0.73	2.47	0.91	**3.54**	0.58	**4.48**	0.67	2.44	0.73
Music	1.86	0.77	2.01	0.99	**3.65**	0.71	**3.83**	0.90	**3.73**	0.85
Visual arts	2.83	0.70	2.55	0.95	**3.39**	0.96	**3.27**	0.98	**3.85**	0.66
Crafts	2.82	0.80	2.98	0.84	**3.28**	0.61	**3.29**	0.74	2.79	0.74
Total	2.72	0.88	2.64	0.98	**3.27**	0.82	**3.44**	1.02	2.87	0.99

Note: Highest means are bold (M ≥ 3.2).

The boxplots in Figures 1 and 2 show the distribution of the data. The outliers and extremes show that in many subject teacher groups there were individual teachers who did not share the general views of that group.

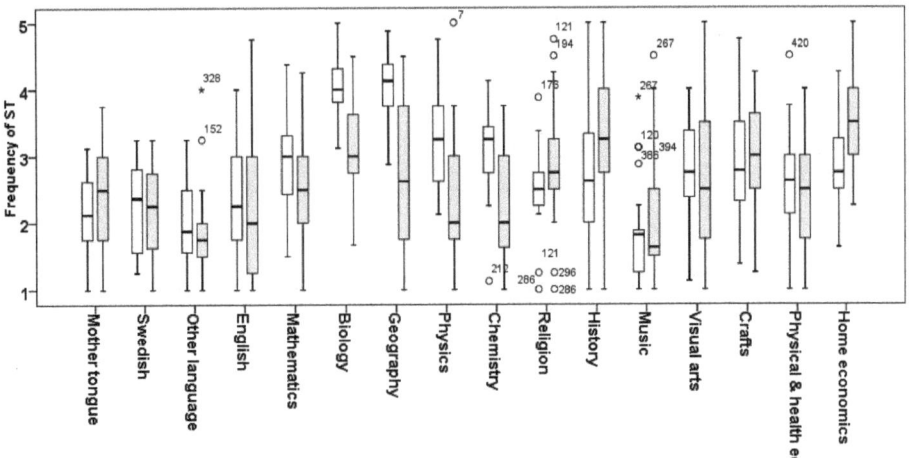

Figure 1. The frequency of ecological and economic ST of the different subject teachers. White bars = ecological sustainability; gray bars = economic sustainability. Boxplots show the median, interquartile range, outliers (circles), and extreme cases (stars) of individual variables.

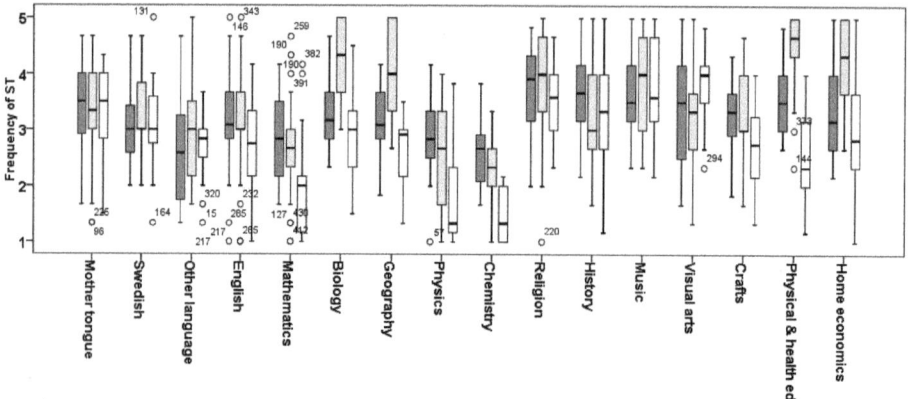

Figure 2. The frequency of social, well-being, and cultural ST of the different subject teachers. Dark gray bars = social sustainability; light gray bars = well-being; white bars = cultural sustainability.

3.4. Differences between the Teachers

There seemed to be clear differences in teachers' ST (Table 3, Figures 1 and 2); thus, univariate analysis of variance (ANOVA) was used to determine which of the independent variables (age, subject of the teacher, or location of the school) were important (Table 4). To test the differences between the teachers, Levene's test indicated that the variances between the teacher groups did not differ significantly ($p > 0.05$) from each other. The results show that the teacher's subject was the most important factor explaining the frequency of ST, accounting 20%–43% of the variance ($SS_{effect} + SS_{error}$) (Table 4).

Table 4. Results of the ANOVA testing the significance of dependent variables.

Dimensions of ST	F	df	p	Partial Eta Squared
Ecological sustainability				
Subject	16.95	15	<0.001	0.40
Age	6.22	3	<0.001	0.04
Economic sustainability				
Subject	7.34	15	<0.001	0.22
Age	8.43	3	<0.001	0.06
Social sustainability				
Subject	6.24	15	<0.001	0.20
Age	3.85	3	NS	-
Well-being				
Subject	14.47	15	<0.001	0.36
Age	3.00	3	NS	-
Cultural sustainability				
Subject	18.99	15	<0.001	0.43
Age	2.65	3	0.049	0.02

The reasons for the results can be seen in Figures 1 and 2, in which the boxplots show large variations between the teachers. Multiple comparisons of ANOVA showed that, for instance, biology and geography teachers considered ecological sustainability issues significantly more often in their teaching than most other teacher groups (Tukey's test, $p < 0.001$). Language teachers were different from other teachers in that they thought significantly less about ecological issues than the teachers in biology, physics, chemistry, and mathematics (Tukey's test, $p < 0.001$). The home economics teachers considered economic sustainability significantly more often than, for instance, language, mathematics, physics, chemistry and music teachers (Tukey's test, $p < 0.001$). In ecological sustainability, the distribution was the largest among history teachers and in economic sustainability among visual arts teachers (Figure 1).

In social, well-being, and cultural sustainability, the overall picture was different from that of ecological and economic ST (Table 3, Figure 2). In teaching on social sustainability the teachers did not differ as much from each other as in ecological and economic sustainability. For instance, in social sustainability, religion teachers were significantly different (Tukey's test, $p < 0.001$) only from mathematics, other language, and chemistry teachers. Well-being was most often considered by the teachers of physical/health education, home economics, biology, and geography. For instance, the teachers of physical/health education differed significantly from all language, mathematics, physics, chemistry, and crafts teachers (Tukey's test, $p < 0.001$). Likewise, music and visual arts teachers considered cultural sustainability more often than mathematics, physics, chemistry, and English teachers (Tukey's test, $p < 0.001$). Well-being and cultural dimensions were the least frequently considered by mathematics, physics, and chemistry teachers, and they differed significantly from most other teacher groups (Tukey's test, $p < 0.001$).

3.5. Holistic Approach in SE

The teachers were asked how often they used more holistic ST dimensions in their teaching. (Table 5). In these six items interactions between sustainability dimensions (ecological, economic, social, and cultural) were described. The challenges between different SD dimensions can be considered in various ways in ST; in Table 5 only reduced relations are named.

Table 5. Relationships between different possible sustainability challenges.

Main Type of Challenge Relation	Items
Ecological–Social (Eco.–Soc.)	The challenges caused by the environmental changes to human living conditions (e.g., refugees, conflicts, famine).
Ecological–Economic (Eco.–Econ.)	The challenges caused by the environmental changes to the economy (devolution of economic activity, poverty).
Social–Ecological (Soc.–Eco.)	The challenges caused by human activities to the condition of the environment (e.g., climate change).
Social–Economic (Soc.–Eco.)	The challenges caused by human activities to the stability of the economy (e.g., market crash, warfare).
Economic–Ecological (Econ.–Eco.)	The challenges caused by the economic growth to the condition of environment (e.g., exhaustion of natural resources).
Economic–Social (Econ.–Soc.)	The challenges caused by economic growth to human wellbeing (e.g., the uneven distribution of material wellbeing).

The frequency with which the teachers used holistic approaches in their teaching varied and the teachers differed significantly from each other (ANOVA $F = 8.7–11.4$, $df = 15$, $p < 0.001$) (Figure 3). Overall, holistic approaches were used rather seldom by most teacher groups, except science, history, and religion teachers. Human activity as a cause of challenges in ecological sustainability (Soc.–Eco.) was considered mostly by mathematics and science teachers. In general, biology, geography, history, and religion teachers used several holistic approaches. These teachers used holistic approaches equally or even more often than they used some of the unidimensional sustainability aspects (Figure 3, Table 1). Overall, the challenges caused to economic sustainability by other sustainability aspects were rather rarely considered by most subject teacher groups. A holistic teaching approach in which the ecological aspect was included as the main cause or effect tended to be most commonly used in ST. Only biology, geography, religion, and history teachers reported that they consider an economic–social combination (Econ.–Soc.) at least sometimes in their teaching (Figure 3).

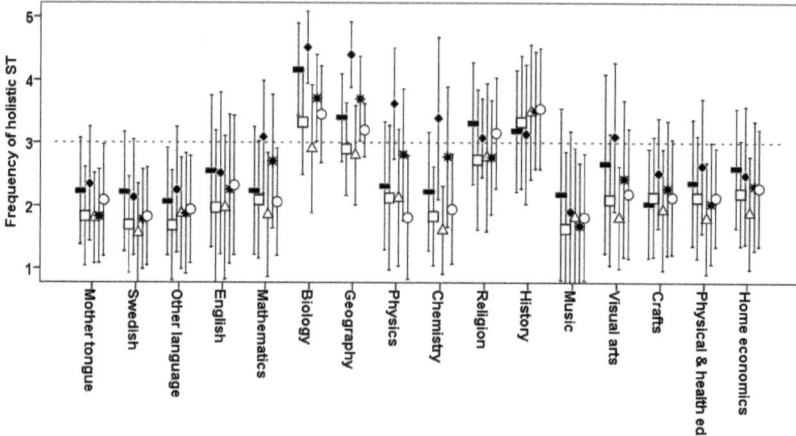

Figure 3. The frequency of holistic approaches in ST (challenges between ecological, economic, and social SD) carried out by different teacher groups. Black rectangle = Eco.–Soc.; White square = Eco.–Econ.; Black square = Soc.–Eco.; White triangle = Soc.–Econ.; Black star = Econ.–Eco.; White circle = Econ.–Soc.

3.6. Teachers' Perceptions of Their SE Competencies

Teachers' perceptions of their general competence in SE were assessed using five items by using a five-point Likert scale. On average, teachers rated their knowledge of the cross-curricular theme "Responsibility for the environment, wellbeing and sustainable future" satisfactory or higher (Figure 4). There were still differences between the teachers (one-way ANOVA, $F = 4.1$, $df = 15$, $p < 0.001$). For instance, biology and geography teachers' responses indicated that their conceptions on their knowledge of the cross-curricular theme was higher than among most other subject teachers, especially physics, chemistry, mathematics, language, and physical and health education teachers (Tukey's test, $p < 0.05$).

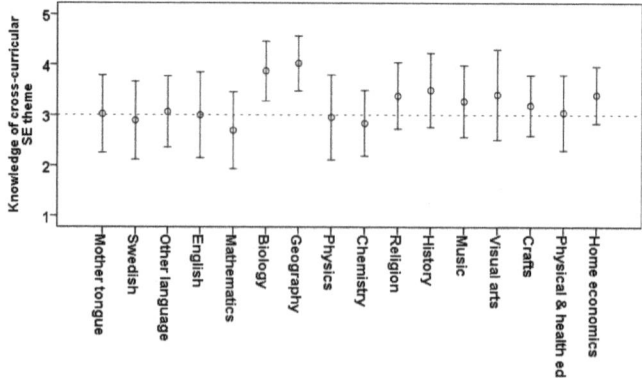

Figure 4. Teachers' conceptions of their knowledge about the cross-curricular theme "Responsibility for the environment, wellbeing and sustainable future".

Teachers' belief in their competence to teach different dimensions of sustainability (ecological, economic, social, and cultural) was examined using four items. The average competence in different dimensions varied from 2 ("rather poorly" in economic and cultural sustainability by mathematics, physics and chemistry teachers) to nearly 5 ("very well" in ecological sustainability by biology and geography teachers) (Figure 5). To study how much each subject teacher group differed in their competence perceptions, the average SE competence was calculated as the mean of the four SE competence items and analyzed with a one-sample t-test. The analysis indicates that there were significant differences ($p < 0.01$) in SE competence perceptions within the subject teacher groups (Figure 5). Mathematics, biology, physics, and chemistry teachers felt significantly more competent in teaching ecological dimensions when compared to their average sustainability competence ($p < 0.01$). Mother tongue and visual arts teachers felt significantly more competent in the economic dimension ($p < 0.01$), while mathematics and home economics teachers felt less competent, respectively. In addition, the competence in the social dimension was rated significantly lower ($p < 0.01$) by mother tongue teachers when compared to their average competence. Similar trends, although not significant, could be found among other teachers (Figure 5).

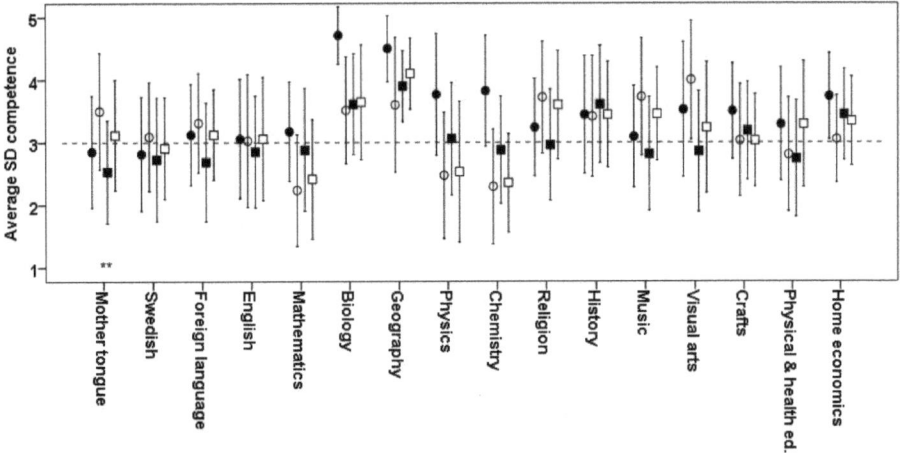

Figure 5. Teachers' perceptions of their competence (means and standard deviations) to manage different aspects of sustainability in their teaching. Black circle = ecological, white circle= economic, black square = social, and white square = cultural sustainability.

When calculated from the whole sample, teachers' contributions in different dimensions and holistic approaches in ST, perceptions of their SE competence, and knowledge of cross-curricular goals were in most cases significantly correlated ($p < 0.01$) with each other (Table 6). In most cases the relationship was moderate (rho = 0.3–0.49) or strong (rho ≥ 0.5), cf. [23]. For instance, the frequency of the ecological dimension used in ST correlated very strongly with all holistic dimensions in ST. The relationship was similar in the economic dimension, but in this case the correlations were mostly moderate. There were also strong correlations between different types of holistic dimensions in ST (Table 6). In some combinations the correlations represent a rather small association (rho = 0.17–0.27), for instance between the social, wellbeing, and cultural sustainability dimensions and holistic approaches of ST that emphasize the combination of ecological, economic, and social aspects (Soc.–Ecol., Econ.–Ecol., see Table 6). Likewise, there were non-significant or rather small correlations between the frequency of social, wellbeing, and cultural sustainability dimensions and the ecological, economic, or curricular competences in ST. On the contrary, ST in the ecological and economic dimensions correlated weakly with the social and cultural competence dimensions.

Small correlations were also found between some holistic approaches in ST and social and cultural SE competence. Overall, the correlations reflect at least three types of ST activity, one being strongly related to ecological-holistic-economic dimensions, another to social-economic-holistic dimensions, and the third to well-being-social-cultural dimensions (Table 6).

Table 6. Spearman's correlation coefficients (rho, $p < 0.01$) between different SE dimensions, holistic SE approaches in ST, and SE competences of all subject teachers.

	1	2	3	4	5	6	7	8	9	10	11	12	13	14	15
						SE dimensions									
1 Ecological															
2 Economic	0.57														
3 Social	0.30	0.51													
4 Well-being	0.32	0.41	0.59												
5 Cultural	0.15	0.40	0.58	0.33											
						Holistic approaches in ST									
6 Ecol.–Soc.	0.57	0.49	0.46	0.41	0.39										
7 Ecol.–Econ.	0.57	0.61	0.45	0.31	0.36	0.75									
8 Soc.–Ecol.	0.70	0.42	0.27	0.26	0.17	0.68	0.66								
9 Soc.–Econ.	0.50	0.52	0.48	0.31	0.42	0.68	0.78	0.58							
10 Econ.–Ecol.	0.64	0.49	0.32	0.19	0.23	0.67	0.73	0.74	0.70						
11 Econ.–Soc.	0.50	0.51	0.43	0.31	0.41	0.70	0.75	0.60	0.77	0.76					
						SE competences									
12 Ecological	0.52	0.30	NS	0.22	NS	0.40	0.32	0.46	0.29	0.40	0.33				
13 Economic	0.39	0.36	0.20	0.20	0.15	0.36	0.38	0.31	0.39	0.36	0.36	0.61			
14 Social	0.21	0.24	0.37	0.36	0.35	0.33	0.27	0.20	0.29	0.18	0.30	0.47	0.59		
15 Cultural	0.15	0.22	0.37	0.29	0.52	0.30	0.26	0.16	0.25	0.14	0.28	0.33	0.41	0.73	
16 Curricular	0.48	0.37	0.24	0.28	0.22	0.35	0.37	0.36	0.35	0.34	0.33	0.52	0.52	0.45	0.44

Note: Strongest correlations (rho ≥ 0.5) are presented in bold; NS, Not significant.

To classify the different subject teachers into larger subgroups, a decision tree analysis was also carried out with CHAD as the growing method to summarize the results (Table 7). The analysis ($F = 37$–81, $p < 000.1$) showed which subject teacher groups answered the questionnaire most similarly. The decision tree analysis classified subject teachers into roughly three or four different subgroups within each of the five sustainability dimensions. The largest averages in Table 7 indicate the highest subgroup activity within a SE dimension. For instance, in the ecological dimension mathematics, biology, physics, geography, chemistry, history, visual arts, crafts, and home economics formed one subgroup. On some occasions, only two or three subject teachers were classified into the same subgroup, such as history and home economics teachers to the economic dimension and biology, physical & health education, and home economics to the well-being dimension. The pattern varied according to the SE dimension, indicating that although subject teachers could be roughly classified into different SE subgroups, the classification strongly depends on the SE dimension in question. Mathematics, physics, chemistry, and language teachers formed the most distinct groups relating to their perceptions to ST, but for other teachers the main factor was their perception of different aspects of SE (Tables 6 and 7).

Table 7. Summary of classification of the decision tree analysis.

SE Dimensions/ Subgroups	Ecological	Economic	Social	Wellbeing	Cultural
1	3.08 (0.82)	2.48 (0.91)	2.75 (0.80)	2.52 (0.82)	1.78 (0.77)
	MA, BG, PH, GE, CH, HI, VIA, CR, HOE	MA, PH, MOT, GE, VIA, PHE	MA, PH, OL, CH	MA, PH, CH	MA, PH, CH
2	2.14 (0.71)	2.96 (0.82)	3.27 (0.75)	**4.31 (0.67)**	2.99 (0.80)
	MOT, SW, OL, EN, MU	BG, RE, CR	BG, MOT, SW, EN, GE, VIA, CR, HOE	BG, PHE, HOE	BG, SW, HOE
3	2.54 (0.66)	2.12 (0.91)	**3.67 (0.70)**	3.20 (0.86)	**3.52 (0.78)**
	RE, PHE	SW, OL, EN, CH, MU	RE, HI, MU, PHE	MOT, SW, OL, EN, HI, VIA, CR	MOT, RE, HI, MU, VIA
4	-	**3.38 (0.81)**	-	3.87 (0.91)	2.68 (0. 78)
		HI, HOE		GE, RE, MU	OL, EN, GE, CR, PHE

Note: MOT = mother tongue; SW = Swedish; EN = English; OL = other language; MA = mathematics; PH = physics; CH = chemistry; BG = biology; GE = geography; HI = history; RE = religion; MU = music; VA = visual arts; CR = crafts; HOE = home economics; PHE = physical & health education. Values are means and standard deviations (in parentheses).

3.7. Differences in Demographical Factors

In general, economic and ecological sustainability were the least frequently considered topics in the ST, and the well-being was the most often considered sustainability dimension for all age groups (Figure 6). There were significant differences between the teachers' age groups in the ST frequency only in the ecological and economic dimensions ($F = 8.4$, *df* = 3, $p < 0.01$) (Table 2). The oldest age group used ecological sustainability topics significantly more often in their teaching than any of the younger age groups (Tukey's test, $p < 0.01$). They also used economic and social topics significantly more in their teaching that the youngest age group (Tukey's test $p < 0.01$). In well-being and cultural sustainability, there were no significant differences between the age groups (Figure 6).

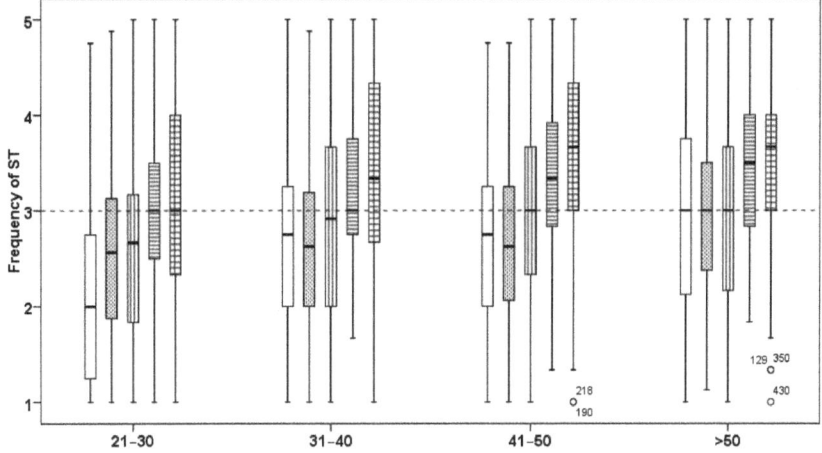

Figure 6. Frequency of different ST dimensions taught by four age groups of the teachers. White = economic, gray = ecological, vertical lines = cultural, horizontal lines = social, checked = wellbeing.

Due to the large number of schools and the varying number of teachers attending the study, the comparisons were carried out using only a non-parametric independent samples Kruskal–Wallis test. The results indicated that there were no differences between the schools in terms of how often the teachers used different dimensions of sustainability in their teaching. Differences between rural, densely populated, and urban areas could be studied with ANOVA, and the results showed that there were no significant differences between the different residential areas in any of the studied factors. The independent samples *t*-test also indicated no overall gender differences in any of the studied variables.

4. Discussion

4.1. Teachers' Main Subject Influence SE

In this study, the perceptions of lower secondary school subject teachers on SE were studied. The results indicated that there were large differences between the subject teachers in how they used ecological, economic, social, well-being, and cultural aspects, as well as holistic approaches, in their ST. Subject teachers also differed from each other in their perception of their competence to teach different dimensions of sustainability and their awareness of the cross-curricular theme "Responsibility for the environment, wellbeing and sustainable future" [5].

The most interesting result of this study was that the teachers' subject was the most important factor explaining their contribution in ST, their age being of only minor importance. Teachers' gender, school, or the location in different types of residential areas did not explain the differences between the subject teachers' perceptions. Teachers' professional development was likely the reason for the finding that older teachers used more ST than younger teachers. In a Swedish study [16] similar results were found; recently qualified teachers' perceptions of SD indicated a poorer understanding of SD than teachers who had been working longer than five years. The results of these studies contradict a British study, which found that student teachers have a more comprehensive understanding of SD than their mentors, the experienced teachers [24].

The lack of difference between the subject teachers in different schools is an interesting result, as in an earlier study, the data for which were collected in the same schools as in this study [9], ninth-grade students' pro-environmental behaviors could be explained by their personal factors, especially self-efficacy beliefs, which in turn was connected to their sustainability-related experiences in the school. In another Finnish survey on ninth-grade students' environmental interests, values, and attitudes, school-related differences were found [8]. Therefore, although subject teachers' perceptions of SE may not differ among schools, students' knowledge of sustainability issues, positive attitudes, and skills to act in sustainable ways may be promoted, for instance, by individual SE enthusiastic teachers and schools' sustainability-oriented action culture.

4.2. Subject Teachers' Strengths and Limitations in ST

On average, social sustainability and well-being were the aspects most often considered by teachers, and the cultural dimension was used more often than ecological and economic dimensions. The results are not in line with the studies that have investigated teachers' understanding of different aspects of SD in teaching [3,15,16]. These studies found that teachers' understanding was mostly focused on the ecological dimension. In our study, only mathematics, physics and chemistry teachers were clearly focused on the ecological dimension alone. The emphasis of teaching on ecological or environmental issues is attributed to the tradition of environmental education, which is more focused on environmental issues than SE [4,25].

There were also large differences in the frequency with which the teachers considered sustainability issues in their teaching. Our results suggest that although teachers may be uncertain what the different SD and SE dimensions are [14,16], they still consider sustainability-related issues in their subject-specific teaching. In general, as regards the ST frequencies, three different teacher groups could be roughly distinguished: those who considered at least three sustainability dimensions rather often and used several types of holistic approaches in their teaching (biology, geography, and history); those who considered two or three dimensions often but were not especially active in holistic teaching (mother tongue, religion, visual arts, crafts, music, physical/ health education, and home economics), and those who used only one SE dimension or considered only one holistic approach (mathematics, physics, chemistry, and language). The perceptions of the biology, geography, and history teachers of their SE competence and awareness of the sustainability curricular theme were higher when compared to the perceptions of other teachers. The results are partially in line with the Swedish study [14], which found that upper secondary school teachers differ in their understanding of the holistic perspective of SD, including economic, ecological, and social dimensions. As in this study, the Swedish study suggested that subject traditions are important factors that influence teaching, so that social science teachers emphasize social dimensions and science teachers emphasize ecological dimensions [14].

In the Swedish study [16] it was found that the teachers were unsure of their understanding of the economic dimension, which is in accordance with our study, in that the economic dimension was the least considered sustainability dimension in ST by some subject teacher groups. However, it is important to note that, in this study, more detailed differences between the subject teachers could be found as all subject teachers were studied separately. For instance, history and home economics teachers used economic aspects relatively often in their teaching. This is understandable, as sustainability issues are included in the curricula of these disciplines [5]. Home economics, biology and geography teachers consider lifestyles, consumption habits, and environmentally responsible behaviors often in their teaching. The second discipline of history teachers is social studies, and thus social and economic issues are often considered by history teachers.

Subject teachers had different strengths in their competence to teach on different sustainability themes. Due to the national curriculum [5] and teaching traditions, biology and geography teachers are often active in their teaching of the ecological dimension [2]. Also in this study, when compared to other teacher groups, biology and geography teachers most often taught ecological sustainability, but they also taught other sustainability dimensions often and used holistic viewpoints in their teaching. They were also very aware of the cross-curricular sustainability theme and generally felt very competent in ST, especially in the ecological dimension and well-being. The results cannot be fully compared with the Swedish studies [14,16], which found that the science teachers, including biology teachers, focused mostly on the ecological dimension. In Finland biology teachers most often teach geography as a second discipline and geography teachers most often have biology as a second discipline, thus influencing each other. The Finnish biology and geography curricula also shared related content, "The common environment" [5,6], so that more holistic and integrated environmental courses could be implemented.

This study shows that teachers in religion, home economics, history, and crafts used social, well-being, and cultural SE dimensions rather often in their teaching, because of the characteristics of their discipline. History and religion teachers did not often use the ecological aspect of sustainability in their teaching, but history teachers combined the ecological dimension into holistic approaches.

Overall, mathematics, physics, chemistry and language teachers used sustainability issues the least in teaching, considering only the ecological or social-cultural dimensions, respectively. For language teachers, the results of this study are in line with the Swedish findings [14] that many language teachers did not use sustainability issues in their teaching, because they did not see any relevance of SD to their subject. This is understandable, as mathematics, physics, chemistry and language teachers focus largely on subject-specific procedural knowledge and problem-solving skills. Recently it was suggested [15,26] that sustainability aspects can easily be included in science education. For instance, the relevance of scientific knowledge and skills can be considered in individual and societal contexts, together with different SE aspects.

4.3. Implications for Teacher Training and Education

On a global scale, it is widely accepted that SE is an important part of formal education, and it also forms an important part of school curricula. Researchers have argued that subject teachers' competence to teach sustainability issues is not very high, and they feel unsure about SE [3,11,14–16,24]. This study indicated that subject teachers had their own strengths and limitations in SE, which should be taken into account when planning and implementing SE in secondary schools. Subject teachers should become aware of their SE competences through their disciplines. Many in-service teachers already consider sustainability-related issues in their teaching, but do not combine them in a more holistic view of sustainability. Thus, subject teachers would benefit from courses considering the holistic and cross-curricular backgrounds of SD and SE, and how the teachers can combine SE aspects in their pedagogical content knowledge. In-service and student teachers would need training in SE, as suggested by many studies [11,15,16]. In teacher education, SE contexts should be readily included. Recently, teacher education is actively developing SE, for instance in different contexts of formal and non-formal science education [27,28].

In the renewed curriculum of basic education [6], transversal competences are emphasized in all subjects. One of these main competence areas is "Participation, agency and building of a sustainable future", which requires SE competences. The implementation of multidisciplinary learning content and the integration of different subjects is also a new cross-curricular goal in basic education, providing teachers with a context to cooperate and plan teaching, in which SE can be the main interdisciplinary approach. It is important that teachers are helped to recognize their strengths in SE, and can take other teachers' SE expertise into account.

4.4. Implications for SE Research

In general, the external validity of the study is very good, because a well-planned stratified sampling was used when gathering the data. When developing the questionnaire, the internal validity was confirmed by using the practices and research-based documents that describe the characteristics of SE in the school [5,18–22]. However, SE is a whole-school approach [29]; thus, the implications of its educational effectiveness are challenging to study. For instance, in this study the variation within the teachers in each school was so large that it may have exceeded the potential variation between the schools. The number of teachers varied from five to 14 in the participating schools and thus all subjects were not presented from every school. The subject of participating teachers also varied. In general, the comparisons of schools with the survey based on teachers' or students' responses to a limited number of Likert-scale items may be a rather rough measure of the complexity of SE. The comparative results between the schools should be interpreted with caution and the sources of variation. The differences between the schools had to be quite large to appear in teachers and students' average responses to Likert scales. Thus, although the statistical significance of differences between the schools or areas may be small, these differences can be important.

The results also reflect the methodological approach of the study, as sustainability-related issues in teaching were examined as such. It is obvious that these dimensions are considered by subject teachers without planned linkage to SE.

To find more detailed information about educational effectiveness in SE, teachers' and students' perceptions of sustainability issues should be studied with questionnaires that assess a range of versatile aspects of SE. This study was carried out in a research project, in which several aspects of educational effectiveness was studied (see e.g. [7,9,17]). In this study only teachers' perceptions of their teaching was investigated. Other SE aspects, such as teachers' sustainability-related values, self-efficacy beliefs and impacts on schools action culture will be published in another research papers.

5. Conclusions

The perceptions of lower secondary school subject teachers about their ST and competence to teach different aspects of sustainability were studied. The teacher's subject was the most important factor explaining teachers' contribution to ST, while their age had little importance. Teachers' general educational experience was likely related to the result that ST increased with age. Gender, school, or the location of the school in different residential areas did not have any effect on SE teaching. As groups, subject teachers differed from each other when teaching ecological, economic, social, well-being, and cultural aspects of SE or considering holistic aspects of SE. They also differed from each other in their perceptions of their competence to teach different dimensions of sustainability.

Every subject teacher group had its specific strengths and limitations in SE. For instance, biology and geography, history and social studies and to some extent also religion and ethics teachers considered several but different sustainability dimensions often and used holistic approaches in their sustainability-related teaching. However, it is likely that subject teachers were not especially aware of their competence in SE. In-service teacher training courses and SE courses in teacher education would be important in clarifying the background and pedagogy of SE. For instance, in mathematics, physics, chemistry, and language teacher education, problem-solving and multi-literacy pedagogy could be practiced using SE contexts. Teachers also need SE competence to carry out multidisciplinary teaching and cooperate with each other, as the whole-school approach has been found to be an effective educational approach in SE [29]. Subject teachers are experts in their discipline; thus, additional teacher training and education have the potential to result in teachers' higher SE competence.

Acknowledgments: The data of this study was collected during the SEED project (Sustainable Food Education for Self-Efficacy Development—SEED—How to encourage future citizens to act for a sustainable society) in Finland, under the auspices of the Academy of Finland, project number 128569. NFBE is acknowledged for their expertise in designing the stratified sampling of the schools.

Author Contributions: Anna Uitto and Seppo Saloranta designed and carried out the survey; Anna Uitto analyzed the data and was responsible in writing the paper; Seppo Saloranta commented different versions of the paper.

Conflicts of Interest: The authors declare no conflict of interest.

References

1. The United Nations Educational, Scientific and Cultural Organization (UNESCO). Shaping the Future We Want. In *UN Decade of Education for Sustainable Development (2005–2014)*; Final Report; UNESCO: Paris, France, 2014; Available online: http://unesdoc.unesco.org/images/0023/002303/230302e.pdf (accessed on 30 October 2016).

2. Rajakorpi, A.; Rajakorpi, H. *Sustainable Development in Schools and Educational Institutions?* Evaluation 7/200; National Board of Education: Helsinki, Finland, 2001; Available online: http://karvi.fi/app/uploads/2014/09/OPH_0501.pdf (accessed on 30 October 2016).

3. Pepper, C.; Wildy, H. Leading for sustainability: Is surface understanding enough? *J. Educ. Adm.* **2008**, *46*, 613–629. [CrossRef]

4. Breiting, S.; Wickenberg, P. The progressive development of environmental education in Sweden and Denmark. *Environ. Educ. Res.* **2010**, *16*, 9–37. [CrossRef]

5. National Core Curriculum for Basic Education (NFBE). *National Core Curriculum for Basic Education Intended for Pupils in Compulsory Education*; Finnish National Board of Education: Helsinki, Finland, 2004; Available online: http://www.oph.fi/english/curricula_and_qualifications/basic_education/curricula_2004 (accessed on 30 October 2016).

6. National Core Curriculum for Basic Education (NFBE). *National Core Curriculum for Basic Education Intended for Pupils in Compulsory Education*; Finnish National Board of Education: Helsinki, Finland, 2014. (In Finnish)

7. Uitto, A.; Saloranta, S. The relationship between secondary school students' environmental and human values, attitudes, interests and motivations. *Procedia Soc. Behav. Sci.* **2010**, *9*, 1866–1872. [CrossRef]

8.   Uitto, A.; Juuti, K.; Lavonen, J.; Byman, R.; Meisalo, V. Secondary school students' interests, attitudes and values concerning school science related environmental issues in Finland. *Environ. Educ. Res.* **2011**, *17*, 167–186. [CrossRef]

9.   Uitto, A.; Boeve-de Pauw, J.; Saloranta, S. Participatory school experiences as facilitators for adolescents' ecological behavior. *J. Environ. Psychol.* **2015**, *43*, 55–65. [CrossRef]

10. Boeve-de Pauw, J.; Gericke, N.; Olsson, D.; Berglund, T. The Effectiveness of Education for Sustainable Development. *Sustainability* **2015**, *7*, 15693–15717. [CrossRef]

11. Hart, P.; Nolan, K. A Critical Analysis of Research in Environmental Education. *Stud. Sci. Educ.* **1999**, *34*, 1–69. [CrossRef]

12. Shulman, L. Those who understand: Knowledge growth in teaching. *Educ. Res.* **1986**, *15*, 4–31. [CrossRef]

13. Jickling, B.; Wals, A.E.J. Globalization and environmental education: Looking beyond sustainable development. *J. Curric. Stud.* **2007**, *40*, 1–21. [CrossRef]

14. Borg, C.; Gericke, N.; Höglund, H.-O.; Bergman, E. The barriers encountered by teachers implementing education for sustainable development: Discipline bound differences and teaching traditions. *Res. Sci. Technol. Educ.* **2012**, *30*, 185–207. [CrossRef]

15. Burmeister, M.; Schmidt-Jacob, S.; Eilk, I. German chemistry teachers' understanding of sustainability and education for sustainable development—An interview case study. *Chem. Educ. Res. Pract.* **2013**, *14*, 169–176. [CrossRef]

16. Borg, C.; Gericke, N.; Höglund, H.-O.; Bergman, E. Subject- and experience-bound differences in teachers' conceptual understanding of sustainable development. *Environ. Educ. Res.* **2014**, *20*, 526–551. [CrossRef]

17. Uitto, A.; Saloranta, S. Contribution of secondary school subject teachers on the education for sustainable development. Part 8: Environmental, health and Informal-Outdoor Science education; Ossevoort, M., Carvalho, G., Co-eds. In *E-Book Proceedings of the ESERA 2011 Conference: Science learning and Citizenship*; Bruguière, C., Tiberghien, A., Clément, P., Eds.; European Science Education Research Association: Lyon, France, 2011; pp. 134–139. Available online: http://www.esera.org/media/ebook/ebook-esera2011. pdf (accessed on 30 October 2016).

18. UNESCO. *Education for Sustainable Development Lens: A Policy and Practice Review Tool*; Education for Sustainable Development in Action Learning & Training Tools No. 2-2010; UNESCO Education Sector: Paris, France, 2010; Available online: http://unesdoc.unesco.org/images/0019/001908/190898e.pdf (accessed on 30 October 2016).

19. Breiting, S.; Mayer, M.; Mogensen, F. *Quality Criteria for ESD-Schools, Guidelines to Enhance the Quality of Education for Sustainable Development*; SEED—Austrian Federal Ministry of Education, Science and Culture: Vienna, Austria, 2005; Available online: http://www.ensi.org/global/downloads/Publications/208/QC-GB.pdf (accessed on 30 October 2016).

20. Eco-School Program. Engaging the youth of today to protect the climate of tomorrow. Available online: http://www.ecoschools.global/ (accessed on 30 October 2016).

21. Loukola, M.-L. *Aihekokonaisuudet Perusopetuksen Opetussuunnitelmassa*; Opetushallitus: Helsinki, Finland, 2004. (In Finnish)

22. OKKA Foundation. Sustainable Development Certification of Educational Establishments. 2016. Available online: http://www.koulujaymparisto.fi/sivu.php?id=1820 (accessed on 30 October 2016).

23. Cohen, J. *Statistical Power Analysis for the Behavioral Sciences*; Erlbaum: Hillsdale, NJ, USA, 1988.

24. Summers, M.; Childs, A.; Corney, G. Education for Sustainable Development in Initial Teacher Training: Issues for Interdisciplinary Collaboration. *Environ. Educ. Res.* **2005**, *11*, 623–647. [CrossRef]

25. Hesselink, F.; van Kempen, P.P.; Wals, A. (Eds.) *ESDebate International Debate on Education for Sustainable Development*; IUCN: Gland, Switzerland; Cambridge, UK, 2000.

26. Stuckey, M.; Hofstein, A.; Mamlok-Naaman, R.; Eilks, I. The meaning of 'relevance' in science education and its implications for the science curriculum. *Stud. Sci. Educ.* **2013**, *49*, 1–34. [CrossRef]

27. Kervinen, A.; Uitto, A.; Kaasinen, A.; Portaankorva-Koivisto, P.; Juuti, K.; Kesler, M. Developing a Collaborative Model in Teacher Education—An Overview of a Teacher Professional Development Project. *LUMAT* **2016**, *4*, 67–86. Available online: http://lumat.fi/index.php/lumat/article/view/33/25 (accessed on 30 December 2016).

28. Tolppanen, S. Creating a Better World: Questions, Actions and Expectations of International Students on Sustainable Development and Its Education. Ph.D. Dissertation, Unit of Chemistry Teacher Education, Department of Chemistry, Faculty of Science, University of Helsinki, Helsinki, Finland, 2015.
29. Henderson, K.; Tilbury, D. *Whole-School Approaches to Sustainability: An International Review of Sustainable School Programs*; Report Prepared by the Australian Research Institute in Education for Sustainability (ARIES) for The Department of the Environment and Heritage; Australian Government: Sydney, Australia, 2004. Available online: http://daten.schule.at/dl/international_review2.pdf (accessed on 30 October 2016).

education sciences

Article

Systems Thinking for Understanding Sustainability? Nordic Student Teachers' Views on the Relationship between Species Identification, Biodiversity and Sustainable Development

Irmeli Palmberg [1,*], Maria Hofman-Bergholm [1], Eila Jeronen [2] and Eija Yli-Panula [3]

1   Education and Welfare Studies, Åbo Akademi University, 65100 Vaasa, Finland; mhofman@abo.fi
2   Faculty of Education, University of Oulu, 90014 Oulu, Finland; eila.jeronen@oulu.fi
3   Faculty of Education, University of Turku, 20500 Turku, Finland; eijyli@utu.fi
*   Correspondence: irmeli.palmberg@abo.fi; Tel.: +358-50-356-4930

Received: 26 May 2017; Accepted: 8 September 2017; Published: 15 September 2017

Abstract: Sustainability is a complex concept including ecological, economic and social dimensions, which in turn involve several aspects that are interrelated in a complex way, such as cultural, health and political aspects. Systems thinking, which focuses on a system's interrelated parts, could therefore help people understand the complexity of sustainability. The aim of this study is to analyse student teachers' level of systems thinking regarding sustainability, especially the ecological dimension, and how they explain the relationship between species identification, biodiversity and sustainability. Nordic student teachers ($N = 424$) participated in a questionnaire and their open answers were content-analysed and categorised. The results indicate the student teachers' low level of systems thinking regarding ecological sustainability. About a quarter of them (25.4%) had a basic level including interconnections (13.7%), additional feedback (8.9%) and also behavioural aspects (2.8%), but none of them reached an intermediate or advanced level. The low level of systems thinking could be explained by two main factors: (1) Systems thinking has not been used as an educational method of developing understanding of sustainability in teacher education programmes; and (2) systems thinking is also a result of life experiences; the older ones showing more systems thinking than the younger ones. Therefore, elementary forms of systems thinking should be an educational method already in primary education.

Keywords: sustainability; biodiversity; species identification; systems thinking; teacher education

---

1. Introduction

"*Sustainable development* cannot be achieved by technological solutions, political regulation or financial instruments alone. We need to change the way we think and act. This requires quality education and learning for sustainable development at all levels and in all social contexts [1]".

Sustainable development (hereafter used synonymously with *sustainability*) is a complex concept including ecological (environmental), economic and social dimensions, which in turn comprise several different aspects, all interrelated in a complex way. For example, cultural and health aspects are parts of the social dimension, and political aspects of the economic dimension. The importance of education for sustainable development (hereafter used synonymously with *sustainability education*) is often highlighted in international policy documents of education. It has been on the agenda for all stages of education since the publication of two documents: 'Brundtland report' [2], and 'Agenda 21' from the Rio de Janeiro conference [3]. Furthermore, the decade 2005–2014 was declared by UNESCO [4] as the United Nations' decade of education for sustainable development. The goal of the declaration was to promote sustainability at all levels of education. Despite all good plans and policy documents, sustainability education has not yet reached the goals for schools and higher education, according to recent research [5–10]. One reason can be the scarcity of sustainability education in teacher education worldwide [11–14]. If teachers have not had any opportunity to think, practise and develop their own understanding of sustainability during their education, they are not expected to do so in their future teaching either [14–16].

Society is still faced with a challenging paradox. Because of the economic growth and development of society towards more market-based economies, many countries have invested in education which prepares their citizens for life in a so-called global knowledge-based economy, whereas sustainability is less emphasised [17]. There is an obvious problem with this development of society, since there is a contradiction between economic growth and sustainability. Economic growth is linked to increased consumption and increased emissions in the atmosphere, which, in turn, are strongly linked to increased environmental impact [18,19]. Consumption and finances, as well as political and social systems, have either direct or indirect impact on Earth's *biodiversity*. Like many policy documents about sustainability education, there are several theories, plans and recommendations about how the education for 'sustainability citizenship' [20] should be arranged. Some of them point out critical pedagogy combined with environmental aspects and ecological politics, involving active participation of teachers and students [21,22].

The importance of integrating *systems thinking* into education has also been emphasised in order to promote understanding of the complex nature of sustainability [23,24]. Systems thinking is a holistic way of analysing how a system's constituent parts are interrelated and how the system works over time and within the context of larger systems [25,26]. Systems thinking could therefore be used to deepen people's holistic thinking about sustainability. It is important to develop a comprehensive understanding of complex casual relationships, as relationships between human systems and natural systems might be. The starting point for managing the complex understanding of sustainability is therefore to develop a holistic understanding of key ecological concepts and the role of biodiversity and species identification. Basic knowledge about species, their identification and life history are important aspects for learning and understanding biodiversity (more in Sections 1.1 and 1.2). Teachers have a central role in providing students with opportunities for understanding sustainability.

Does teacher education give student teachers the necessary tools to understand the importance of everyone's role in the system? The aim of this study is to analyse student teachers' level of systems thinking regarding sustainability, especially the ecological dimension of sustainability, and how they explain the relationship between species identification, biodiversity and sustainable development. Student teachers are university students who study education as their main subject in order to become primary-school teachers (for grades 1–6, 1–4 or 1–7). As a theoretical framework we focus on these main concepts and their role in understanding sustainability.

1.1. Species Identification and Ecological Literacy for Understanding of Sustainability

An undeniable fact is that newly qualified teachers teach about nature and science using the skills they obtained during the obligatory part of their teacher education. Knowledge of species and species' role in the ecosystem constitute an important core of biology teaching [27]. Knowledge of species and identification skills are factors which are also important in developing people's interest in environmental issues and sustainability [28,29]. It is easier to understand abstract processes in ecology when well-known species are included [30–33]. Species identification skills, an interest in nature and outdoor experiences, in turn, develop people's understanding of environmental issues and a sustainable lifestyle [28,29,34–36].

An understanding of ecological key concepts and processes helps people to see more complex relationships in the natural and human systems [36,37]. Unfortunately, the level of people's knowledge of species has decreased significantly during the past 20 years [28,29,38–41]. At the same time, also their knowledge of ecological key concepts and understanding of ecological processes have decreased [37,42–44] to such an extent that the phenomenon has been referred as *ecological illiteracy* [36,45,46].

In the 1980s *environmental literacy* was positioned as an essential goal of environmental education. This education was supposed to develop ecological knowledge, socio-political knowledge, and knowledge of environmental issues, as well as to adopt environmentally responsible behaviour [47]. The concept *ecological literacy* has been used synonymously to environmental literacy by several researchers, while for example Cutter-Mackenzie and Smith [48] emphasise the pedagogical content knowledge and fundamental ideas and approaches in environmental education as a special part of ecological literacy. A person's ecological literacy has been defined as their capacity to understand the systems in nature by understanding key ecological systems and characteristic features of ecology [49,50]. Ecological literacy could therefore form the basis of environmental sustainability as a more positive approach than focusing only on environmental problems [47,51].

The fact that Nordic student teachers possess low levels of species identification [29] and ecological knowledge [37] makes it interesting to study how they think about the relationship between species identification, biodiversity and sustainable development.

1.2. Biodiversity for Understanding of Sustainability

Biodiversity is fundamental for continuous life on Earth. It is also essential for human health and resilience [52], as well as for social and economic development [4,53]. Biodiversity means variation richness among all living organisms at three levels: 1. Genetic diversity (richness of the variety and range of genes within and between populations of organisms); 2. Species diversity (the number of species and number of individuals of each species in a particular location); and 3. Ecosystem diversity (variety of habitats, living communities, and ecological processes). These levels are also important parameters of sustainability, when reflecting the interaction of ecological, economic and social issues [3,54–58].

Biodiversity has been described as one of the major pathways to sustainability [59] and the protection of biodiversity as one of the basic roads to sustainability [60]. Therefore, basic knowledge about species, their identification and life history have been considered to be fundamental components for learning and understanding biodiversity [31,33,57,61]. Biodiversity education in turn can be seen as a model for sustainability education, while sustainability education is one instrument among others (e.g., technical innovations and restrictions by law) for achieving a sustainable future [62].

People's understanding of biodiversity, however, seems to have declined significantly during the past decades [60,62,63]. A global problem today is therefore that all three dimensions of biodiversity have been simplified and homogenised, while species extinction continues, mainly caused by human activities [64]. People take the term biodiversity to refer mostly to the animal kingdom and associate it with words connected with environmental problems [60], or, they only consider the economic values of biodiversity and nature [65]. One reason can be the significant decline in general knowledge of common organisms [29,38,41,66], but also problems in understanding what a sustainable use of biodiversity means [60].

The situation is not better regarding teachers and student teachers. Previous research reveals that they do not understand what biodiversity means and everything it includes [59,60,67–69]. It was, however, easier for student teachers to explain ecology-related concepts when they had relevant knowledge of species occurring in a habitat [70]. Magntorn's idea in learning to 'read nature' [50] is that taxonomy can be linked to systems thinking via the autecology of the species (the ecological relationships of a particular plant or animal species). Although students do not understand the complexity of biodiversity, they do, according to another study [63], have positive attitudes towards it. Previous research emphasises the importance of the preparation of student teachers in biodiversity education [61,71]. Therefore, we find it important to analyse student teachers' understanding of biodiversity, what they include in the concept and how they describe the importance of biodiversity for sustainability.

1.3. Systems Thinking for Understanding of Sustainability

Systems thinking is understood as the ability to see the world as a complex system where everything is connected to everything else [72]. It is an important factor in order to develop thinking in education. The challenge for education is to develop a pedagogy that provides individuals with knowledge about how different choices affect society [73]. Systems thinking, being the capacity of identifying various biophysical and social components in a given environmental context and the interrelations in whole systems [24], should therefore be based at least on critical thinking and reflection, deliberation and action competence [26,74]. Systems thinking is a way of thinking that helps people see their role from a holistic point of view. It is more than causal thinking, which, however, is part of systems thinking [75]. Systems thinking is focused on processes and entirety instead of parts or details [25,76]. System dynamics and systems thinking can be taught without involving sustainability, but sustainability cannot be taught without involving systems thinking [77].

The level of systems thinking can be described, and also assessed, in different ways. Draper [72] associates seven thinking skills with systems thinking: structural, dynamic, generic, operational, scientific, closed-loop, and continuum thinking, whereas Stave and Hopper [78] identify the same skills and several more as seven different levels of activities in systems thinking: recognising interconnections, identifying feedback, understanding dynamic behaviour, differentiating types of flows and variables, using conceptual models, creating simulation models, and testing policies (see Table 1). The levels of activities are based on Bloom's taxonomy [79], and they can be arranged as a continuum from a low (basic) to a high (advanced) level of systems thinking, with the next level always including the previous one. The basic level includes three levels of systems thinking, while the intermediate and advanced levels have two levels of systems thinking each.

Table 1. Skills and levels in systems thinking (Skills according to Draper [72]; levels of systems thinking, indicators and assessment according to Stave and Hopper [78]).

Skills and Their Main Contents	Levels of Systems Thinking and Indicators of Achievement that a Person Should Be Able to Do	Assessment
1. Structural thinking Understanding interrelations	1. Recognising interconnections - identify parts of a system - identify causal connections among parts - recognise that the system is made up of the parts and their connections - recognise emergent properties of the system	- list of systems parts - connections represented in words or diagrams - description of the systems in terms of its parts and connections - definition of emergent properties - description of properties the system has that the components alone do not
2. Dynamic thinking Ability to see and deduce behaviour patterns	2. Identifying feedback - recognise chains of causal links - identify closed loops - describe polarity of a link - determine the polarity of a loop	- representation of causality and loops in words or diagrams - diagram indicating polarity
3. Generic thinking Ability to observe generic system structures	3. Understanding dynamic behaviour - describe problems in terms of behaviour over time - understand that behaviour is a function of structure - explain the behaviour of a particular causal relationship or feedback loop - explain the behaviour of linked feedback loops - explain the effect of delays - infer basic structure from behaviour	- representation of a problematic trend in words or graphs - story of how problematic behaviour arises from interactions among system components - story about what will happen when one piece of the system changes - story of the causal structure likely generating a given behaviour

Table 1. *Cont.*

Skills and Their Main Contents	Levels of Systems Thinking and Indicators of Achievement that a Person Should Be Able to Do	Assessment
4. Operational thinking Understanding how things really work, not in theory	4. Differentiating types of variables and flows - classify parts of the system according to their functions - distinguish accumulations from rates - distinguish material from information flows - identify units of measure for variables and flows	- table of system variables by type - types of variables with units
5. Scientific thinking Ability to quantify relations, hypothesise and test assumptions and models	5. Using conceptual models - use a conceptual model of system structure to suggest potential solutions to a problem	- story of the expected effect of an action on a given problem - justification of why a given action is expected to solve a problem
6. Closed-loop thinking Recognising internal circular causality of cause-effect feedback	6. Creating simulation models - represent relationships between variables in mathematical terms - build a functioning model - operate the model - validate the model	- model equations - simulation model - model run - compare model output to observed behaviour
7. Continuum thinking Recognising continuous processes in real-world phenomena	7. Testing policies - identify places to intervene within the system - hypothesize the effect of changes - use model to test the effect of changes - interpret model output with respect to problem - design policies based on model analysis	- list of policy levers - description of expected output for given change - model output - comparison of output from different hypothesis tests - policy design

Stave and Hopper [78] also developed indicators of achievement and assessment tests for the seven levels. These indicators and tests are used as a basis in the analysis of the level of the student teachers' systems thinking in this study (see Methods). Indicators of achievement also include aspects of behaviour and action, which means a wider perspective of systems thinking than only an organisational level, and for which Flood [80] therefore used the concept 'socio-ecological perspective of systems thinking'. Action orientation, learning how to act and how actions affect human and the environment in turn constitute the basis in an ecosocial approach of education for sustainable lifestyle [81,82].

2. The Aim of the Study and Research Questions

This is the second part of the Nordic-Baltic case studies of student teachers' views of species, biodiversity and sustainable development. The first part [29] provided a comprehensive review of previous research on the theme and an overview of 456 student teachers' species identification skills, their interest in and opinion of the importance of species, biodiversity and sustainable development. Because the student teachers' ability to identify very common species was low, although a majority of them regarded species identification as important or very important in general (55%) and especially for sustainable development (86%), in the same way as biodiversity was for sustainable development (92%), it is fundamental to study further, and in more detail, how the student teachers perceive the relationship between species identification, biodiversity and sustainable development. Do they describe interrelations in the complex system of sustainability? The aim of this study is to analyse student teachers' level of systems thinking regarding sustainability, especially the ecological dimension of sustainability, and how they explain the relationship between species identification, biodiversity and sustainable development.

The following research questions guided the study:

1. How do student teachers describe the relationship between species identification, biodiversity and sustainable development?
2. What level of systems thinking do student teachers' answers reflect?

3.   Are there any differences in student teachers' answers with respect to their backgrounds (the country where they participated in teacher education, their gender or age)?

3. Materials and Methods

In total, 424 second- to fourth-year student teachers in three Nordic countries (225 Finnish, 68 Norwegian, and 131 Swedish) participated in the survey as volunteers. The student teachers had taken the obligatory course/courses in biology or science at least half a year before taking part in the survey. The majority of them (82%) were women, 65 percent were under 25 years old, 24 percent were aged 25–35 and 11 percent were over 35. They thus represented the typical group of student teacher by age, gender and completed obligatory studies in biology or science in the Nordic countries [29]. There were, however, some differences in students' age distribution in the three countries. The majority of the Norwegian students (81%) were under 25, while the corresponding percentages for the Finnish and Swedish students were 70 and 50. Nearly 23 percent of the Swedish students, but only 5 percent of the Finnish and 9 percent of the Norwegian students, were over 35. Age and gender were selected as probable factors affecting understanding of sustainability based on previous research, e.g., [9,15]. An interesting question was also whether the different teacher education programmes in these countries [29] have any effects on their student teachers' ways of thinking about species identification, biodiversity and sustainability.

In addition to the questions about the students' background, the survey consisted of two parts: a species identification test and a comprehensive questionnaire with fixed, multiple-choice and open questions (see more details about the total survey in [29]). All material was collected during one single session, but for this study, an open, summarising question from the questionnaire was chosen as the main question ('Describe your opinion about the relationship between species identification, biodiversity and sustainable development'). The student teachers were asked to describe their own view about the relationship between species identification, biodiversity and sustainable development. They were encouraged to use some kind of mind-map or other sketches in their answer. They could also specify their view about the importance of species identification and biodiversity for sustainable development in two additional questions. These questions were used as a complement to the main question, but also to ensure the researchers' correct interpretations of the main question.

The student teachers' answers were first coded and carefully transcribed together with possible mind-maps and sketches. The sketches and texts were then analysed mainly using inductive content analysis [83,84], but the analysis was also guided by Stave and Hopper's model of the seven levels of systems thinking (see Table 1). The analysis can therefore be considered a mix between inductive and deductive content analysis, i.e., an abductive approach in phenomenological methodology [85].

The inductive content analysis resulted in four categories. The first category, *no answer*, comprises a range of answers from a total lack of attempts to answers where students pointed out that they did not understand the question (e.g., by writing a question mark or sentences such as 'I do not know', 'I do not have enough knowledge to answer', 'I do not understand the question'). Answers where students only repeated the names of the three key concepts (species identification, biodiversity and sustainable development) without describing them are also included in this category. The second category, *answers involving nonsense or cliché*, includes answers which clearly show that students had not understood the relationship but still tried to explain something, and often used some kind of clichés. The third category, *answers involving partial relationships*, includes several kinds of answers about the key words separately, but without indicating systems thinking. The fourth category includes different kinds of systems thinking, and was further categorised according to Stave and Hopper's seven categories of systems thinking [78].

Two researchers read the transcribed answers several times making notes and headings. They then individually categorised the answers and selected descriptive examples for every category. Finally, they compared and discussed their categorising until they could agree to 100 percent. All used categories and corresponding categories in Stave and Hopper's model [78] are summarised in Table 2.

Table 2. Categories used in the analysis of the student teachers' answers about the relationship between species identification, biodiversity and sustainable development, from the lowest to the highest level of possible systems thinking.

Categories Used in This Study	Corresponding Seven Categories in Stave and Hopper's Model [78] (Descriptions in Table 1)
No level of systems thinking	
1. No answer	-
2. Answers involving nonsense or cliché	-
3. Answers involving partial relationships	-
Basic level of systems thinking	Basic level of systems thinking
4. Answers involving interconnections	1. Recognising interconnections
5. Answers involving feedback	2. Identifying feedback
6. Answers involving behavioural aspects	3. Understanding dynamic behaviour
Intermediate level of systems thinking	Intermediate level of systems thinking
7. Answers involving variables and flows	4. Differentiating types of variables and flows
8. Answers involving conceptual models	5. Using conceptual models
Advanced level of systems thinking	Advanced level of systems thinking
9. Answers involving simulation models	6. Creating simulation models
10. Answers involving policy models	7. Testing policies

In the following section we will describe the recognised categories both quantitatively and qualitatively, using rates of responses, and citations and sketches as examples from every category. The citations and sketches are word-for-word translations from Finnish, Swedish or Norwegian into English, and marked with four-digit numbers to guarantee anonymity. The first digit indicates a student's home country: (1) Finland; (2) Sweden; and (3) Norway. The three remaining digits are individual student codes. In addition, the students' gender (F = female and M = male), as well as their age (1 <25, 2 =25–35 and 3 >35 years of age) are indicated after the four-digit numbers. For example, the code 1056F1 indicates a Finnish female student teacher aged 25 or under. Differences in the student teachers' answers with respect to their background (the country in which they participated in teacher education, their gender, or age) were tested for statistical significance by Pearson Chi-Square ($p < 0.001$).

4. Results

The student teachers' answers about the relationship between the species identification, biodiversity and sustainable development were very heterogeneous, including also different views on how important they consider species identification and biodiversity are for sustainable development. According to previous research, systems thinking could be an important way to understand sustainability, and the analysis of student teachers' systems thinking is therefore the main subject here and will be described in detail. We also found differences in the levels of systems thinking depending on the country in which they participated in teacher education or their age.

4.1. Student Teachers' Systems Thinking

The results show that the student teachers have no or just a basic level of systems thinking regarding ecological sustainability. The majority of students (74.6%) showed no systems thinking in their answers about the relationship between species identification, biodiversity and sustainable development. Systems thinking was, however, used by 25.4 percent of the students, but only on a basic level (Figure 1). None of the answers reached an intermediate or advanced level of systems thinking, and all figures are therefore presented here without the categories 7–10 (c.f. Table 2).

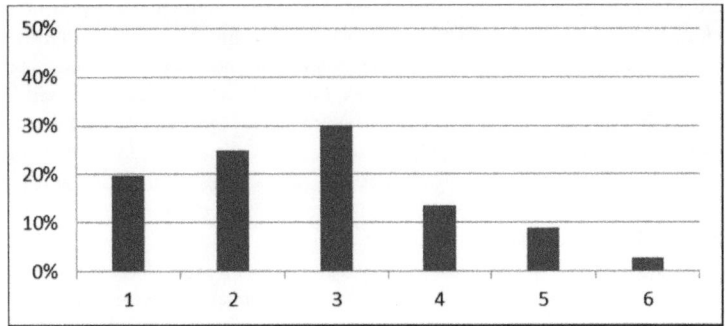

Figure 1. Student teachers' views about the relationship between species identification, biodiversity and sustainable development in six categories (1 = no answer; 2 = answers involving nonsense or cliché; 3 = answers involving partial relationships without systems thinking; 4 = answers involving interconnections; 5 = answers involving interconnections and feedback; 6 = answers involving interconnections, feedback and behavioural aspects). Note: Categories 7–10 were deleted from the figure because there were no answers in these categories.

The answers that lack systems thinking (categories 1–3) were very heterogeneous. Almost a fifth of all answers (19.8%) were placed in Category 1. In addition to many 'empty answers' the category included answers where student teachers explained why they could not answer the question, for example, that they were not familiar enough with the theme, or that they had never before thought about this kind of relationship.

Category 2 included answers with nonsense or clichés (24.8%). Nonsense answers, in this study, were answers which denied, or described something else than the relationship between or about the three given concepts. For example, a female student teacher, who considered biodiversity to be 'neither important nor unimportant' for sustainable development, expressed the relationship in this way: "In my opinion there is no such immediate relationship between these (concepts). Or in my own mind I think of them as separate classes, which I cannot connect" (1135F1). Some other student teachers named only food and protection. A female student, for example, ticked the alternatives 'very important' and 'important' for the importance of species identification respectively biodiversity for sustainable development, and explained the relationship in this way: "If you know plants and animals, you do not eat protected species" (1015F1). Another female student, who claimed to be interested in nature, wrote: "I'm not so familiar with small animals. Big animals, however, I think are important. Birds and frogs are not that important, are they? Snakes and reptiles are disgusting. I think [the relationship] is not that important. If an animal is meant to live, nature itself will take care of it (. . .)" (2081F1). There were also answers which were more like clichés than explanations: "The relationship is important, for us and for the future" (2093F1). The cycle must function and all species have a part in it" (2056F3). What exactly they meant, is unclear, because they did neither explain the importance of species identification nor biodiversity for sustainable development.

Category 3 (30% of the answers) consisted of answers involving many clear and important descriptions of some or all of the three given concepts, but lacking systems thinking. For example, a female student described the relationship in this way: "The three things are related because we humans need knowledge of species in order to maintain diversity. In a society with sustainable development, one must have knowledge of the species" (3049F1). Another female student explained the relationship in the following way: "The relationship is that if one is aware of the plants and animals one can contribute to sustainable development, which means that you are extra careful how you for example choose to deal with nature" (2059F1). Another student pointed out that: "If you want to have a deeper understanding, the importance of species identification increases. Species identification can help you appreciate biodiversity. A decrease in biodiversity makes the living environment and the whole earth more vulnerable. Development, which destroys biodiversity, cannot be sustainable" (1145F3). This category also comprises very short answers where student teachers named some details or topics that are relevant for the relationship, but without explaining how these are connected. Such topics were: endangered species and nature conservation; protection of biodiversity; edible and poisonous species; usefulness and wholesomeness of species for man; sufficiency of food; food chains and webs; indicators of the balance in nature; interest-increasing knowledge; knowledge and a need to do more for protection; knowledge to be familiar with and to appreciate one's own neighbourhood; the development of the relationship to nature.

Answers in categories 4–6 (25.4%) included systems thinking on a basic level. Student teachers in Category 4 (13.7%) recognised interconnections in the relationship between species identification, biodiversity and sustainable development. The relationship was described by a student in this way: "It is important to be able to give names to the species, (and) then it is much easier to register when someone may be missing. Biodiversity is the diversity of species which can most likely ensure sustainable development" (3026M2). Another student put it this way: "Species identification: becoming aware of diversity. Biodiversity: getting a greater understanding. Sustainable development: everything is connected to everything else and even mosquitoes are needed" (2025F3). Some students described the relationship using a concept map, for example this student (1086M1) (Figure 2).

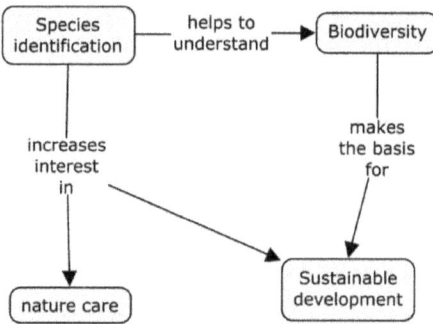

Figure 2. Example of a student's answer as a concept map in Category 4.

Category 5 comprised 8.9 percent of all answers. It included interconnections and additional feedback loops in the described relationships between species identification, biodiversity and sustainable development. A female student produced the following: "All parts of nature are interconnected. If one part disappears, many other parts also disappear. Biodiversity is very important and species identification too is very important for understanding the entirety" (1070F2). Another student explained it by first drawing a loop between the three concepts: biodiversity—species identification—sustainable development, and then explained: "All are interconnected, a 'cause and effect'-relationship; it is good to start from species identification for understanding the biodiversity of the organisms, which in turn affects sustainable development positively. All organisms have their place and meaning, and therefore biodiversity is very important" (...) (1167F3).

Category 6 included also behavioural aspects in addition to interconnections and feedback loops. Only 2.8 percent of the answers were placed in this category. Typical for this category was that all answers included some of the words or meanings: 'choices affect', 'consequences of actions' or 'everything is connected'. Two examples describe this category:

> "Man should base their actions in accordance with the principles of sustainable development. Since our actions do anyway cause changes in nature, the bigger the biodiversity, the better nature can handle it on the whole. When we know species, we can also perceive the

biodiversity of nature, and can therefore better notice the consequences of our actions, [and] appreciate every species as an important part of the big picture (...)" (1182F3).

"Individual species are important for the diversity of living organisms. We use resources so that nature can stay varied and functional. Then we also take care of individual species, know their needs and habitats, and do not destroy species 'by mistake'. Sustainable development: if we take care of comprehensiveness by protecting individual species, our own species remains viable on a viable planet (...)" (1027F3).

Descriptive examples of the categories were mostly given only in words, but the original answers often also included some kind of sketches, where the three key words were 'correctly' placed but not always explained.

4.2. Differences between Finnish, Norwegian and Swedish Student Teachers' Answers

There were several differences between the answers given in the three participating countries. The Finnish student teachers used basic systems thinking much more than their Norwegian and Swedish colleagues when describing the relationship between species identification, biodiversity and sustainable development. About a third of the Finnish answers (34.2%) were placed in categories with systems thinking (categories 4–6), while the corresponding percentages for Norwegian and Swedish answers were 13.3 and 16.8 (Figure 3).

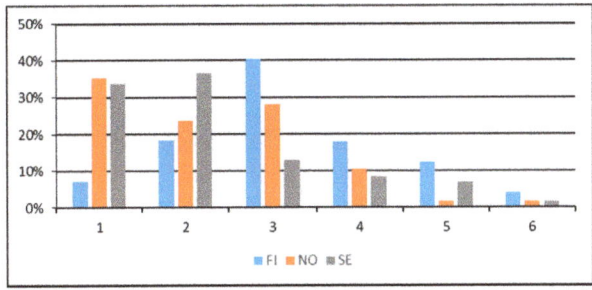

Figure 3. A comparison of Finnish (FI), Norwegian (NO) and Swedish (SE) students' views about the relationship between species identification, biodiversity and sustainable development in six categories (1 = no answer; 2 = answers involving nonsense or cliché; 3 = answers involving partial relationships without systems thinking; 4 = answers involving interconnections; 5 = answers involving interconnections and feedback; 6 = answers involving interconnections, feedback and behavioural aspects). Note: Categories 7–10 were deleted from the figure because there were no answers in these categories.

Only 7.1 percent of the Finnish teacher students did not answer or did not understand the question (Category 1), in contrast with 35.3 respectively 33.6 percent of the Norwegian and Swedish students. The most frequent category for the Finnish students was Category 3 (40.4%), Category 1 (35.3%) for the Norwegian students and Category 2 for the Swedish students. The differences between the countries were statistically significant (Pearson Chi-Square (10, $N = 424$) = 87.7718, $p = 0.000$).

4.3. Gender Differences

There were some differences in the answers as far as gender is concerned. 31.6 percent of the male student teachers showed basic systems thinking (categories 4–6), while the corresponding percentage for the females were 24.1 (Figure 4). However, only 5.3 percent of the males and 2.3 percent of the females described the relationship between species identification, biodiversity and sustainable development using the highest basic level of systems thinking, including interconnections, feedback and behavioural aspects (Category 6).

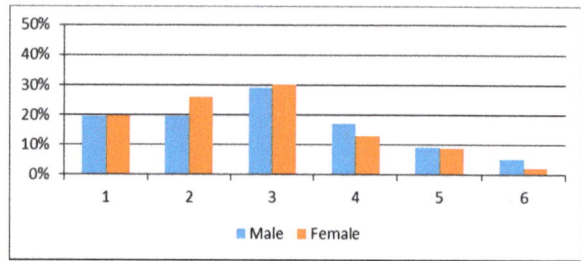

Figure 4. A comparison of female and male student teachers' views about the relationship between species identification, biodiversity and sustainable development in six categories (1 = no answer; 2 = answers involving nonsense or cliché; 3 = answers involving partial relationships without systems thinking; 4 = answers involving interconnections; 5 = answers involving interconnections and feedback; 6 = answers involving interconnections, feedback and behavioural aspects). Note: Categories 7–10 were deleted from the figure because there were no answers in these categories.

The gender differences were not, however, statistically significant (Pearson Chi-Square (5, N = 424) = 3.714, p = 0.591).

4.4. Differences between Age Groups

Another interesting factor is how age, and thus life experience, affects student teachers' ways of understanding and describing the relationship between species identification, biodiversity and sustainable development. To study this, the descriptions were studied regarding three age groups of student teachers: those under 25 years, those aged 25–35, and those over 35 years of age. Descriptions produced by the age group under 25 were mostly found in categories 1, 2 and 3 (78.9%), whereas systems thinking only existed in 21.1 percent of their answers. The corresponding percentage for age group 25–35 was 35.4 and that for those over 35 was 31.3 (Figure 5).

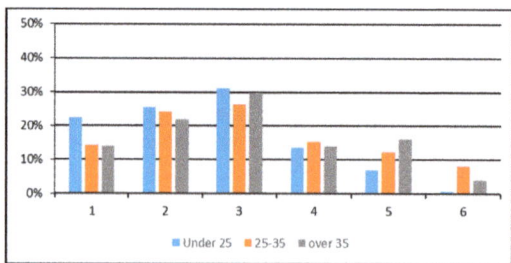

Figure 5. A comparison of student teachers' views about the relationship between species identification, biodiversity and sustainable development in three age groups (<25; 25–35; >35) and six categories (1 = no answer; 2 = answers involving nonsense or cliché; 3 = answers involving partial relationships without systems thinking; 4 = answers involving interconnections; 5 = answers involving interconnections and feedback; 6 = answers involving interconnections, feedback and behavioural aspects). Note: Categories 7–10 were deleted from the figure because there were no answers in these categories.

The differences between the age groups were statistically significant (Pearson Chi-Square $(10, N = 422) = 22.472, p = 0.013$).

5. Discussion and Conclusions

In this study, focus was directed towards student teachers' systems thinking about the ecological dimension of sustainability, and especially their views about the relationship between species identification, biodiversity and sustainable development. According to previous research [28,29,33], knowledge of species and species identification skills are important factors in developing people's interest in environmental issues and sustainability. Furthermore, an understanding of ecological key concepts, such as biodiversity, helps people to see and understand more complex relationships in natural systems [36,37], especially if also well-known species [32,33] and nature experiences are included [34,35,86]. People's ability to identify the separate components in ecological sustainability however, is only a starting point. Systems thinking could therefore help them to identify and understand how everything is connected to everything else in the complex system of sustainability [24]. As far as we know, however, there are no major investigations of people's level of systems thinking concerning sustainability. This study contributes to the improving of the situation in several ways. Firstly, it investigated the level of systems thinking regarding one complex dimension of sustainability, i.e., ecological sustainability. Secondly, it studied a large group of student teachers from three countries who are future primary-school teachers, and therefore have a central role in the education of sustainability in the Nordic countries. Moreover, this study describes the actual level of student teachers' understanding of ecological sustainability, which can be used as a base for further development of sustainability in teacher education programmes. Education is seen as a key strategy to help people understand the complexity of sustainability, which in turn could help them to make more sustainable lifestyle decisions [15,24].

Because the majority of student teachers (about 75%) did not show any signs of systems thinking when describing ecological sustainability, systems thinking as an educational method seems not to have been used very much in teacher education programmes. Furthermore, there was a statistically significant difference between the three age groups; the older ones (25–35 and >35) showing more systems thinking than the younger ones (<25), especially when it comes to the Norwegian student teachers. This indicates that their systems thinking could be more a result of life experiences than that of education. On the other hand, there are several reports of teacher education programmes that totally lack, or have only few, sustainability subjects [12–14,87,88]. The student teachers' low level of systems thinking in ecological sustainability also reflects minor volumes of nature studies and ecological aspects among the more extensive pedagogical and other subject studies in teacher education [37,44,70,72].

The low level of student teachers' systems thinking and the many insufficient answers in the two lowest categories, nearly half of all answers (44.6%), could hardly depend on a methodological factor. The main question of this study ('Describe your opinion about the relationship between species identification, biodiversity and sustainable development') was placed as the last question of the survey because of its summarising character. This means that some student teachers might have left this particular question unanswered because of time constraints or that they did not put too much effort answering the question in a very detailed way, because of loss of interest or energy. However, the two former questions, which dealt specifically with the importance of species identification and biodiversity for sustainable development, also had corresponding deficiencies. Several of the student teachers wrote that they had never thought of this kind of relationship or that they did not know enough to be able to answer the question. Some of them just wrote anything to fill the empty space or, even worse, had no idea of what the question was all about. Because the answers were anonymous, further interviews with these students were unfortunately impossible.

There are several studies [36,37,42,60] which point out that many student teachers (such as those in this study) do not understand the key concepts of ecology. One of the most important key concepts is biodiversity. However, people's understanding of biodiversity, and particularly the importance of biodiversity for sustainability, is often incomplete and includes misunderstandings [60–63]. In this study, and our previous study [29], most of the student teachers considered biodiversity to be important or very important for sustainable development, but many of them could not explain why. Their views of the importance of species identification for sustainable development may explain something of their difficulties to understand biodiversity. They perceived species as either useful or harmful to themselves (e.g., eatable or poisonous), not as an important part of the whole. This anthropocentric view and economic valuation of nature are often given priority compared to other types of values, and can therefore threaten biodiversity conservation and sustainability [65]. It is, therefore, important to include other values and also emotional aspects in sustainability education [89]. Student teachers need to develop their understanding of ecological key concepts at the latest in teacher education, in order to avoid spreading their own misconceptions as teachers.

Another interesting fact is that there was a statistically significant difference in the levels of systems thinking between student teachers from the different countries. The Finnish student teachers had a higher percentage of basic systems thinking than their Norwegian or Swedish colleagues. In fact, the same group of Finnish student teachers also had better species identification skills (detail knowledge) than the corresponding groups of Norwegian and Swedish students in our previous study [29]. However, the differences are small and cannot be explained only by the differences in the respective country's teacher education programme, or by the different number of participating students from the three countries. In addition, there exist several studies where Finnish teacher education is criticised for failing in sustainability [9,14,87]. The Finnish programme for teacher education for primary schools is, however, very attractive and draws many more applicants than the corresponding Norwegian or Swedish programmes [88], which is why only high-performance students are accepted. Teacher education authorities in these countries probably follow the same recommendation from Unesco [90] in order to implement sustainability in teacher education. Sustainability is strongly connected to ecological literacy and also value-dependent, and applications of sustainability are therefore complicated [14]. Education of good quality requires teachers to have knowledge and skills to be able to plan and carry out meaningful teaching [91]. Student teachers may find it difficult to teach about sustainability and all its dimensions and aspects. They need training in sustainability education, which has also been suggested in many other studies [13,14,87,92].

The results of this study showed that the majority of student teachers in Finland, Norway and Sweden have not developed any form of systems thinking through their education. It is also obvious that those student teachers who have a basic level of systems thinking, have developed it mainly through their own life experiences. Systems thinking needs to be incorporated in the education of teachers, because there is a necessity to develop an educational programme that provides individuals with knowledge about how different actions and choices affect the whole society. In other words, teacher education programmes should include such a form of systems thinking that is based on critical thinking, negotiation and action competence. Sustainability cannot be taught without involving systems thinking [23,77].

Since systems thinking is a way of thinking the starting point is to focus more on the process than the content of teaching. Instead of education which is limited to instruction and transfer of knowledge, education should comprise dynamic, activity-based and participatory training based on generating knowledge and meaning in relation to the circumstances in the local society and the world. Problem-solving in such education is thus based on real events [74]. Integrating systems thinking in sustainable education in teacher education can be made by using interdisciplinary and multidisciplinary projects, where the main goal is to make participants think in holistic ways by identifying and analysing possible components in their project, and then critically reflect on how everything is connected to everything else in the complex system. Since systems thinking is also a result of life experiences, elementary forms of systems thinking should be an educational method already in primary education.

Acknowledgments: Our thanks go to our colleagues in Finland, Norway and Sweden for their help with collecting the material. The following foundations have supported the research: Högskolestiftelsen i Österbotten, Svenska Kulturfonden and Aktiastiftelsen.

Author Contributions: Irmeli Palmberg is the responsible project leader and wrote all sections of this paper. Irmeli Palmberg, Eila Jeronen and Eija Yli-Panula designed and carried out the survey. Irmeli Palmberg and Maria Hofman-Bergholm analysed and categorised the material, and Maria Hofman-Bergholm made the statistical analyses. All authors checked and commented on the manuscript after the language check.

Conflicts of Interest: The authors declare no conflict of interest.

References

1. UNESCO. Education for Sustainable Development. 2017. Available online: http://en.unesco.org/themes/education-sustainable-development (accessed on 15 March 2017).
2. Wolff, L.-A.; Sjöblom, P.; Hofman-Bergholm, M.; Palmberg, I. High performance education fails in sustainability? – A reflection on Finnish primary teacher education. *Educ. Sci.* **2017**, *7*, 1–22. [CrossRef]
3. WCED (World Commission on Environment and Development). *Our Common Future*; University Press: Oxford, UK, 1987.
4. UNCED (United Nations Conference on Environment and Development). The Final Text of Agreements Negotiated by Governments at United Nation's Conference on Environment and Development, In Agenda 21: Programme of Action for Sustainable Development: Rio Declaration on Environment and Development; Statement of Forest Principles. In Proceedings of the UNCED (United Nations Conference on Environment and Development), Rio de Janeiro, Brazil, 3–14 June 1992; United Nations Department of Public Information: New York, NY, USA, 1993.
5. UNESCO (United Nations Educational, Scientific and Cultural Organization). *UN Decade of Education for Sustainable Development 2004–2005*; UNESCO: Paris, France, 2005.
6. Alexandar, R.; Poyyamoli, G. The Effectiveness of environmental education for sustainable development based on active teaching and learning at high school level—A case study from Puducherry and Cuddalore regions, India. *JSE* **2014**, *7*. Available online: http://www.jsedimensions.org/wordpress/content/the-effectiveness-ofenvironmental-educationfor-sustainable-development-based-on-active-teaching-and-learning-at-high-school-level-a-case-studyfrom-puducherry-and-cuddalore-regions-india_2014_12/ (accessed on 27 May 2016).
7. Amaral, L.P.; Martins, N.; Gouveia, J.B. Quest for a sustainable university: A review. *Int. J. Sustain. High. Educ.* **2015**, *16*, 155–172. [CrossRef]
8. Beringer, A.; Adomßent, M. Sustainable university research and development: Inspecting sustainability in higher education research. *Environ. Educ. Res.* **2008**, *14*, 607–623. [CrossRef]
9. Olsson, D.; Gericke, N.; Chang ·Rundgren, S.-N. The effect of implementation of education for sustainable development in Swedish compulsory schools—Assessing pupils sustainability consciousness. *Environ. Educ. Res.* **2016**, *22*, 176–202. [CrossRef]
10. Pathan, A.; Bröckl, M.; Oja, L.; Ahvenharju, S.; Raivio, T. Kansallisten Kestävää Kehitystä Edistävien Kasvatuksen Ja Koulutuksen Strategioiden Toimeenpanon Arviointi. [Evaluation of the Implementation of the Strategies on Education for Sustainable Development]. Gaia Consulting Oy: Helsinki, 2012. Available online: http://www.ym.fi/download/noname/%7B7A0AC771-670C-48B8-B7F8-8FB0B173236F%7D/78365 (accessed on 20 Mars 2017).
11. Scott, W.; Gough, S. Sustainable development within UK higher education: Revealing tendencies and tensions. In *Education for Sustainable Development. Papers in Honour of the United Nations Decade of Education for Sustainable Development (2005–2014)*; Chalkley, B., Haigh, M., Higgitt, D., Eds.; Routledge: London, UK, 2009; pp. 141–153.
12. Àlvarez-Garcia, O.; Sureda-Negre, J.; Comas-Forgas, R. Environmental education in pre-service teacher training: A literature review of existing evidence. *JTEFS* **2015**, *17*, 72–85. [CrossRef]
13. Borg, C.; Gericke, N.; Höglund, H.-O.; Bergman, E. The barriers encountered by teachers implementing education for sustainable development: Discipline bound differences and teaching traditions. *Res. Sci. Technol. Educ.* **2012**, *30*, 185–207. [CrossRef]
14. Falkenberg, T.; Babiuk, G. The status of education for sustainability in initial teacher education programmes: A Canadian case study. *Int. J. Sustain. High. Educ.* **2014**, *15*, 418–430. [CrossRef]

15. Birdsall, S. Measuring student teachers' understandings and self-awareness of sustainability. *Environ. Educ. Res.* **2014**, *20*, 814–835. [CrossRef]

16. Borg, C.; Gericke, N.; Höglund, H.-O.; Bergman, E. Subject-and experience-bound differences in teachers' conceptual understanding of sustainable development. *Environ. Educ. Res.* **2014**, *20*, 526–551. [CrossRef]

17. Stevenson, R.B. Schooling and environmental/sustainability education: From discourses of policy and practice to discourses of professional learning. *Environ. Educ. Res.* **2007**, *13*, 265–285. [CrossRef]

18. IPCC. *Climate Change 2014: Impacts, Adaptation, and Vulnerability. Working Group II Contribution to the Fifth Assessment Report of the Intergovernmental Panel on Climate Change*; Cambridge University Press: Cambridge, UK, 2014.

19. Stern Review on the Economics of Climate Change. 2006. Available online: http://www.sternreview.org.uk (accessed on 20 January 2017).

20. Dobson, A. *Sustainability Citizenship*; Greenhouse: London, UK, 2011.

21. Huckle, J.; Wals, A.E.J. The UN decade of education for sustainable development: Business as usual in the end. *Environ. Educ. Res.* **2015**, *21*, 491–505. [CrossRef]

22. Kahn, R. *Critical Pedagogy, Ecoliteracy and the Planetary Crisis: The Ecopedagogy Movement*; Peter Lang: New York, NY, USA, 2010.

23. Lewis, E.; Mansfield, C.; Baudains, C. Ten tonne plan: Education for Sustainability from a whole systems thinking perspective. *Appl. Environ. Educ. Commun.* **2014**, *13*, 128–141. [CrossRef]

24. Sterling, S. Whole Systems Thinking as a Basis for Paradigm Change in Education: Explorations in the Context of Sustainability. 2003. Available online: http://www.bath.ac.uk/cree/sterling/sterlingthesis.pdf (accessed on 20 January 2017).

25. Bunge, M. Systemism: The alternative to individualism and holism. *J. Socio-Econ.* **2000**, *29*, 147–157. [CrossRef]

26. Sterling, S. Sustainable Education. In *Science, Society and Sustainability: Education and Empowerment for an Uncertain World*; Gray, D., Colucci-Gray, L., Camino, E., Eds.; Routledge: New York, NY, USA, 2009; pp. 105–118.

27. Mayr, E. *What Makes Biology Unique? Considerations of the Autonomy of a Scientific Discipline*; Cambridge University Press: Cambridge, UK, 2004.

28. Palmberg, I. Artkännedom och artintresse hos blivande lärare för grundskolan. *NorDiNa Nord. Stud. Sci. Educ.* **2012**, *8*, 244–257.

29. Palmberg, I.; Berg, I.; Jeronen, E.; Kärkkäinen, S.; Norrgård-Sillanpää, P.; Persson, C.; Vilkonis, R.; Yli-Panula, E. Nordic–Baltic student teachers' identification of and interest in plant and animal species: The importance of species identification and biodiversity for sustainable development. *J. Sci. Teach. Educ.* **2015**, *26*, 549–571. [CrossRef]

30. Helldén, G.; Helldén, S. Students' early experiences of biodiversity and education for sustainable future. *Nord. Stud. Sci. Educ.* **2008**, *4*, 123–131.

31. Lindemann-Matthies, P. "Loveable" mammals and "lifeless" plants: How children's interest in common local organisms can be enhanced through observation of nature. *IJSE* **2005**, *27*, 655–677. [CrossRef]

32. Magntorn, O.; Helldén, G. Reading nature from a "bottom-up" perspective. *JBE* **2007**, *41*, 68–75. [CrossRef]

33. Randler, C. Teaching species identification—A prerequisite for learning biodiversity and understanding ecology. *Eurasia J. Math. Sci. Technol. Educ.* **2008**, *4*, 223–231.

34. Palmberg, I.; Kuru, J. Outdoor activities as a basis for environmental responsibility. *JEE* **2000**, *31*, 32–36. [CrossRef]

35. Palmer, J.A.; Suggate, J.; Robottom, I.; Hart, P. Significant life experiences and formative influences on the development of adults' environmental awareness in the UK, Australia and Canada. *Environ. Educ. Res.* **1999**, *5*, 181–200. [CrossRef]

36. Puk, T.G.; Stibbards, A. Systemic ecological illiteracy? Shedding light on meaning as an act of thought in higher learning. *Environ. Educ. Res.* **2012**, *18*, 353–373. [CrossRef]

37. Palmberg, I.; Jonsson, G.; Jeronen, E.; Yli-Panula, E. Blivande lärares uppfattningar och förståelse av baskunskap i ekologi i Danmark, Finland och Sverige. *NorDiNa Nord. Stud. Sci. Educ.* **2016**, *12*, 197–217.

38. Balmford, A.; Clegg, L.; Coulson, T.; Taylor, J. Why conservationists should heed pokemon. *Science* **2002**, *295*, 2367. [CrossRef] [PubMed]

39. Bebbington, A. The ability of A-level students to name plants. *JBE* **2005**, *39*, 63–67. [CrossRef]

40. Kaasinen, A. Kasvilajien Tunnistaminen, Oppiminen ja Opettaminen Yleissivistävän Koulutuksen Näkökulmasta. [Plant Species Recognition, Learning and Teaching from Viewpoint of General Education]. Dissertation Thesis, Helsingin yliopisto, Käyttäytymistieteellinen tiedekunta, Soveltavan kasvatustieteen laitos, Tutkimuksia, Helsinki, Finland, 2009.
41. Randler, C. Pupils' factual knowledge about vertebrate species. *JBSE* **2008**, *7*, 48–54.
42. Krall, R.M.; Lott, K.H.; Wymer, C.L. Inservice elementary and middle school teachers' conceptions of photosynthesis and respiration. *JTE* **2009**, *20*, 41–55. [CrossRef]
43. Pe'er, S.; Goldman, D.; Yavetz, B. Environmental literacy in teacher training: Attitudes, knowledge, and environmental behavior of beginning students. *JEE* **2007**, *39*, 45–59. [CrossRef]
44. Zak, K.M.; Munson, B.H. An exploratory study of elementary preservice teachers' understanding of ecology using concept maps. *JEE* **2008**, *39*, 32–46. [CrossRef]
45. Jucker, R. *Our Common Illiteracy: Education as if the Earth and People Mattered*; Environmental Education, Communication and Sustainability; Peter Lang: Frankfurt am Main, Germany, 2002; Volume 10.
46. Orr, D.W. *Ecological Literacy: Education and the Transition to a Postmodern World*; State University of New York Press: Albany, NY, USA, 1992.
47. McBride, B.B.; Brewer, C.A.; Berkowitz, A.R.; Borrie, W.T. Environmental literacy, ecological literacy, ecoliteracy: What do we mean and how did we get here? *Ecosphere* **2013**, *4*, 67. [CrossRef]
48. Cutter-Mackenzie, A.; Smith, R. Ecological literacy: The "missing paradigm" in environmental education (part one). *Environ. Educ. Res.* **2003**, *9*, 497–524. [CrossRef]
49. Berkowitz, A.R.; Ford, M.F.; Brewer, C.A. A framework for integrating ecological literacy, civics literacy, and environmental citizenship in environmental education. In *Environmental Education and Advocacy: Changing Perspectives of Ecology and Education*; Johnson, E.A., Mappin, M.J., Eds.; Cambridge University Press: New York, NY, USA, 2005; pp. 227–266.
50. Magntorn, O. Reading Nature: Developing Ecological Literacy through Teaching. Studies in Science and Techology Education; Dissertation Thesis, Department of Social and Welfare Studies, Linköping University, Norrköping, Sweden, 2007.
51. Fleischer, S. Emerging beliefs frustrate ecological literacy and meaning-making for students. *CSSE* **2011**, *6*, 235–241. [CrossRef]
52. Sala, O.E.; Mayerson, L.A.; Parmesan, C. (Eds.) *Biodiversity Change and Human Health: From Ecosystem Services to Spread of Diseases*; SCOPE 69; Island Press: Washington, DC, USA, 2009.
53. UNESCO. Learning about Biodiversity—Multiple-Perspective Approaches; Education for Sustainable Development in Action. Learning and Training Tools, 6; UNESCO Education Sector. United Nations Decade of Education for Sustainable Development (2005–2014), UNESCO, 2014. Available online: http://unesdoc.unesco.org/images/0023/002311/231155e.pdf (accessed on 15 March 2017).
54. Van Weelie, D.; Wals, A.E.J. Making biodiversity meaningful through environmental education. *IJSE* **2002**, *24*, 1143–1156. [CrossRef]
55. Dreyfus, A.; Wals, A.; van Weelie, D. Biodiversity as a postmodern theme for environmental education. *CJEE* **1999**, *4*, 155–175.
56. Menzel, S.; Bögeholz, S. The loss of biodiversity: How do students in Chile and Germany perceive resource dilemmas and what solutions do they see? *RISE* **2009**, *39*, 429–447.
57. Gaston, K.J.; Spicer, J.I. *Biodiversity*; Blackwell: Oxford, UK, 2004.
58. Kassas, M. Environmental education: Biodiversity. *Environmentalist* **2002**, *22*, 345–351. [CrossRef]
59. Gayford, C. Biodiversity education: A teacher's perspective. *Environ. Educ. Res.* **2000**, *6*, 347–362. [CrossRef]
60. Dikmenli, M. Biology student teachers' conceptual frameworks regarding biodiversity. *Education* **2010**, *130*, 479–489.
61. Lindemann-Matthies, P.; Constantinou, C.; Lehnert, H.-J.; Nagel, U.; Raper, G.; Kadji-Beltran, C. Confidence and perceived competence of preservice teachers to implement biodiversity education in primary schools—Four comparative case studies from Europe. *IJSE* **2011**, *33*, 2247–2273. [CrossRef]
62. Lude, A. The spirit of teaching ESD—Biodiversity in educational projects. In *Biodiversity in Education for Sustainable Development—Reflection on School-Research Cooperation*; Ulbrich, K., Settele, J., Benedict, F.F., Eds.; Pensoft Publishers: Moscow, Russia, 2010; pp. 17–29.
63. Nisiforou, O.; Charalambides, A.G. Assessing undergraduate university students' level of knowledge, attitudes and behaviour towards biodiversity: A case study in Cyprus. *IJSE* **2012**, *34*, 1027–1051. [CrossRef]

64. Speth, J.G. *The Bridge at the Edge of the World: Capitalism, the Environment, and Crossing from Crisis to Sustainability*; Yale University Press: New Hawen, CT, USA, 2008.

65. Kopnina, H. Forsaking Nature? Contesting 'Biodiversity' through competing discourses of sustainability. *J. Educ. Sustain. Dev.* **2013**, *7*, 51–63. [CrossRef]

66. Randler, C. Animal related activities as determinants of species knowledge. *Eurasia J. Math. Sci. Technol. Educ.* **2010**, *6*, 237–243.

67. Dresner, M. Teachers in the woods: Monitoring forest biodiversity. *JEE* **2002**, *34*, 26–31. [CrossRef]

68. Summers, M.; Kruger, C.; Childs, A.; Mant, J. Primary school teachers' understanding of environmental issues: An interview study. *Environ. Educ. Res.* **2000**, *6*, 293–312. [CrossRef]

69. Summers, M.; Kruger, C.; Childs, A.; Mant, J. Understanding the science of environmental issues: Development of a subject knowledge guide for primary teacher education. *IJSE* **2001**, *23*, 33–53. [CrossRef]

70. Magntorn, O.; Helldén, G. Student-teachers' ability to read nature: Reflections on their own learning in ecology. *IJSE* **2005**, *27*, 1229–1254. [CrossRef]

71. Lindemann-Matthies, P.; Constantinou, C.; Junge, X.; Köhler, K.; Mayer, J.; Nagel, U.; Raper, G.; Schüle, D.; Kadji-Beltran, C. The integration of biodiversity education in the initial education of primary school teachers: Four comparative case studies from Europe. *Environ. Educ. Res.* **2009**, *15*, 17–37. [CrossRef]

72. Draper, F. A proposed sequence for developing systems thinking in a grades 4–12 curriculum. *Syst. Dyn. Rev.* **1993**, *9*, 207–214. [CrossRef]

73. Salonen, A.O. Kestävä Kehitys Globaalin Ajan Hyvinvointiyhteiskunnan Haasteena. [Sustainable Development and its Promotion in a Welfare Society in Global Age]. Dissertation Thesis, Helsingin yliopiston Tutkimuksia, Helsinki, Finland, 2010.

74. Hofman, M. What is an education for sustainable development supposed to achieve—A question about what, how and why. *J. Educ. Sustain. Dev.* **2015**, *9*, 213–228. [CrossRef]

75. Sheehy, N.; Wylie, J.; McGuinnes, C.; Orchard, G. How children solve environmental problems: Using computer simulations to investigate systems thinking. *Environ. Educ. Res.* **2000**, *6*, 109–126. [CrossRef]

76. Blewitt, J. *Understanding Sustainable Development*; Earthscan: London, UK, 2008.

77. Cloud, J.P. Some systems thinking concepts for environmental educators during the decade of education for sustainable development. In *Education for Sustainable Development*; Chalkley, B., Haigh, M., Higgitt, D., Eds.; Routledge: New York, NY, USA, 2009; pp. 225–229.

78. Stave, K.A.; Hopper, M. What Constitutes Systems Thinking? A Proposed Taxonomy. In Proceedings of the 25th International Conference of the System Dynamics Society, Boston, MA, USA, 29 July–2 August 2007. Available online: https://www.systemdynamics.org/conferences/2007/proceed/papers/STAVE210.pdf (accessed on 20 January 2017).

79. Krathwohl, D.R. A revision of Bloom's taxonomy: An overview. *TIP* **2002**, *41*, 212–218. [CrossRef]

80. Flood, R.L. The relationship of 'Systems thinking' to action research. *SPAR* **2010**, *23*, 269–284. [CrossRef]

81. Salonen, A. An ecosocial approach in education. In *Schooling for Sustainable Development: Concepts, Policies and Educational Experiences of the End of the UN Decade of Education for Sustainable Development*; Jucker, R., Mathar, R., Eds.; Springer: Berlin/Heidelberg, Germany, 2014; pp. 231–233.

82. Salonen, A.; Konkka, J. An ecosocial approach to well-being: A solution to the wicked problems in the era of Anthropocene. *Foro Educ.* **2015**, *13*, 19–34. [CrossRef]

83. Creswell, J.W. *Educational Research: Planning, Conducting, and Evaluating Quantitative and Qualitative Research*; Pearson Prentice Hall: Upper Saddle River, USA, 2008.

84. Elo, S.; Kyngäs, H. The quantitative content analysis process. *JAN* **2008**, *62*, 107–115. [CrossRef]

85. Tuomi, J.; Sarajärvi, A. *Laadullinen Tutkimus ja Sisällönanalyysi*. [Qualitative Analysis and Content Analysis]; Tammi: Helsinki, Finland, 2009.

86. Bögeholz, S. Nature experience and its importance for environmental knowledge, values and action: Recent German empirical contributions. *Environ. Educ. Res.* **2006**, *12*, 65–84. [CrossRef]

87. Hofman, M. Hållbar Utveckling i den Finländska Lärarutbildningen—Politisk Retorik eller Verklighet? 2012. Available online: https://www.doria.fi/bitstream/handle/10024/134034/MariaHofman_lic.pdf?sequence=1 (accessed on 15 January 2012).

88. Rasmussen, J.; Dorf, H. Challenges to Nordic teacher education programmes. In *Advancing quality cultures for Teacher Education in Europe: Tensions and Opportunities*; Hudson, B., Zgaga, P., Åstrand, B., Eds.; Umeå School of Education, Umeå University: Umeå, Sweden, 2010; pp. 51–67. [CrossRef]

89. Ojala, M. Emotional awareness. On the importance of including emotional aspects in education of sustainable development (ESD). *J. Educ. Sustain. Dev.* **2013**, *7*, 167–182. [CrossRef]

90. UNESCO. Guidelines and Recommendations for Reorienting Teacher Education to Address Sustainability. Education for Sustainable Development in Action, Technical Paper. 2005. Available online: http://unesdoc. unesco.org/images/0014/001433/143370E.pdf (accessed on 20 January 2017).

91. Abell, S.K. Research on science teacher knowledge. In *Research on Science Teacher Education*; Abell, S.K., Lederman, N.G., Eds.; Routledge: New York, NY, USA, 2007; pp. 1105–1149.

92. Uitto, A.; Saloranta, S. Subject teachers as educators for sustainability: A survey study. *Educ. Sci.* **2017**, *7*. [CrossRef]

Article

An On-Campus Botanical Tour to Promote Student Satisfaction and Learning in a University Level Biodiversity or General Biology Course

Harish H. Ratnayaka

Department of Biology, Xavier University of Louisiana, 1 Drexel Drive, New Orleans, LA 70125, USA;
hratnaya@xula.edu; Tel.: +1-504-520-5709

Academic Editor: Eila Jeronen
Received: 22 November 2016; Accepted: 13 January 2017; Published: 24 January 2017

Abstract: Outdoor, hands-on and experiential learning, as opposed to instruction-based learning in classroom, increases student satisfaction and motivation leading to a deeper understanding of the subject. However, the use of outdoor exercises in undergraduate biology courses is declining due to a variety of constraints. Thus, the goal of this paper is to describe a convenient, no-cost and flexible exercise using an on-campus botanical tour for strengthening specific knowledge areas of major plant groups. Its assessment on conduct and coverage, and student-perceived and actual knowledge gain is also described. Data presented derived from traditional biology undergraduates in sophomore year over nine fall and three spring semesters. Conduct and coverage was assessed using a summative survey including open-ended questions administered to 198 students. A pre- and post-exercise survey addressing 10 knowledge categories was administered to 139 students to evaluate student-perceived knowledge gain. Quiz grades from the on-campus tour exercise were compared with average quiz grades from two in-class plant-related labs of 234 students to assess actual knowledge gain. Each student reporting on the conduct and coverage indicated either one or a combination of outcomes of the exercise as positive engagement, experiential learning, or of interest. Student-perceived improvement was evident in all ten knowledge categories with a greater improvement in categories learned anew during exercise compared to subjects reviewed. Quiz grades from the exercise were >11% greater than quiz grades from the two in-class plant-related labs. Active learning with interest likely contributed to the increased perceived and actual knowledge gains. Suggestions for adoption of the exercise in different settings are presented based on both student comments and instructor's experience.

Keywords: teaching biology outdoors; student engagement; experiential learning; plant classification; biodiversity

---

1. Introduction

Student satisfaction, the favorability of students' subjective evaluation of the experience and outcome of what they learned [1], and motivation are positively correlated to a variety of learning measures [2]. However, finding a match between what makes students satisfied and motivated and what needs to be covered in a specific biology course to meet program goals and standards is a challenge. Such matches, if found, will increase student-driven learning, rather than passive reception. Pleasurable experiences with our outdoors and resulting curiosity are among the reasons why many of us, today's biology teachers, chose to be biologists. Thus, exercises that enable today's students to understand structure, function and benefits of outdoor world may stimulate their curiosity as well, and help sustain their satisfaction and interest in biology. Merits and impacts of outdoor teaching have also been well-recognized in a variety of scopes such as camping education [3], extension and enrichment of curriculum [4], and experiential [5] and collaborative [6] learning. Furthermore, dedicated outdoor learning is found to increase enthusiasm and attendance, decrease behavioral problems [7,8], and improve cognitive function and academic achievement [9]. However, a large proportion of the U.S. population today has abandoned the natural world mainly due to lack of early experience with nature [10], and the same trend is experienced in the UK [11]. A variety of limitations including lack of teacher preparedness, limited encouragement by schools, differences in curricular priorities and inaccessibility to field sites in and around especially urban universities [12], time, cost of transport, risk [13], etc. underlie this decline in student exposure to the outdoors. Scott, Boyd, Scott and Colquhoun grouped the barriers that prevent outdoor learning into two main categories, teacher confidence and school culture [14]. Future biologists, today's biology undergraduates in particular, need the opportunities to experience outdoor learning that impart curiosity, joy and enrichment of the subject.

At the university level, this decline in teaching and learning field biology and dilemmas associated with it are also well-recognized, particularly with regard to identification of plants and animals, which is fundamental to the appreciation and understanding of natural history and our surroundings [15, 16]. It is, however, possible to engage students in an effective outdoor learning experience on our campus premises in the U.S. and elsewhere without travelling long distances to field sites, especially in the study of plant diversity. This article describes how we have accomplished that at Xavier University of Louisiana (XULA) located in the city of New Orleans, LA, USA, and provides examples of strategies and assessments used with the expectation that biology instructors elsewhere will make necessary adjustments to develop similar exercises using suitable botanical stations available on their campuses. XULA is a mainly minority-serving institute with a nationally renowned biology pre-med program [17]. Despite the success of the program, only up to a third of the graduating class enters medical school annually. Given the unacceptably low minority representation in biology Ph.D.s, Doctors of Philosophy, nationally [18], including in organismal biology [19], a large proportion of the minority biology graduates not entering medical school from pre-med programs may also be an opportunity. This outdoor exercise may also help enhance chances of their participation in non-medical biological sciences at the postgraduate level. Objectively planned outdoor exercises can also help integrate biology core concepts with eventual competencies [20,21] while adding value to the everyday classroom experience [22] of students in any undergraduate biology program, minority-serving or other.

Thus, the broad goal of this exercise was to develop a non-medical, no-cost and convenient activity to help fulfill the need for outdoor exposure of undergraduate Biology majors. The specific objectives of the exercise were: (a) to provide students with a hands-on experience and a deeper understanding of how the local botanicals of *Bryophytes*, *Pteridophytes*, *Gymnosperms* and *Angiosperms* contribute to the existence of other life forms in their surroundings in an outdoor setting and (b) to evaluate student-perceived and actual knowledge gain from the exercise by summative assessments. Conduct, assessment and suggestions for implementation of the exercise are discussed.

2. Methods

2.1. Course Content and Accommodations

The Biodiversity course at XULA covers fundamentals of evolution, a survey of eukaryotic kingdoms and principles of ecology taught in sequence. A survey of eukaryotic kingdoms covers cladograms to discuss evolution of major clades and Linnaean taxa with their major characteristics and representatives. Students taking the course are approximately 19-year-old sophomore biology majors. By the time of taking this on-campus tour exercise as part of their lab, students were familiar with the basics of plant systematics such as the cladogram showing four major plant groups (nonvascular *Bryophytes*, vascular seedless *Pteridophytes*, seed non-flowering *Gymnosperms*, and flowering *Angiosperms*), their phyla and few common names of their major representatives. The exercise was introduced following the two Biodiversity labs in which students use a combination of preserved samples, microscopic slides and occasional potted live specimens of the four major plant groups to draw pictures and label structures. Time for the exercise was found by consolidating four other lab periods to follow into three labs which covered animals using preserved specimens in class and a review for the final exam without replacing any content. Biodiversity being the third biology core course in the sequence, fall semester had a higher number of class sections and students per section than spring. This exercise has been conducted continuously for the past 11 years while the data presented in this paper were collected over a period of six years.

2.2. Worksheet and Map

Ten tree species including *Gymnosperms* and *Angiosperms*, and four other botanical groups, namely, parasitic plants, lichens, epiphytes and herbaceous plants, which included *Bryophytes*, *Pteridophytes* and *Angiosperms* in close vicinity on campus, were identified for the exercise. Trees were listed as numbered stations according to the planned sequence of visits to them, and the discussion topics were included in a note-taking column as shown in Table 1 to cover the specific objective (a). The four non-tree botanical groups were numbered following ten trees on the worksheet and were planned to be covered between visits to the trees based on the proximity of the group to a visiting tree station. A Google Earth map with the stations labeled was prepared (Figure 1) to accompany the worksheet. While the sequence of stations to visit during a class tour was determined considering the blockades on the path due mainly to construction activities on campus, the most recent tours started at station 1 and ended at 11. Since botanical groups 12 and 13 were on the tree number 2, all three were covered together while the botanical group 14 was covered between trees, 4 and 5 (Figure 1). In the worksheet, Phylum *Magnoliophyta* meant the most inclusive plant phylum, all flowering plants. Economic benefits discussed included mainly the food for people from different tree species, timber, ornamental or shade value in landscaping, medicinal or other industrial uses, etc. Ecological benefits included air and soil quality improved and sustained by trees; food for animals with examples such as squirrels, other rodents and birds eating seeds, moth and butterfly caterpillars feeding on leaves; shelter for many animal species; trees hosting epiphytes and lichens; poisonous compounds in some trees, etc. Morphological characteristics included appearance of the tree in the winter, its stature and architecture, leaf shapes (e.g., deciduous or evergreen, relative size to which the tree grows, branching patterns of the main trunk and presence of simple/lobed/compound leaves, etc.) and simple flower morphology. In the non-tree botanical groups, nutritional meant nutritional habits of these groups or their components such as fungi and algae in the case of lichens. A quiz used for the assessment of actual knowledge gain was prepared based on the discussion had during the tour, and, therefore, the notes to be written by students in the worksheet. For the purpose of adoption, the design of the worksheet, therefore the map, could be changed, considering the specific course objectives, material already covered, types of trees and other botanical groups present on the given campus premises and the length of the time available for the exercise.

Table 1. Format of the worksheet used by students to take notes during the on-campus tour exercise. Numbers 1–10 = trees; 11–14 = other botanical groups.

Tree/Botanical Group No.	Common Name	Botanical Name	Basic Classification (Major Group, Phylum—Class in *Magnoliophyta*), Ecological and Economic Benefits/Uses, Morphology (Seasonal Appearance, Relative Size and Architecture, Leaf Shapes, Flower Characteristics), Native Land of Trees; Nutritional Habits of Non-Tree Botanicals, etc.
1	Bald cypress	*Taxodium distichum*	
2	Live oak	*Quercus virginiana*	
3	Crape myrtle	*Lagerstroemia indica*	
4	Sweet gum	*Liquidamber styraciflua*	
5	Pear	*Pyrus communis*	
6	Arbor vitae	*Thuja occidentalis*	

Table 1. *Cont.*

Tree/Botanical Group No.	Common Name	Botanical Name	Basic Classification (Major Group, Phylum—Class in *Magnoliophyta*), Ecological and Economic Benefits/Uses, Morphology (Seasonal Appearance, Relative Size and Architecture, Leaf Shapes, Flower Characteristics), Native Land of Trees; Nutritional Habits of Non-Tree Botanicals, etc.
7	Sago palm	*Cycas revoluta*	
8	Callery pear	*Pyrus calleryana*	
9	Pine	*Pinus spp.*	
10	Oleander	*Narium oleander*	
11	Parasitic Dodder plant	*Cuscuta sp.*	
12	Lichens		
13	Epiphytes (e.g., resurrection fern, mosses, Spanish moss)		
14	Herbaceous plants (e.g., clover, dandelion, broadleaved plantain, common purslane, spotted spurge, nutsedge, grasses)		

Figure 1. Google Earth map of the locations of trees (1 through 10) and other botanical groups (11 through 14) used for the exercise. Numbers of trees and other botanical groups are the same as in the worksheet.

2.3. Botanical Tour

A mock tour was taken first to approximately estimate and adjust the time needed to walk to each station, complete the discussion of the station, and take notes (Table 1). The tour was restricted to the coverage mentioned in the worksheet considering that the total time allocated for the lab was 1 h and 50 min, and students (a) would spend ~20 min in class for taking a short quiz from the previous lab and listening to a directive to the conduct of the exercise; (b) would take approximately another 20 min for walking between stations shown in Figure 1; and (c) would be dismissed ~10 min before the end of the lab period allowing them to go to their next class from the last station of the exercise. During the in-class directive, use of both worksheet and the map were briefed on. Students were asked to use the map during the tour and again later if they wanted to re-visit any station and review the materials discussed during the tour. They were reminded to stay together as one group and bring the worksheet and something to keep under it as support while writing but not the book bags. Both during the in-class directive and while on the tour, students were encouraged to observe, touch, take pictures and ask questions about the trees and other botanical groups that they would visit on tour. Photographs presented (Figure 2) were taken by students.

(a)   (b)

Figure 2. Students writing notes for Live Oak tree (*Quercus virginiana*) (**a**). Observations and discussions on moth eggs on oak leaves; seeds used as food by rodents; epiphytic lichens, mosses, resurrection fern and Spanish moss on the bark allowed students to appreciate multiple ecological benefits of the tree. A student writing notes using a flower picked from the pear tree (*Pirus communis*) and checking if it is *Monocot* or *Eudicot* (**b**).

2.4. Qualitative Assessment

Two summative student surveys were conducted over a period of six years (Table 2). Survey 1 was administered to each student pre- and post-exercise in six class sections in fall and three sections in spring to determine student-perceived improvement in 10 knowledge areas covered by the exercise. Data collected from the second survey (Table 2) conducted in eight fall and three spring sections served as student feedback on the conduct of the exercise. Rankings of survey 1 data were used to calculate the percentage student-perceived improvement as, ((post-exercise rating —pre-exercise rating)/pre-exercise rating) × 100. Survey 2 responses were processed using the pivot table feature on Microsoft Excel 2010.

Table 2. Two surveys administered to assess the student-perceived improvement in specific knowledge areas (survey 1, administered pre- and post-exercise) and the conduct of the exercise (survey 2).

Survey 1. Circle One Number as the Answer for Each Question.				Name		
Question	Response (1 = not knowledgeable; 5 = very knowledgeable)					
1	How knowledgeable are you of the four major plant groups?	1	2	3	4	5
2	How knowledgeable/familiar are you of the trees in local parks, campuses or other man-made landscapes?	1	2	3	4	5
3	How knowledgeable are you of the ecological benefits/contributions of the local trees?	1	2	3	4	5
4	How knowledgeable are you of the economic benefits/uses of the local trees?	1	2	3	4	5
5	Are you aware of the state trees of your and neighboring states?	1	2	3	4	5
6	Do you know the different leaf forms (morphologies) of local trees?	1	2	3	4	5
7	Are you familiar/knowledgeable with the major *Gymnosperms* in and around campus?	1	2	3	4	5
8	Are you knowledgeable of the representatives of *Monocots* and *Eudicots* in the local landscape?	1	2	3	4	5
9	Are you knowledgeable of the visible symbiotic relationships that local plants harbor?	1	2	3	4	5
10	Are you knowledgeable of the non-woody (herbaceous) plants in the local landscape?	1	2	3	4	5
Survey 2 Please Answer the Following Questions Regarding the on-Campus Tour Last Week.						
1	Given the time allocated to the lab, was the coverage of subject material (e.g., number of items on the handout) adequate? (please also comment, if desired).					
2	Was the time used effectively? (please also comment if desired).					
3	Did the exercise help strengthen your knowledge/experience of the plant kingdom? Please circle one, A. Yes, a great deal B. Yes, to some extent C. Yes, only marginally D. No and reason out your above answer with examples, if possible, below.					
4	Based on the overall exercise (educationally, logistically or in any other aspect), please indicate what worked well.					
5	Based on the overall exercise (educationally, logistically or in any other aspect), please indicate what did not work well? Please suggest improvements, if possible?					

2.5. Quantitative Assessment

Student grades from a ten question post-exercise quiz were compared with the averaged grades of two quizzes from other plant-related labs conducted in-class previously to determine the actual knowledge gain in eight fall and three spring sections. Each quiz had the same format with 10 multiple choice questions each with equal points. Since both quiz types were administered to the same individual students the mean comparison for quiz grades was performed with "repeated measure" under "general linear model" using SPSS V. 19.0.0.1 [23,24].

3. Results

3.1. Student-Perceived Knowledge Improvement

Students reported that their knowledge improved in all 10 areas investigated. The lowest improvement, 66%, was reported for the knowledge of four major plant groups while the highest, 200%, for the knowledge of major local *Gymnosperms* (Figure 3). Four knowledge areas, namely: (a) four major plant groups; (b) trees in local campuses and parks; (c) ecological benefits and (d) economic benefits of trees had lower (111%) self-reported improvement, averaged across the two semesters, than the other six knowledge areas. These six areas included: (a) state trees of neighboring states; (b) leaf morphologies; (c) local *Gymnosperms*; (d) local *Angiosperms* (*Monocots* and *Eudicots*); (e) symbiotic relationships of plants with other organisms; and (f) herbaceous plants, which showed 187% improvement. Students' self-reported improvement in each knowledge area showed no difference between semesters.

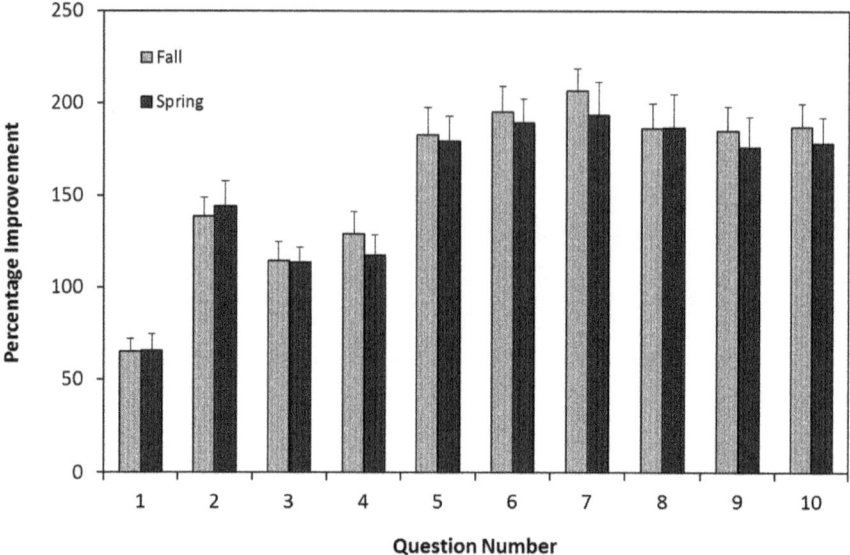

Figure 3. Improvement of student-perceived knowledge in ten subject areas questioned in survey 1. N = 95 and 44 for fall and spring, respectively. Error bars are SE.

3.2. Conduct

Student engagement was evident by consistently observing, touching and picking parts of specimens visited; frequent commenting on what they saw; questioning and note taking etc. (Figure 2). In survey 2, each student reported that the content covered was adequate and time was used efficiently (Table 3). Largest proportion of students, $\geq 50\%$, in each semester, responded "a great deal" while none responded "no" to the question, "Did the exercise help strengthen knowledge/experience of the plant kingdom?". Moreover, every student had responses to the question, "What worked?". Most students identified visual, hands-on and experiential learning as the reason why the exercise strengthened their knowledge of the plant kingdom followed by the information learned about each tree or botanical group. Organization of the tour and the coverage of material were cited most frequently as "what worked" followed by studying or being outdoors. In each semester, at least 50% of the students had no responses to the question, "What didn't work—suggest improvements" (Table 3). Students who responded to this question most frequently cited worksheet-related concerns. More than 50% of the worksheet-related concerns were about "too much information to write" followed by "an item was missing" and "sequence was not followed exactly". The most frequent comment under the season/weather-related concerns was "flowers (or leaves) were not there" followed by "weather too hot".

3.3. Actual Knowledge Gain

Performance on the quiz from the on-campus tour was 11.2 and 18.5% greater ($p < 0.001$), resulting in 0.82 and 1.16 points higher grade out of 10, compared to the average performance on the other two plant-related quizzes from the labs conducted in-class in fall and spring, respectively (Figure 4, descriptive statistics in Table 4 and results of the mean comparison in Table 5). Although the quiz grade from the on-campus tour was 9.5% higher in fall than spring ($p < 0.01$), improvement in the grade by on-campus tour was the same in each semester ($p = 0.14$).

Table 3. Percentage student responses for different categories covered in survey 2. $N = 154$ and 44 for fall and spring, respectively.

Semester	Coverage Adequate?		Time Used Effectively?		Strengthened Knowledge or Experience of the Plant Kingdom?				What Helped Strengthen Knowledge or Experience?				What Worked During the Tour?		What Didn't Work? Suggest Improvements to the Tour.						
	Y	N	Y	N	YG	YS	YM	N	VH	IT	KL	NA	TO	SO	WS	CW	SD	SW	DH	TW	NA
Fall	100	0	100	0	50	42	8	0	61	30	4	5	51	49	28	6	0.06	4	7	3	51
Spring	100	0	100	0	53	47	0	0	64	36	0	0	75	25	17	0	7	15	11	0	50

Y—Yes; N—No; YG—Yes a great deal; YS—Yes to some extent; YM—Yes marginally; VH—Visual/hands-on experience; IT—Information on each tree/botanical group; KL—Knowledge on local landscape; NA—Not available; TO—Tour organization/coverage; SO—Studying/being outdoor; WS—Worksheet-related; CW—Construction work on campus; SD—Student distractions; SW—Season/weather-related; DH—Difficulty hearing; TW—Tiring/boring walk.

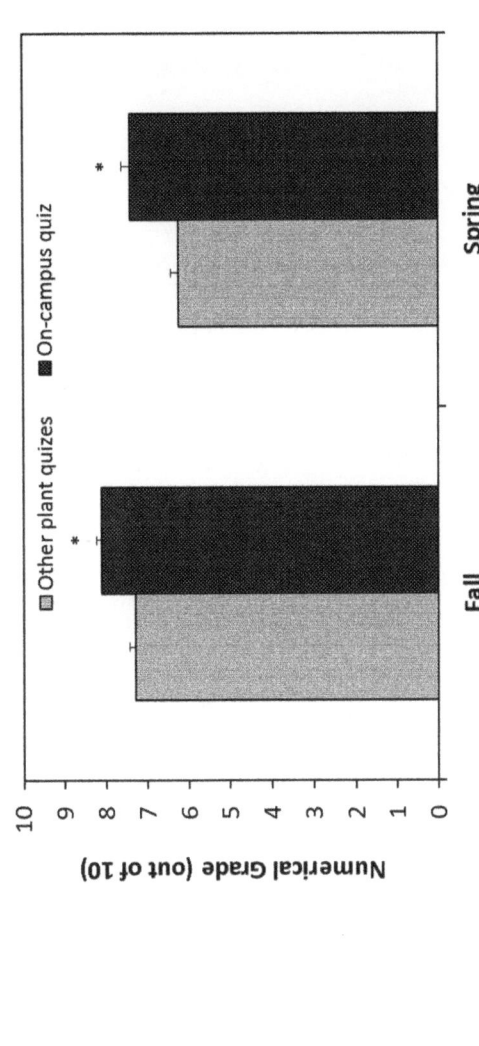

Figure 4. Student performance on the quiz from the on-campus tour exercise compared to the average performance on the two other quizzes from plant-related labs conducted in the classroom. The asterisk above a bar indicates statistical significance compared with the other value in a semester ($p < 0.001$). $N = 164$ and 70 for fall and spring, respectively. Error bars are SE.

Table 4. Descriptive statistics for the quiz comparison shown in Figure 4.

Semester/Descriptive Statistic	Fall		Spring	
	On-Campus Quiz	Other Plant Quizes	On-Campus Quiz	Other Plant Quizes
Mean	8.11	7.30	7.40	6.24
Median	8.25	7.50	8.00	6.25
Mode	10.00	7.50	9.00	6.00
Standard Error	0.13	0.14	0.22	0.19
Kurtosis	0.21	−0.57	−0.10	0.14
Maximum	10.00	10.00	10.00	9.00
Minimum	3.00	2.50	3.00	2.00
Range	7.00	7.50	7.00	7.00
Sample Variance	2.88	3.07	3.29	2.65
Skewness	−0.85	−0.43	−0.62	−0.61
Standard Deviation	1.70	1.75	1.81	1.63
Count	164	164	70	70

Table 5. Results of the general linear model used for the quiz comparison shown in Figure 4.

Semester	Source	Sum of Squares	Degrees of Freedom	Mean Square	F	Significance
Fall	Intercept	19,472.54	1	19,472.54	4079.76	0.000
	Error	777.99	163	4.77		
Spring	Intercept	6514.46	1	6514.46	1445.16	0.000
	Error	311.04	69	4.51		

3.4. Discussion and Educational Implications

Assessment showed that the exercise enhanced both student-perceived knowledge and actual knowledge gain. Student-perceived improvement of knowledge, while not an effective measure of knowledge gain [25], is indicative of student satisfaction, which is a predictor of quality of learning outcome [26]. Interestingly, students felt that the on-campus tour exercise strengthened their knowledge substantially (111% improvement) even in the subject areas that had already been covered in previous indoor labs and lecture, such as the subjects addressed in the first four questions of survey 1. Unsurprisingly, students reckoned that the exercise more markedly strengthened (187% improvement) their knowledge of the subjects that they were not directly taught prior to the exercise, the subjects addressed in questions five through ten of survey 1. Thus, this outdoor exercise shows promise for increasing student satisfaction in both reviewed and newly introduced subject areas. Student satisfaction and engagement were also evidenced by the results presented under conduct. For instance, every student had favorable comments about either outdoor experiential learning or tour organization/coverage under "what helped strengthen knowledge/experience" and "what worked", while the largest proportion of students had no response to "what didn't work, suggest improvements" even when asked to "suggest improvements". Furthermore, frequent questioning, sharing ideas freely among peers, following directions including note-taking and staying together as one group observed during the tour testified to the relaxed engagement of students in the exercise. Increased note-taking and verifying with me if the notes were correct, and more frequent group discussion among students compared to in-class labs was also evident. Students themselves identified "opportunities for group discussion" as part of "what worked" in survey 2. Research shows that learning in a group setting transforms the learning experience from competitive to collaborative, makes students engaged who otherwise might not become actively engaged [27], and improves grades in STEM fields [28]. In this exercise, students' awareness that the information covered during the tour was not available from the lab manual or textbook may also have contributed to their deeper engagement. Thus, one main outcome of the exercise was the student satisfaction, which translated into their engagement with what they handled eventually instigating effective experiential learning. Dedicated exposure to the local outdoors also encourages students to map their bioregion and understand the ecological and socioeconomic benefits of the world [29]. Students' experiences that (a) initiate interest in biology-at-work outdoors; (b) motivate them to ask questions and (c) engage them with the material they work with, may also strengthen their will to seek undergraduate research opportunities, which is the turning point for many to pursue careers in research [30,31]. Subsequently, a career in research is perceived by most students to be associated with high job satisfaction and social status [32].

Knowledge gain shown by higher quiz grades from the on-campus tour exercise compared to the two in-class labs that mainly used preserved specimens may result from the increased understanding and remembrance of the material learned as a result of hands-on, experiential and engaged learning that happened with a greater satisfaction during the on-campus tour. With the exception of basic taxonomy, much of the material covered during the on-campus tour exercise was not covered in previous plant labs or the lecture. For instance, ecological and economic uses, state trees of adjacent states, herbaceous plants, leaf morphologies, poisonous trees, native lands, botanical names, etc. learned during the on-campus tour as opposed to the overall cladogram, names of taxa and the common names of few representatives of those taxa learned in the previous labs or lecture. Moreover, the quiz from the on-campus tour did not include any question directly related to the previously covered materials. Therefore, the higher quiz grade from the on-campus tour exercise is most likely due to the attributes of outdoor experiential learning rather than due to the knowledge from materials covered already. The Biodiversity course in the fall semester is comprised mostly of students directly progressing from previous biology core courses, General Biology 1 and 2 (regular sequence) compared to the spring, which tends to enroll a sizeable number of students repeating the course or transferring from a different program (off sequence). Interestingly, although this difference between the two cohorts was manifested as a greater quiz grade in fall than spring, the on-campus tour exercise imparted the same degree of improvement in knowledge gain in either cohort.

Assessments by the surveys and the quiz testified that the students acknowledged and experienced the influence of the exercise on their learning of multiple areas of the main subject, the study of plants in Biodiversity. For instance, discussion on social recognition of trees by way of naming state trees, experiencing the fundamental biological principles such as symbiosis, becoming aware of local representatives of major plant groups, knowing that herbaceous plants are immediately important as most of the human food, being able to recognize trees by names using morphological characteristics, etc. were either reported as knowledge/skill areas that were highly improved or commented as reasons why the exercise was interesting. Thus, the findings of this study show that given the proper exposure and guide, students can be motivated to appreciate outdoor experience, a core meaning of biology. Such planned guidance is increasingly significant today due to (a) poor representation of organismal diversity in current biology curricula [33]; (b) inadequate basic systematics skills of biology students [15,16]; (c) student perception that biology curricula are detached from their lives and interests [34] and (d) general public perception that modern biology students are distracted from the nature. The opportunity for students to apply what they learn in class to the local outdoor environment, and to work interactively as a team may also help them develop improved study habits.

4. Conclusions

Assessment of this on-campus tour exercise showed that it (a) instigated student satisfaction and engagement in learning plant-related biodiversity of the local environment; and (b) enhanced the knowledge of selected subject areas of the curriculum that can be connected to outdoors. Findings testified that, given the opportunity, students willingly engage in and apply what they experience in the outdoor world contrary to the general perception that today's biology students are inadequately interested in the outdoor environment. Teaching outdoors was useful for both review and introduction of new material notwithstanding the inherent differences in academic performance of student cohorts of different semesters. Thus, an on-campus tour exercise is both an academically effective and a practically convenient alternative when organized field trips with the class are not possible.

Educ. Sci. **2017**, *7*, 18

Acknowledgments: The author thanks Peter Martinat, the coordinator of the Biodiversity course at Xavier University of Louisiana, for granting permission to incorporate this exercise into the course, and students who participated in the study.

Conflicts of Interest: The author declares no conflict of interest.

References

1. Elliott, K.M.; Shin, D. Student satisfaction: An alternative approach to assessing this important concept. *J. High. Educ. Policy Manag.* **2002**, *24*, 197–209. [CrossRef]
2. Pintrich, P.R.; Schunk, D.H. *Motivation in Education: Theory, Research and Applications*, 2nd ed.; Merrill: Upper Saddle River, NJ, USA, 2002.
3. Sharp, L.B. Outside the classroom. *Educ. Forum.* **1943**, *7*, 361–368. [CrossRef]
4. Hammerman, W.M. *Fifty Years of Resident Outdoor Education, 1930–1980: Its Impact on American Education*; American Camping Association: Martinsville, IN, USA, 1980.
5. Hammerman, D.R.; Hammerman, W.M.; Hammerman, E.L. *Teaching in the Outdoors*, 5th ed.; Interstate Publishers: Danville, IL, USA, 2001.
6. Boes, K.E. Campus Eco Tours—An integrative & interactive field project for undergraduate biology students. *Am. Biol. Teach.* **2013**, *75*, 330–334.
7. Lieberman, G.A.; Hoody, L. *Closing the Achievement Gap: Using the Environment as an Integrating Context for Learning*; California Student Assessment Project: Poway, CA, USA, 1998.
8. Barrows, R.M.; Silver, E.J.; Stein, R.E. School recess and group classroom behavior. *Pediatrics* **2009**, *123*, 431–436. [CrossRef] [PubMed]
9. Fägerstam, E.; Blom, J. Learning biology and mathematics outdoors: Effects and attitudes in a Swedish high school context. *J. Advent. Educ. Outdoor Learn.* **2013**, *13*, 56–75. [CrossRef]
10. Weigl, P.D. The natural history conundrum revisited: Mammalogy begins at home. *J. Mamm.* **2009**, *90*, 265–269. [CrossRef]
11. Barker, S.; Slingsby, D.; Tilling, S. *Teaching Biology Outside of the Classroom: Is It Heading for Extinction? A Report on Biology in the 14–19 Curriculum*; Field Studies Council Occasional Publication 72; Preston Montford: Shropshire, UK, 2002.
12. Zettler, J.A.; Collier, A.; Leidersdorf, B.; Sanou, M.P. Plants in your ants; using ant mounds to test basic ecological principles. *Am. Biol. Teach.* **2010**, *72*, 173–176. [CrossRef]
13. Lock, R. Biology fieldwork in schools and colleges in the UK: An analysis of empirical research from 1963 to 2009. *J. Biol. Edu.* **2010**, *44*, 58–64. [CrossRef]
14. Scott, G.W.; Boyd, M.; Scott, L.; Colquhoun, D. Barriers to biological fieldwork: What really prevents teaching out of doors? *J. Biol. Edu.* **2015**, *49*, 165–178. [CrossRef]
15. Scott, G.W.; Goulder, R. Conflicting perceptions of the status of field biology and identification skills in UK education. *J. Biol. Edu.* **2016**, *50*, 233–238.
16. Bilton, D.T. What is in a name? What have taxonomy and systematics ever done for us? *J. Biol. Edu.* **2014**, *48*, 116–118. [CrossRef]
17. Hannah-Jones, N. *A prescription for More Black Doctors*; New York Times: New York, NY, USA, 2015.
18. Rath, K.A.; Peterfreuand, A.R.; Xenos, S.P.; Bayliss, F.; Carnal, N. Supplemental instruction in introductory biology I: Enhancing the performance and retention of underrepresented minority students. *CBE-Life Sci. Edu.* **2007**, *6*, 203–216. [CrossRef] [PubMed]
19. Baker, B. Recruiting minorities to the biological sciences: Biologists are trying a range of approaches to diversify their field. *Bioscience* **2000**, *50*, 191–195. [CrossRef]
20. Ksiksi, T.S. Teaching introductory Biology courses: What works and what does not work. *Am. Eurasian J. Sci. Res.* **2006**, *1*, 46–48.
21. American Association for the Advancement of Science. *Vision and Change in Biology Education, a Call to Action*; American Association for the Advancement of Science: Washington, DC, USA, 2011.
22. Dillon, J.; Rickinson, M.; Teamey, K.; Morris, M.; Choi, M.Y.; Sanders, D.; Benefield, P. The value of outdoor learning: Evidence from research in the UK and elsewhere. *School Sci. Rev.* **2006**, *87*, 107–111.
23. International Business Machines. *SPSS version 19.0.0.1 Statistical Program*; IBM Co.: Armonk, NY, USA, 2010.

24. Sokal, R.R.; Rohlf, F.J. *Biometry, the Principles and Practice of Statistics in Biological Research*, 3rd ed.; W.H. Freeman and Co.: New York, NY, USA, 1997.
25. Bacon, D.R. Reporting actual and perceived student learning in education research. *J. Market. Edu.* **2016**, *38*, 3–6. [CrossRef]
26. Eom, S.B.; Wen, H.J.; Ashill, N. The determinants of students' perceived learning outcomes and satisfaction in university online education: An empirical investigation. *Decision Sci. J. Innov. Edu.* **2006**, *4*, 215–235. [CrossRef]
27. Tanner, K.; Chatman, L.S.; Allen, D. Approaches to cell biology teaching: Cooperative learning in the science classroom—Beyond students working in groups. *Cell Biol. Educ.* **2003**, *2*, 1–5. [CrossRef] [PubMed]
28. Freeman, S.; Eddya, S.L.; McDonougha, M.; Smithb, M.K.; Okoroafora, N.; Jordta, H.; Wenderotha, M.P. Active learning increases student performance in science, engineering, and mathematics. *PNAS* **2014**, *111*, 8410–8415. [CrossRef] [PubMed]
29. Oberbillig, D.; Randle, D.C.; Middendorf, G.; Lardelús, C.L. Outdoor learning in formal ecological education: Looking to the future. *Front. Ecol. Environ.* **2014**, *12*, 419–420. [CrossRef]
30. Gavin, R. The Role of Research at Undergraduate Institutions: Why is it necessary to defend it? In *Academic Excellence. The Role of Research in the Physical Sciences at Undergraduate Institutions*; Doyle, M.P., Ed.; Research Corporation: Tucson, AZ, USA, 2000; pp. 9–16.
31. National Research Council (U.S.) Committee on Undergraduate Biology Education to Prepare Research Scientists for the 21st Century. In *Bio2010: Transforming Undergraduate Education for Future Research Biologists*; National Academies Press: Washington, DC, USA, 2003.
32. Henderson, D.; Stanisstreet, M.; Boyes, E. Who wants a job in biology? Student aspirations and perceptions. *J. Biol. Edu.* **2007**, *41*, 156–161. [CrossRef]
33. Greene, H.W. Organisms in nature as a central focus for biology. *Trends Ecol. Evol.* **2004**, *20*, 23–27. [CrossRef] [PubMed]
34. Hagay, G.; Baram-Tsabari, A. A shadow curriculum: Incorporating students' interests into the formal biology curriculum. *Res. Sci. Edu.* **2011**, *41*, 611–634. [CrossRef]

education
sciences

Review

Teaching Methods in Biology Education and Sustainability Education Including Outdoor Education for Promoting Sustainability—A Literature Review

Eila Jeronen [1,*], Irmeli Palmberg [2] and Eija Yli-Panula [3]

[1]   Faculty of Education, University of Oulu, 90014 Oulu, Finland
[2]   Faculty of Education and Welfare Studies, Åbo Akademi University, 20500 Turku, Finland;
      irmeli.palmberg@abo.fi
[3]   Faculty of Education, University of Turku, 20500 Turku, Finland; eijyli@utu.fi
*   Correspondence: eila.jeronen@oulu.fi; Tel.: +358-40-577-9103

Academic Editor: James Albright
Received: 31 October 2016; Accepted: 14 December 2016; Published: 22 December 2016

Abstract: There are very few studies concerning the importance of teaching methods in biology education and environmental education including outdoor education for promoting sustainability at the levels of primary and secondary schools and pre-service teacher education. The material was selected using special keywords from biology and sustainable education in several scientific databases. The article provides an overview of 24 selected articles published in peer-reviewed scientific journals from 2006–2016. The data was analyzed using qualitative content analysis. Altogether, 16 journals were selected and 24 articles were analyzed in detail. The foci of the analyses were teaching methods, learning environments, knowledge and thinking skills, psychomotor skills, emotions and attitudes, and evaluation methods. Additionally, features of good methods were investigated and their implications for teaching were emphasized. In total, 22 different teaching methods were found to improve sustainability education in different ways. The most emphasized teaching methods were those in which students worked in groups and participated actively in learning processes. Research points toward the value of teaching methods that provide a good introduction and supportive guidelines and include active participation and interactivity.

Keywords: biology education; sustainability education; environmental education; education for sustainable development; outdoor education; primary schools; secondary schools; pre-service teacher education; literature review

---

1. Introduction

One of the international goals for the future is the construction of a sustainable society [1]. A sustainable society is considered to be a society that has reached sustainability through a process called sustainable development. Sustainable development as a concept is heavily context-dependent in social, cultural, and environmental situations [2]. Brundtland's report defines sustainability as "development that meets the needs of the present without compromising the ability of future generations to meet their own needs" [3]. According to Diesendorf [4], this definition emphasizes the long-term aspect of the concept of sustainability and introduces the ethical principle of achieving equity between the present and future generations. It does not mention the natural environment explicitly, focusing only upon human needs or wants. However, the report makes it clear that these "needs" include the conservation of the natural environment. More recently, it has been given a broader definition which conveys that there are three principal dimensions: an ecological, economic and social one [5]. In the teaching and learning of sustainable development, the ecological dimension refers to the natural one and includes all living things, resources and life-supporting systems. Its goal is conservation. The economic dimension comprises jobs and income, and its goal is appropriate development. The social dimension involves people living together. Its goal is peace, equality and human rights. In addition to these three dimensions, there is also a fourth one, the political dimension. It has to do with politics, policy and decision-making as a goal of democracy [5]. The ecological issues are important in biology education, e.g., in Finland, Sweden and Denmark, they form the core content in the curricula of biology for basic education. All biology curricula emphasize different biotopes and ecosystems, lifecycles of plants and animals, and life-supporting processes, such as photosynthesis, respiration and biodiversity, but they do not mention the other dimensions of sustainability [6–8]. For this reason, we stress the ecological aspect in this study. Our aim is to find out and describe useful teaching methods in biology education and sustainability education (SE) including outdoor education (OE) for promoting sustainability in primary and secondary schools and teacher education. As far as we know, there are no previous studies from these perspectives.

An ongoing debate over the last three decades has been how the role of education should be conceptualized when creating sustainability and a sustainable future. Sustainability and a sustainable future are here understood as the goals of sustainable development. The relationships between environmental education, education for sustainable development, and sustainable development education have been discussed. Environmental education and education for sustainable development are interpreted in different ways around the world, according to context [9]. Some authors argue that education for sustainable development is a part of environmental education [10] or a perspective of environmental education [11], or that environmental education has developed into education for sustainable development [12]. In Agenda 21, it has been stated that environmental education is a continual, life-long learning process to raise public awareness and action globally, nationally and locally in every area in which humans impact the environment [13]. Important distinctions between the goals of environmental education were made by Lucas [14]—"in," "about" or "for" the environment—in order to avoid misunderstandings about the intended type of environmental education.

According to UNESCO [15], education for sustainable development is about enabling people to constructively and creatively address present and future global challenges and create more sustainable and resilient societies. Learning in education for sustainable development often includes only knowledge, values and theories related to sustainable development. However, it also means "learning to ask critical questions; learning to clarify one's own values; learning to envision more positive and sustainable futures; learning to think systematically; learning to respond through applied learning; and learning to explore the dialectic between tradition and innovation" [13]. Thus it offers learners a context for developing active citizenship and participation, embracing the complexity of the interdependencies of ecological, societal, and economic systems [16]. The overall goal of the UN Decade of Education for Sustainable Development (2005–2014) was to integrate the principles, values, and practices of sustainable development into all aspects of education and learning [17]. In Finland, sustainability is included in the curriculum for basic education at all educational levels. How this has been done is described in more detail in another article of this special issue [18].

Sustainable development education again is based particularly on environmental and ecological sciences and focuses on the interaction between ecological and social systems. It encourages students to critically reflect on the ideas of sustainable development and the values that underlie them, and to create solutions to achieve concrete goals in a variety of unpredictable situations [19].

As noted above, both environmental education, education for sustainable development, and sustainable development education share a vision of quality education and a society that lives in balance with Earth's carrying capacity. They are thus integrated and represented in all dimensions of sustainable development. In this study, we use the term sustainability education (SE) [20] because it catches all forms of environmental education, education for sustainable development, and sustainable development education.

2. Theoretical Background

Many of the topics in biology education are closely linked to the content of SE. These kinds of contents exist especially in the fields of ecology, biodiversity, conservation and system biology. According to Palmberg et al. [21], the ability to identify species is important for a better understanding of biodiversity and issues concerning the environment and sustainability, not only for comprehension of certain branches of biology (e.g., ecology, evolution, genetics). However, taxonomy is often a forgotten field in school curricula. Biological phenomena connected to socio-scientific issues, such as climate change, need to have an integrative and interdisciplinary approach to be thoroughly taught and learned. When biology education is given in connection to SE, teaching methods such as experiential, collaborative, process-based and problem-based experimental learning and computer-assisted methods can be useful.

2.1. Common Educational Principles Promoting Sustainability

To achieve the goals of SD, active teaching methods such as the process-based instruction, problem-based learning, and OE are recommended by several researchers [19,22,23]. Process-based instruction focuses upon developing students' independence in learning and problem solving by providing a framework into which curriculum activities can be placed [24]. In problem-based learning, students use "triggers" from a problem case or scenario to define their own learning objectives. Subsequently they do independent, self-directed study before returning to the group to discuss and refine their acquired knowledge [25]. Problem-based learning and experience-based learning in authentic environments are main ideas also in OE [22,26]. There is, however, no definitive description of authentic learning. Educators must make their own interpretations of what creates meaning for students in the classroom [27]. In this study, we do not take the term authentic environment to mean only environments outside the classroom; instead we take it to mean teaching strategies which make student experiences as authentic as possible compared to what happens in real life. In order to do so, the information to be studied and the environment in which learning takes place must be meaningful to the students. In addition, it also means that teachers should support the students to be reflective. Different learning environments and current and contextual tasks used in problem-based learning and OE support self-efficacy, autonomy, engagement, and meaningful learning as well as foster creativity and flexibility [28]. Collaborative learning can be supported e.g., by searching information [29] and producing knowledge in groups [30], by evaluating learning, action, and knowing together [31].

The ever-growing importance of complex problem solving and knowledge construction in modern society emphasizes the need for collaborative activities and settings in schools to foster learning and collective competencies [32]. Collaborative learning is seen as an active process resulting in jointly processed knowledge better than the knowledge produced by an individual (e.g., [33]). This is especially the case concerning environmental issues, which should be solved to support sustainable development. Recently, the collaborative and inquiry-based study approaches have been investigated in the computer-assisted study environments in science. Studies have indicated that inquiry-based learning can be applied to the context of computer-assisted collaborative learning and that collaborative technology facilitates high-level cognitive and social interaction while students work together toward deeper understanding (e.g., [34,35]). These skills are important when solving multifaceted environmental problems in order to work toward a more sustainable lifestyle.

2.2. Teaching Principles and Methods in Biology Promoting Sustainability

Biodiversity, climate change, the sustainable use of natural resources, health, cultural heritage, multiculturalism, and global welfare are important contents in the planning of a sustainable future. The effects of students' own behavior should be discussed and sustainable actions practiced in local surroundings. An important goal is to learn negotiation, problem solving and decision-making skills through discussions about ecological, social, economic, and ethical principles concerning local and global responsibility in their own life. Through memorable, experiential, and active processes, students learn to discuss their own value selection and to evaluate phenomena and sources of information critically [36–38].

In biology education, selected teaching methods should support learning biology, learning to do biological science and learning about biological science [39]. Several biological topics require approaches promoting experimental problem-solving and process-based skills [40,41]. The focus is on science investigation processes and the goal is to reach valuable learning results, and students therefore need crucial science content knowledge as well as autonomous learning [42]. This, however, seems to create difficulties for the so-called working memory, which again impairs the self-regulation competencies [43]. Therefore it is important to implement teaching methods including both autonomous learning and instructional activities, and to vary the level of openness of experimental tasks. The implementation of problem-based active learning models have positive effects on students' academic achievements and their attitudes to science courses [44], while implementation of problem-based learning and group investigation encourages students to think critically through planning, arguing, stating questions and problems, and providing solutions to environmental problems [45].

Biological field-based activities, e.g., fieldwork and field trips, provide students with authentic and interactive experiences and experiential learning opportunities, which increase students´ interest and enhance their learning [46]. Students´ engagement in field-based activities plays an essential role in learning biological issues. Fieldwork provides students with a chance to observe nature and the environment and to use scientific inquiry to test ideas and concepts they have learned in the classroom. According to Hart and Nolan [47], fieldwork had a positive effect on students´ knowledge, attitude and behavior, crucial factors also in promoting sustainability.

2.3. Teaching Principles and Methods in Sustainability Education Promoting Sustainability

According to the World Bank [48], "[t]he achievement of sustained and equitable development remains the greatest challenge facing the human race." Recently, the sustainable development goals represented a focus on the role of education in achieving a more humane world [49]: "education for sustainable development and sustainable lifestyles, human rights, gender equality, promotion of a culture of peace and non-violence, global citizenship, and appreciation of cultural diversity and of culture's contribution to sustainable development." This requires an ecological or participatory worldview [50]. It is important to understand the interlinkages between the three pillars of sustainable development (economic growth, social development, and environmental protection) and the consequences of human choices. It means that people's ways of thinking should change toward more holistic, systemic and integrative modes [51].

Human societies and ecological systems are interconnected so that they are co-adaptive, reacting to each other and to previous interactions and reactions in a network of feedbacks [19]. Consequently, the approach of education must be complex, transdisciplinary, and broad [52]. However, current learning processes and practices are generally not aligned with this kind of education [53] (p. 21); [54].

The focus of SE is on the interaction between social and ecological systems requiring interdisciplinary thinking skills [21]. Practical problem-based learning develops this kind of understanding [52]. SE aims to foster students' ability to apply knowledge in a variety of unpredictable situations. Students are encouraged to critically reflect on the ideas of sustainable development and the values that underlie them, and create solutions to achieve concrete goals in their unique situation [21]. Typical for SE is that educators offer a wide range of conceptual and material content, illustrate interconnections and interdependence, and stress dynamic rather than fixed structures and processes [55]. Furthermore, hands-on experiences can be incorporated into the curricula [52]. OE is seen as an effective way of getting hands-on experiences because it integrates concrete experiences, interests, emotions, and values [56].

2.4. Outdoor Education and Meaning of the Place Promoting Sustainability

Fieldwork and field trips in biology involve many different goals, contents and learning environments [57–59] and therefore also vary in effectiveness and learning outcomes. A common feature, however, is that all activities are arranged in authentic, often natural environments, where students can connect their theoretical thinking with experiences of various kinds of real nature. Fieldwork and field trips are examples of outdoor learning, or its synonyms outdoor learning activities and outdoor activities [22,28]. In addition to outdoor activities, outdoor education includes overall interdisciplinary aspects of the world outside the school. It can be arranged, e.g., as adventure education, adventure/wilderness therapy, experiential education, outdoor leadership, outdoor environmental education, outdoor recreation or expeditions (e.g., [22,28,60]).

Developing a relationship with nature is an important precursor to understanding sustainability (e.g., [61,62]). This is why different approaches to outdoor education and outdoor learning (see overview in [26]), and especially fieldwork, field trips and nature studies, are important ways of improving ecological literacy [57,58], i.e., "understanding the key ecological systems using sound ecological thinking, and also understanding the nature of ecological science and its interface with society" [63]. Other important outcomes of outdoor learning are, e.g., connectedness to nature [64,65], positive environmental attitudes [66,67], and environmental consciousness [22,68]. Outdoor nature experiences then again are the most important factor connecting with interest in biology [69]. Several research results confirm significantly better learning results for students when they get first-hand experiences and studies in authentic learning environments, like farms [70] and natural environments [57,59,61,62].

3. Research Aim and Questions

An important question concerning biology education and SE including OE is how they can promote sustainability. As far as we know, there are no previous studies discussing this question based on comparison and evaluation of different teaching methods. The aim of this study is therefore to identify and describe useful teaching methods in biology education and SE including OE for promoting sustainability. The results are used for developing curricula and instructions of biology education in basic and teacher education.

The research is guided by the following research questions:

(1) What are the teaching methods used in biology education and SE including OE for achieving the sustainable development goals in primary and secondary schools and in teacher education?

To get answers to the first research question, we analyzed described teaching methods, objectives for the development of psychomotor skills, emotions and attitudes, knowledge and thinking skills to be learned, learning environments, and how achievements were evaluated.

(2) What are the features of the useful teaching methods in biology education and SE including OE for achieving sustainable development goals?

To get answers to the second research question, we analyzed features of useful teaching methods and what kind of implications there were for developing curricula and the teaching of biology.

4. Material

The material was selected applying the method presented by Àlvarez-Garcia et al. [71]. For a systematic review, we identified peer-reviewed journal articles using a consistent search strategy, established the criteria for the selection of articles to be considered, and analyzed them based on clear and precise criteria and dimensions [72].

The articles were searched using scientific databases such as ERIC, Web of Science, and SCOPUS. The search strategy was based on a systematical organization, categorization and selection of keywords related to biology education and SE. A word search was thus conducted in relation to the terms biology education, teaching methods, sustainable development, environmental education, education for sustainable development, outdoor education, fieldwork, excursions and study trips, problem-based learning, project-based learning, experimental learning, experiential learning, game-based learning, value-based learning, place-based learning, collaborative learning, computer-supportive learning, inquiry-based learning, and teacher training. All searches were done in English, Finnish, Swedish and German. Using these keywords, a common search strategy was developed for the various databases consulted, adapting it to the characteristics of the given platform. For each database, a hierarchical search strategy was applied, starting from the simplest expression (one term) to the most complex form (combinations of terms). Depending on the requirements of each database, the search fields were basically limited to the title and abstract of the articles. Also manual examinations of key research journals in biology education and SE including OE were used as well as reviews and bibliographies.

The following criteria were used to select material for the more detailed analyses of teaching methods:

(a)   Scope: National and international research;
(b)   Type of research: Empirical research on teaching methods in biology education and SE including OE;
(c)   Period: 2006–July 2016;
(d)   Target groups: students in primary schools, secondary schools and pre-service teacher education;
(e)   Languages: Finnish, Swedish, English or German;

Although we are well aware of the existence of other types of documents that could have been analyzed, such as dissertation theses, research reports, books and book chapters and conference proceedings, we limited the review to academic papers published in peer-reviewed journals because they have been subjected to rigorous review and are, therefore, high-quality documents. We also eliminated articles that do not specifically refer to teaching methods in biology education or SE including OE.

(f)   Quality: Academic papers published in peer-reviewed journals.

5. Methods

The study is a qualitative survey with quantitative features [73,74]. At first, we examined the selected 17 journals concerning biology education and SE. They included in total 29 articles that mentioned teaching methods. From these, we selected 16 journals with 24 articles to be analyzed in detail (Table 1).

Table 1. The selected journals and the analyzed articles.

The Selected Journals	The Analyzed Articles
Environmental Education Research	[75–77]
Eurasia Journal of Mathematics, Science & Technology Education	[78]
International Journal of Environmental and Science Education	[79]
International Journal of Science Education	[80–82]
International Research in Geographical and Environmental Education	[83]
Journal of Adventure Education & Outdoor Learning	[84]
Journal of Biological Education	[85]
Journal of Education for Sustainable Development	[86]
Journal of Environmental Education	[87]
Journal of Science Teacher Education	[88–92]
Journal of Sustainable Development	[93]
Journal of Sustainability Education	[94]
Journal of Teacher Education for Sustainability	[95]
Nordic Studies in Science Education	[96]
PLoS ONE	[97]
Sustainability—Open Access Journal	[98]

In the analysis, we followed the method of qualitative content analysis [99–102]. Inductive content analysis was used to analyze teaching methods, learning environments and features of useful teaching methods and implications [99,101]. Deductive content analysis was used to analyze psychomotor skills, emotions and attitudes, knowledge and thinking skills and also evaluation methods [99].

In order to ensure the reliability of the process, all three members of the research team first conducted the selection of information units, the categorization and the subsequent analysis independently. The analysis process was dialogical by nature. The final decisions were made through e-mail discussions where each researcher argued why the content of the article should be placed into a certain category or categories. The discussion continued until consensus was reached and clear arguments were found. The generalizability of our results relates to the selection of analyzed data. To ensure that our categorization decisions were based on comprehensive understanding of the article, we decided to read the whole article before categorizing it. We also based our analysis on what the authors of the articles had explicitly written rather than what we in some cases thought we could read between the lines as being the authors' intentions. As such decisions always include elements of subjective interpretation, joint discussions about each article were essential in deciding which aspects of the instructional process the article emphasized. This procedure ensured that decisions were not based on a single person's first impression of an article but on well-argued joint discussions. Because of the dialogical nature of the analysis, we did not see a need for calculating an inter-rater reliability. Researcher triangulation was an essential part of our analysis process. Our research group consisted of experts from biology education, environmental education, sustainable development education, and educational sciences, and all researchers are experienced teacher educators and researchers.

6. Findings and Discussion

There are many articles concerning studies and comparisons of teaching methods in relation to other issues in the studies of biology and sustainability education. Teaching methods can be seen as objective-oriented activities and flow of information between teachers and students. Studies of teaching methods are important because teaching methods influence all types of learning in the cognitive, affective and psychomotor domains [103,104]. The choice of teaching methods depends on what kind of teaching approach is preferred. Traditional instruction in biology is deductive and comprises the principles and methods used for instruction to be implemented by teachers to achieve the desired learning or memorization by students. In this kind of teacher-centered approach to learning, teachers are authorities and students' primary role is to passively receive information through lectures and direct instruction. Learning is measured using objectively scored tests and assessments [104,105]. Alternative teaching approaches are inductive where instruction begins e.g., with observations, experimental data to interpret or a real-world problem to be solved. In this student-centered approach to learning, teachers and students play an equally active role in the learning process. The teacher's primary role is to coach and facilitate student learning and overall comprehension of material. Learning is continuously measured using both formal and informal forms of assessment, including group projects, student portfolios, and class participation [104]. The selection of teaching methods is affected by the learning objectives. The clearly specified learning objectives also provide the goals at which the curriculum is aimed, they facilitate the selection and organization of content, and they make it possible to evaluate the outcomes of the learning [105]. Several good features are emphasized in the analyzed teaching methods and have implications especially for developing curricula and teaching for sustainability.

6.1. Teaching Methods

In total, 22 different teaching methods were found in the analyzed articles (Figure 1). The most common teaching method was students working in groups and participating actively in learning processes. Nowadays, this is also used in science education [44]. The most frequently mentioned teaching methods were outdoor education and fieldwork, experimental, interactive and experiential learning. Teachers' presentations and teaching discussions were also popular. They were used mostly when introducing students to the work and toward objectives.

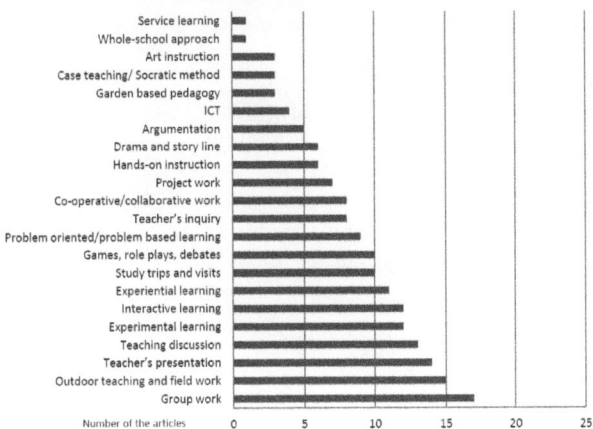

Figure 1. Teaching methods found in the analyzed articles.

Previous studies have shown that in active teaching-learning processes, retention of knowledge is significantly increased [106,107], there is enhanced motivation and higher-order learning [108] and development of practical skills [27]. Substantial evidence also exists that indicates that well-planned, taught, and guided outdoor teaching and fieldwork can have a positive impact on long-term memory due to memorable experiences. Residential experience can lead to individual growth and improvements in social skills. More importantly, there can be reinforcement between the affective and the cognitive domains. However, students are different: some of them like fieldwork and some do not. Poor fieldwork is likely to lead to poor learning. Some researchers also present a health warning concerning OE [27].

There are also barriers and opportunities for OE and fieldwork at schools and in teacher education. These include e.g., fear and concern about health and safety, teachers' lack of confidence in teaching outdoors, curriculum requirements limiting opportunities for outdoor learning, and shortage of time, resources and support. Research into students' experiences of outdoor learning activities suggests that there are several factors that can facilitate and/or impede learning in outdoor settings. These include the structure, duration and pedagogy of OE programs, the characteristics, interests and preferences of students, and the nature and novelty of the outdoor learning settings [28].

Problem-oriented/problem-based, co-operative/collaborative and argumentation as teaching methods were emphasized in more than one-fifth of the articles. These teaching methods are important in students learning processes and can enhance learning when they are used together and connected to information and communications technology. Collaboration supports students to make their own thinking visible [109,110] and helps them to learn from argumentation [111]. Argumentation has been shown to support higher-order and critical thinking, and engagement in science learning [112]. Higher-order and critical thinking is important to enhance understanding of socio-scientific issues connected to biology and sustainable development education. Collaborative reading within an argumentative discussion supports students to understand the text in more depth [113].

Whole-school approaches and service-learning approaches can be seen as part of place-based learning in local environments and communities through the use of local features, phenomena, and issues as context and scaffolding for content [114,115]. These were scarcely represented in the reviewed literature. However, they should be taken more into account also in biology education because they can generate a broader public interest and perhaps motivate local, state, and national policy makers to advocate for the integration of SE within the school curriculum [116]. They can also produce greater confidence, stronger motivation toward learning, and a greater sense of belonging and responsibility. In addition, through these, students can develop more positive relationships with each other, with their teachers and with the surrounding communities [28].

6.2. Objectives for the Development of Psychomotor Skills, Emotions and Attitudes

Learning in the psychomotor domain is associated with physical skills such as speed, dexterity, grace, the use of instruments, expressive movement, and the use of the body in dance or athletics. The psychomotor domain addresses skill development relating to manual tasks and physical movement as well as the operation of equipment, such as computers and laboratory tools [117,118]. Its subdomains are perception, set, guided response, mechanism, and complex overt reaction. Perception refers to the ability to apply sensory information to motor activity and set to the readiness to act [117,119]. Guided response comprises the ability to imitate a displayed behavior or to utilize trial and error [117]. Mechanism refers to the ability to use learned skills intendedly in different actions without supervision [117,119]. Complex overt reaction has to do with the ability to skillfully perform complex patterns of actions [117,119]. The three first subdomains were well represented in the articles (Figure 2) whereas the two last ones were not.

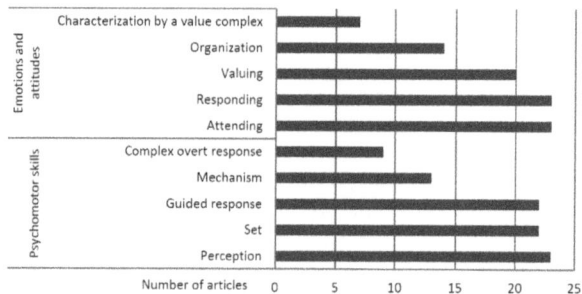

Figure 2. The objectives for the development of the psychomotor skills (categorized according to the model of [117,119]) and objectives for development of emotions and attitudes (categorized according to the model of [119,120]).

Kearney [121] defined affective learning as "an increasing internalization of positive attitudes toward the content or subject matter." Feelings, emotions, and attitudes belong to the affective domain which has five subdomains. The lowest subdomain has to do with attending or receiving. It includes the awareness of feelings and emotions as well as the ability to utilize selected attention. The next subdomain involves responding or reacting to phenomena, which means active participation of the student. The third subdomain has to do with the ability to see the value of something and to express it. The fourth subdomain, organization, includes the ability to prioritize values and to create a unique value system. The uppermost subdomain is characterization. It is the ability to internalize values and let them control one's behavior [119,120]. Rodriguez et al. [122] suggest affective learning subsumes student motivation and promotes greater learning because "affective learning motivates students to engage in task-relevant behaviors."

The three lower subdomains were well represented in the articles, but the upper ones were not taken into account as often. A deficiency concerns the pedagogies. It is easy to assert that the affective domain is important in science education. However, it is usually not clear what types of behavior should be looked for in students when their feelings, appreciations, attitudes, and values are evaluated. Compounding the difficulty is the general uncertainty about the definition or specification of the phenomena related to science education that we expect students to exhibit feelings and attitudes about [123]. Research shows that teachers are not familiar with student-centered teaching methods. They often think that students understand content knowledge of science subjects without any theoretical background or support given by a teacher [124]. Good quality learning demands that the teacher has knowledge and competency to plan and carry out meaningful instruction.

According to Kärnä et al. [123], having students work together in a carefully structured environment of cooperation and support can allow feelings to emerge and both cognitive and affective changes to begin [125]. Emotionally supportive environments can be fostered by creating a community of learners, providing helpful feedback, and creating opportunities for peer interactions that limit competition [126]. Although positive emotions such as enjoyment of learning, hope for success, and pride of a given task are commonly associated with positive learning outcomes, recent research indicates that this connection is much more complicated than initially proposed [127]. According to Kärnä et al. [123], Finnish pupils' attitudes toward biology correlated with different performance levels. Pupils' perceptions of their own competence had the highest correlation with successful performance in the assessment. Attitudes became even more positive with better grades in different natural sciences. Pupils with the poorest performance levels in a subject liked the subject the least and did not perceive it to be as useful as those of their peers who performed the best in the assessment. One reason can be that students with negative emotions such as anxiety, anger, and shame may learn less, because they are more likely to use poor processing skills such as memorization or rehearsal of content, and also more likely to withdraw from a class when faced with difficulties and failure [128].

6.3. Knowledge and Thinking Skills to Be Learned

According to Krathwohl [129] there are four kinds of knowledge: fact (factual) knowledge, concept (conceptual) knowledge, method (procedural) knowledge, and metacognitive knowledge. Factual knowledge includes basic elements (knowledge of terminology and knowledge of specific details) that students must know to be acquainted with a discipline or solve problems in it. Conceptual knowledge means interrelationships among basic elements within a larger framework that enable them to function together. It includes knowledge of classifications and categories, knowledge of principles and generalizations, and knowledge of theories, models, and structures. Procedural knowledge means understanding how to do something. It includes methods of inquiry, and criteria for using skills, algorithms, techniques, and methods, knowledge of subject-specific skills and algorithms, knowledge of subject-specific techniques and methods and knowledge of criteria for determining when to use appropriate procedures. Metacognitive knowledge means knowledge of cognition in general as well as awareness and knowledge of one's own cognition. It includes strategic knowledge, knowledge about cognitive tasks, including appropriate contextual and conditional knowledge, and self-knowledge. Of these types of knowledge, metacognitive knowledge was the least represented one in the reviewed articles (Figure 3).

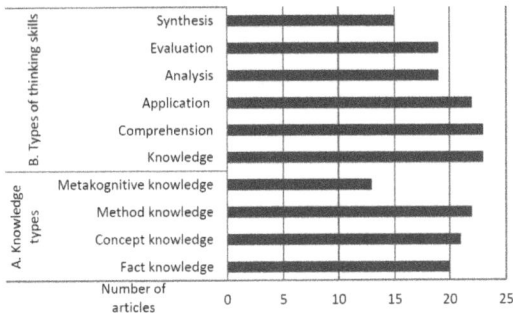

Figure 3. Types of knowledge (categorized according to the model of [129]) and types of thinking skills (categorized according to the model of [129,130]).

Types of thinking skills were analyzed using the hierarchy of the cognitive domain. Bloom [118] defined cognitive learning as dealing with "recall or recognition of knowledge and the development of intellectual abilities and skills." The cognitive domain comprises six subdomains concerning the development of our mental skills and the acquisition of knowledge. The subdomain of knowledge has to do with the ability to recall data and/or information. Comprehension means the ability to understand the meaning of what is known and to demonstrate understanding by describing, paraphrasing, etc. The subdomain of application is the ability to utilize an abstraction or to use knowledge in a new situation. Analysis involves the ability to differentiate facts and opinions and to break down a problem into its constituent parts. The subdomain of synthesis means the ability to integrate different elements or concepts in order to form a sound pattern or structure so that new meaning can be established. The uppermost subdomain, evaluation, includes the ability to make judgments about the importance of concepts [118,129,130]. In dealing with the cognitive domain, it is relatively easy to specify desired types of student behavior and the phenomena on which they impinge, i.e., the subject-matter content of science instruction. Teachers and researchers are also used to specifying the types of behavior desired of the student in acquiring and using science content [123].

The subdomains of knowledge, comprehension, and application were well represented in the articles, as well as those of analysis and evaluation (Figure 3). Synthesis was taken into account the least. It requires creativity: putting elements together to form a coherent or functional whole, reorganizing elements into new patterns or structures through generating, planning, or producing. It involves the generating of new ideas, products, or ways of viewing things. It is considered the most complex form of thinking [118]. Studies analyzing classroom tests have found that most teacher-made tests require only recall of information [122]. However, when teachers are asked how often they assess application, reasoning, and higher-order thinking, both elementary [37,131] and secondary [38] teachers claim that they assess these cognitive levels quite often. The reason that recall-level test questions are so prevalent is that they are the easiest kind to create. They are also the easiest kind of questions to ask spontaneously in the classroom.

6.4. Learning Environments

Since learning environments have been developed to support the selected teaching methods, they both have an effect on learners' achievements. The most often used learning environment were classrooms, which were mentioned in 22 out of 24 articles. Introductions, guidelines, and discussions concerning learning experiences and results of observations and experiments were often carried out in the classrooms, in addition to traditional teacher presentations and inquiries. Outdoor and field environments were mentioned in 14 articles. Different visiting places, such as museums, gardens, and nature parks, were the third most common learning environments (mentioned in 11 articles). Such places appear to be good learning environments because students' learning results are significantly better when they get first-hand experiences and studies in authentic learning environments [57,59,62,70]. One reason can be that emotionally supportive learning environments engage students in adaptive learning strategies such as elaboration, organization, and critical thinking [114].

Laboratory environments were found in only five articles, although laboratories are places where students can meet real scientists and learn how research is done. In school laboratories, students can develop their experimentation skills when planning and carrying out small studies. The internet and electronic discussion forums were mentioned in two articles. Computer-assisted teaching-learning processes offer a useful way for cognitive process-oriented instruction, during which the teacher's role is to activate students' mental activities and to support self-regulatory strategies for learning [130,132].

6.5. Evaluation Methods

Evaluation methods were analyzed using a common categorization of the teaching and learning evaluation types [119,133]. Summative and diagnostic evaluations were the most popular methods (found in 18 and 17 articles, respectively). Formative evaluation was used only in 10 articles. Comprehensive evaluation is an important part of teaching and learning processes, and summative assessment should be complemented by formative and diagnostic assessment. The prevailing evaluation culture should develop from a measuring culture to a development and supporting culture [121,134,135]. Evaluation comprises values and beliefs, which affect conceptions of evaluation goals and aims that guide evaluation practices [136]. Instead of teacher-centered evaluation, more such methods where students can learn actively should be used [135,137,138].

6.6. Features of Useful Teaching Methods and Implications

The most emphasized feature of useful teaching methods was the activity, participation, and interactivity of the students (Figure 4).

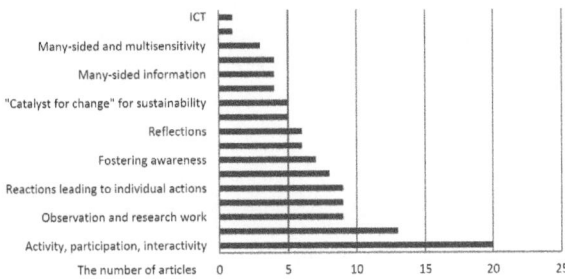

Figure 4. The features of useful teaching methods.

The review gives a clear endorsement for the provision of a certain kind of biology education approach. This research emphasizes the value of teaching methods which have a good introduction and supportive guidelines and include active participation and interactivity (Figure 5). The results support Rickinson's research [26]. First-hand experiences, locality and place-based education, and OE are also emphasized. Conversely, systematic teaching of sustainable development, teachers as role models, continuing development of EESD (Environmental Education for Sustainable Development), positive feedback, and whole-school approaches were not popular (mentioned only twice). Moreover, neither continuous teacher and staff education nor differentiation were popular, having been mentioned only in one article together with the ideas that SE should be taken into account at all education levels, and that there should be enough time for SE. The reason could be similar to those that Rickinson reported in his study, e.g., that the aims of SE are not always realized in practice, the different types of barriers faced by individual students and teachers in learning and teaching SE, and familiarity with the SE setting [26].

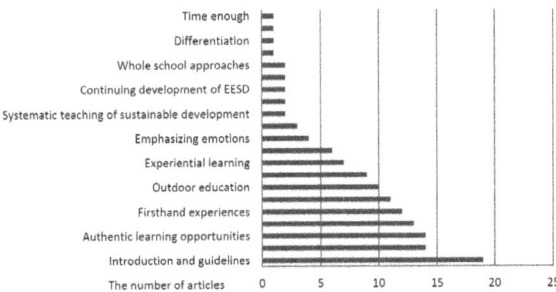

Figure 5. Implications concerning the analyzed teaching methods (EESD = Environmental Education for Sustainable Development).

7. Main Conclusions and Implications

The study aimed to identify and describe useful teaching methods in biology education and sustainability education (SE) including outdoor education (OE) for promoting sustainability. Although our analyses of recent research on teaching methods and their evaluation included several details, a holistic view of the educational processes is needed for the understanding of all effects. All teaching methods are, of course, context- and subject-dependent, and cannot therefore be arranged as a list of the most or least effective methods. The analyses, however, provide ideas of how to use these methods together for promoting sustainability aspects in teaching, and also of how to evaluate the whole process for the purpose of curricula development. The study emphasizes especially the value of inductive teaching methods with student-centered approaches in authentic environments with first-hand experiences. Like previous research [44,46,47], the analyses also emphasized fieldwork and field trips, including problem-based activities, as factors increasing students' interest in and knowledge of sustainability. Fieldwork appeared to have positive effects also on students' attitudes and behavior concerning sustainability [66,67]. Students' relationships with and connectedness to nature [64–66], environmental consciousness [23,59,68], and interest in biology [69] are all important factors in any attempt to create a sustainable future [57,58,61,62].

An issue to be taken more into account is the whole-school approach. According to Wyn et al. [49], it can bring benefits to school communities, enhancing the development of school environments where students feel safe, have a sense of belonging and develop the skills needed to participate fully. The results of the analyses also emphasized a great need for several comparative studies of teaching methods and their careful evaluations in relation to the expected results.

Author Contributions: Eila Jeronen: Abstract and keywords; Introduction; Theoretical background: Teaching principles and methods in sustainability education promoting sustainability; Conclusions and Implications. Irmeli Palmberg: Theoretical background: Outdoor Education and meaning of the place promoting sustainability. Eija Yli-Panula: Theoretical background: Teaching principles and methods in biology promoting sustainability; Figures. All authors: Design of the research; Theoretical background: Common educational principles promoting sustainability; Research aim and questions; Collecting and analyzing of material; Methods; Findings and discussion; References; Checking and correcting the manuscript in the different phases of the writing process, and completing of the manuscript.

Conflicts of Interest: The authors declare no conflict of interest.

References

1. Gladwin, T.N.; Kennelly, J.J.; Krause, T.-S. Shifting paradigms for sustainable development: Implications for management theory and research. *AMR* **1995**, *20*, 874–907.
2. Kopnina, H. Education for sustainable development (ESD): The turn away from 'environment' in environmental education? *Environ. Educ. Res.* **2012**, *18*, 699–717. [CrossRef]
3. United Nations. Report of the World Commission on Environment and Development: Our Common Future. 1987. Available online: http://www.un-documents.net/our-common-future.pdf (accessed on 26 May 2016).
4. Diesendorf, M. Sustainability and sustainable development. In *Sustainability: The Corporate Challenge of the 21st Century*; Dunphy, D., Benveniste, J., Griffiths, A., Sutton, P., Eds.; Allen & Unwin: Sydney, Australia, 2000; pp. 19–37.
5. Fien, J.; Maclean, R.; Park, M.G. *Work, Learning and Sustainable Development: Opportunities and Challenges*; Springer: Berlin, Germany, 2009.
6. Opetushallitus. Perusopetuksen Opetussuunnitelman Perusteet [Curriculum for Basic Education]. 2016. Available online: http://www.oph.fi/download/163777_perusopetuksen_opetussuunnitelman_perusteet_2014.pdf (accessed on 18 December 2016).
7. Skolverket. Grundskolans Kursplaner och Betygskriterier [Course Plans for Basic Education]. 2000. Available online: http://www.skolverket.se/laroplaner-amnen-och-kurser/grundskoleutbildning (accessed on 18 December 2016).

8. Utdanningsdirektoraten. Generell del av Læreplanen. Det Miljømedvitne Mennesket [Curriculum]. Available online: http://www.udir.no/laring-og-trivsel/lareplanverket/generell-del-av-lareplanen/det-miljomedvitne-mennesket/ (accessed on 4 December 2016).
9. Wesselink, R.; Wals, A.E.J. Developing competence profiles for educators in environmental education organisations in the Netherlands. *Environ. Educ. Res.* **2011**, *17*, 69–90. [CrossRef]
10. McKeown, R.; Hopkins, C. EE ≠ ESD: Defusing the worry. *Environ. Educ. Res.* **2003**, *9*, 117–128. [CrossRef]
11. Sauvé, L. Currents in environmental education: Mapping a complex and evolving pedagogical field. *JEE* **2005**, *10*, 11–37.
12. Eilam, E.; Trop, T. ESD pedagogy: A guide for the perplexed. *JEE* **2010**, *42*, 43–64. [CrossRef]
13. General Assembly. United Nations A 58/210. Activities undertaken in implementation of Agenda 21, the programme for the implementation of Agenda 21 and the outcomes of the World summit on sustainable development. Report of the Secretary-General. 2003. Available online: https://documents-dds-ny.un.org/doc/UNDOC/GEN/N03/451/88/PDF/N0345188.pdf?OpenElement (accessed on 16 December 2016).
14. Lucas, A.M. *Environment and Environmental Education: Conceptual Issues and Curriculum Implications*; Australian International Press and Publications: Melbourne, Australia, 1979.
15. UNESCO. Education for sustainable development—An expert review of processes and learning. 2011. Available online: http://unesdoc.unesco.org/images/0019/001914/191442e.pdf (accessed on 26 May 2016).
16. Pigozzi, M. Quality in education defines ESD. *JESD* **2007**, *1*, 27–35. [CrossRef]
17. UNESCO. United Nations Decade of Education for Sustainable Development (DESD, 2005–2014). Review of Contexts and Structures for Education for Sustainable Development. 2009. Available online: http://www.unesco.org/education/justpublished_desd2009.pdf (accessed on 27 May 2016).
18. Wolff, L.-A.; Hofman-Bergholm, M.; Palmberg, I.; Sjöblom, P. High performance education fails in sustainability?—A reflection on Finnish primary teacher education. *Educ. Sci.* **2016**, *6*. in press.
19. Dale, A.; Newman, L. Sustainable development, education and literacy. *IJSHE* **2005**, *6*, 351–362.
20. Sterling, S. Learning for resilience, or the resilient learner? Towards a necessary reconciliation in a paradigm of sustainable education. *Environ. Educ. Res.* **2010**, *16*, 511–528. [CrossRef]
21. Palmberg, I.; Berg, I.; Jeronen, E.; Kärkkäinen, S.; Norrgård-Sillanpää, P.; Persson, C.; Vilkonis, R.; Yli-Panula, E. Nordic–Baltic student teachers' identification of and interest in plant and animal species: The importance of species identification and biodiversity for sustainable development. *JSTE* **2015**, *26*, 549–571. [CrossRef]
22. Palmberg, I.; Kuru, J. Outdoor activities as a basis for environmental responsibility. *JEE* **2000**, *31*, 32–36. [CrossRef]
23. Jeronen, E.; Jeronen, J.; Raustia, H. Environmental education in Finland—A case study of environmental education in nature schools. *IJESE* **2009**, *4*, 1–23.
24. Ashman, A.F.; Conway, N.F. Teaching students to use process-based learning and problem solving strategies in mainstream classes. *Learn. Instr.* **1993**, *3*, 73–92. [CrossRef]
25. Wood, D.F. ABC of learning and teaching in medicine Problem based learning. *BMJ* **2003**, *326*, 328–330. [CrossRef] [PubMed]
26. Rickinson, M.; Dillon, J.; Teamey, K.; Morris, M.; Choi, M.Y.; Sanders, D.; Benefield, P. A Review of Research on Outdoor Learning. 2004. Available online: http://www.field-studies-council.org/media/268859/2004_a_review_of_research_on_outdoor_learning.pdf (accessed on 27 May 2016).
27. Kent, M.; Gilbertsson, D.D.; Hunt, C.O. Fieldwork in geography teaching: A critical review of the literature and approaches. *JGHE* **1997**, *21*, 313–332. [CrossRef]
28. Turner, J.C.; Fulmer, S.M. Observing interpersonal regulation of engagement during instruction in middle school classrooms. In *Interpersonal Regulation of Learning and Motivation: Methodological Advances*; Volet, S., Vauras, M., Eds.; Routledge: New York, NY, USA, 2013; pp. 147–169.
29. Volet, S.E.; Summers, M.; Thurman, J. High-level co-regulation in collaborative learing: How does it emerge and how is it sustained? *Learn. Instr.* **2009**, *19*, 128–143. [CrossRef]
30. Khosa, D.K.; Volet, S.E. Productive group engagement in cognitive activity and metacognitive regulation during collaborative learning: Can it explain differences in students' conceptual understanding? *Metacogn. Learn.* **2014**, *9*, 287–307. [CrossRef]
31. Volet, S.; Vauras, M.; Khosa, D.; Iiskala, T. Metacognitive regulation in collaborative learning: Conceptual developments and methodological contextualizations. In *Interpersonal Regulation of Learning*

and Motivation: Methodological Advances; Volet, S., Vauras, M., Eds.; Routledge: New York, NY, USA, 2013; pp. 67–101.

32. Vauras, M.; Volet, S. The study of interpersonal regulation in learning challenges the research methodology. In *Interpersonal Regulation of Learning and Motivation: Methodological Advances*; Volet, S., Vauras, M., Eds.; Routledge: New York, NY, USA, 2013; pp. 1–13.

33. Häkkinen, P. Collaborative learning in networked environments: Interaction through sharedworkspaces and communication tools. *JET Int. Res. Pedagog.* **2003**, *29*, 279–281. [CrossRef]

34. Hakkarainen, K. Progressive inquiry in a computer-supported biology class. *JRST* **2003**, *40*, 1072–1088. [CrossRef]

35. Hakkarainen, K.; Sintonen, M. The interrogative model of inquiry and computer supported collaborative learning. *Sci. Educ.* **2002**, *11*, 25–43. [CrossRef]

36. Maina, F.W. Authentic learning: Perspectives from contemporary educators. *J. Authentic Learn.* **2004**, *1*, 1–8.

37. McMillan, J.H.; Myron, S.; Workman, D. Elementary teachers' classroom assessment and grading practices. *JER* **2002**, *95*, 203–213. [CrossRef]

38. McMillan, H.J. Secondary Teachers' Classroom Assessment and Grading Practices. *NCME* **2001**, *20*, 20–32. [CrossRef]

39. Spörhase, U. Welche allgemeinen Ziele verfolgt Biologieunterricht. In *Biologie Didaktik, Praxishandbuch fur die Sekundarstufe I und II*, 5th ed.; Spörhase, U., Ed.; Cornelsen Verlag: Berlin, Germany, 2012; pp. 24–61.

40. Keselman, A. Supporting inquiry learning by promoting normative understanding of multivariable causality. *JRST* **2003**, *40*, 898–921. [CrossRef]

41. Ehmer, M. Förderung von Kognitiven Fähigkeiten Beim Experimentieren Im Biologieunterricht der 6. Klasse: Eine Untersuchung zur Wirksamkeit von Methodischem, Epistemologischem und Negativem Wissen [Promoting Cognitive Abilities with Experimenttion in Grade Six Biology Teaching. An Investigation of the Effectiveness of Methodological, Epistemological, and Negative Knowledge]. Ph.D. Thesis, University of Kiel, Kiel, Germany, 11 July 2008. Available online: http://eldiss.unikiel.de/macau/servlets/MCRFileNodeServlet/dissertation_derivate_00002469/diss_ehmer.df;jsessionid=AA40217F5511C865E4BBCE4B53020415?host=&o (accessed on 28 October 2016).

42. Hof, S. Wissenschaftsmethodischer Kompetenzerwerb durch Forschendes Lernen. Entwicklung und Evaluation einer Interventionsstudie [Science Methodical Acquisition of Competency by Inquiry Based Learning. Development and Evaluation of an Intervention Study]. Ph.D. Thesis, Universität Kassel, Kassel, Germany, 2011.

43. Kirschner, P.A.; Sweller, J.; Clark, R.E. Why minimal guidance during instruction does not work: An analysis of the failure of constructivist, discovery, problem-based, experiential, and inquiry-based teaching. *Educ. Psychol.* **2006**, *41*, 75–86. [CrossRef]

44. Akınoğlu, O.; Tandoğan, R.Ö. The Effects of problem-based active learning in science education. *Eurasia J. Math. Sci. Technol. Educ.* **2007**, *3*, 71–81.

45. Asyari, M.; Al Muhdhar, M.H.I.; Ibrohim, S.H. Improving critical thinking skills through the integration of problem based learning and group investigation. *Int. J. Lesson Learn. Stud.* **2016**, *5*, 36–44. [CrossRef]

46. Simmons, M.; Wu, X.; Knight, S.; Lopez, R. Assessing the influence of field- and GIS-based inquiry on student attitude and conceptual knowledge in an undergraduate ecology lab. *CBE Life Sci. Educ.* **2008**, *7*, 338–345. [CrossRef] [PubMed]

47. Hart, P.; Nolan, K. A critical analysis of research in environmental education. *Stud. Sci. Educ.* **1999**, *34*, 1–69. [CrossRef]

48. The World Bank. *World Development Report 1992: Development and the Environment*; Oxford University Press: New York, NY, USA, 1992; p. 1.

49. Wyn, J.; Cahill, H.; Holdsworth, L.; Rowling, L.; Carson, S. MindMatters, a whole school approach promoting mental health and wellbeing. *Aust. N. Z. J. Psychiatry* **2000**, *34*, 594–601. [CrossRef] [PubMed]

50. Reason, P.; Bradbury, H. Introduction: Inquiry and participation in a search of a world worthy of human aspiration. In *Handbook of Action Research—Participative Practice and Enquiry*; Reason, P., Bradbury, H., Eds.; SAGE: London, UK, 2001; pp. 1–14.

51. Sterling, S. An analysis of the development of sustainability education internationally: Evolution, interpretation and transformative potential. In *The Sustainability Curriculum—Facing the Challenge in Higher Education*; Blewitt, J., Cullingford, C., Eds.; Earthscan: London, UK, 2004; pp. 43–62.

52. Jucker, R. Sustainability? Never heard of it! Some basics we shouldn't ignore when engaging in education for sustainability. *IJSHE* **2001**, *3*, 8–18.

53. United Nations. Transforming Our World: The 2030 Agenda for Sustainable Development, A/RES/70/1. Available online: https://sustainabledevelopment.un.org/content/documents/21252030%20Agenda%20for%20Sustainable%20Development%20web.pdf (accessed on 24 November 2016).

54. Lotz Sisitka, H. Enabling environmental and sustainability education in South Africa's national curriculum: Context, culture and learner aspirations for agency. In *Environmental Education and Geographical Education for Sustainability: Cultural Contexts*; Lee, C.K., Williams, M., Eds.; Nova Science Publishers: New York, NY, USA, 2006.

55. Warburton, K. Deep learning and education for sustainability. *IJSHE* **2003**, *4*, 44–56. [CrossRef]

56. Bogner, F.X. The influence of short-term outdoor ecology education on longterm variables of environmental perspective. *JEE* **1998**, *29*, 17–29.

57. Brody, M. Learning in nature. *Environ. Educ. Res.* **2005**, *11*, 603–621. [CrossRef]

58. Puk, T.G.; Stibbards, A. Systemic ecological illiteracy? Shedding light on meaning as an act of thought in higher learning. *Environ. Educ. Res.* **2012**, *18*, 353–373. [CrossRef]

59. Lavie Alon, N.L.; Tal, T. Student self-reported learning outcomes of field trips: The pedagogical impact. *IJESE* **2015**, *37*, 1279–1298. [CrossRef]

60. Gairn, N. *Outdoor Education: Theory and Practice*; Cassel: London, UK, 1997.

61. Palmer, J.A.; Suggate, J. Influences and experiences affecting the pro-environmental behavior of educators. *Environ. Educ. Res.* **1996**, *2*, 109–122. [CrossRef]

62. Bögeholz, S. Nature experience and its importance for environmental knowledge, values and action: Recent German empirical contributions. *Environ. Educ. Res.* **2006**, *12*, 65–84. [CrossRef]

63. Berkowitz, A.R.; Ford, M.F.; Brewer, C.A. A framework for integrating ecological literacy, civics literacy, and environmental citizenship in environmental education. In *Environmental Education and Advocacy: Changing Perspectives of Ecology and Education*; Johnson, E.A., Mappin, M.J., Eds.; Cambridge University Press: New York, NY, USA, 2005; pp. 227–266.

64. Arnold, H.E.; Cohen, F.G.; Warner, A. Youth and environmental action: Perspectives of young environmental leaders on their formative influences. *JEE* **2009**, *40*, 27–36. [CrossRef]

65. Ernst, J.; Theimer, S. Evaluating the effects of environmental education programming on connectedness to nature. *Environ. Educ. Res.* **2011**, *17*, 577–598. [CrossRef]

66. Liefländer, A.K.; Fröhlich, G.; Bogner, F.X.; Schultz, P.W. Promoting connectedness with nature through environmental education. *Environ. Educ. Res.* **2013**, *19*, 370–384. [CrossRef]

67. Rios, J.M.; Brewer, J. Outdoor education and science achievement. *Appl. Environ. Educ. Commun.* **2014**, *13*, 234–240. [CrossRef]

68. Nazir, J.; Pedretti, E. Educators' perceptions of bringing students to environmental consciousness through engaging outdoor experiences. *Environ. Educ. Res.* **2016**, *22*, 288–304. [CrossRef]

69. Uitto, A.; Juuti, K.; Lavonen, J.; Meisalo, V. Students' interest in biology and their out of-school experiences. *JBE* **2006**, *40*, 124–129. [CrossRef]

70. Smeds, P.; Jeronen, E.; Kurppa, S. Farm education and the value of learning in an authentic learning environment. *IJESE* **2015**, *10*, 381–404.

71. Àlvarez-Garcia, O.; Sureda-Negre, J.; Comas-Forgas, R. Environmental education in pre-service teacher training: A literature review of existing evidence. *JTEFS* **2015**, *17*, 72–85. [CrossRef]

72. Higgins, J.P.T.; Green, S. (Eds.) *Cochrane Handbook for Systematic Reviews of Interventions, Version 5.1.0. [Updated March 2011]*; University of Oxford: Oxford, UK, 2011.

73. Morse, J.M. Procedure and practice of mixed method design. Maintaining control, rigor and complexity. In *Handbook of Mixed Methods in Social and Behavioural Research*; Tashakkori, A., Teddlie, C., Eds.; SAGE Publications: London, UK, 2010; pp. 339–352.

74. Collins, K.M. Advanced sampling designs in mixed research. Current practices and emerging trends in the social and behavioral sciences. In *Handbook of Mixed Methods in Social and Behavioural Research*; Tashakkori, A., Teddlie, C., Eds.; SAGE Publications: London, UK, 2010; pp. 353–378.

75. O'Gorman, L.; Davis, J. Ecological footprinting: Its potential as a tool for change in preservice teacher education. *Environ. Educ. Res.* **2013**, *19*, 779–791. [CrossRef]

76. Baur, A.; Haase, M.-H. The influence of active participation and organisation in environmental protection activities on the environmental behaviour of pupils: Study of a teaching technique. *Environ. Educ. Res.* **2015**, *21*, 92–105. [CrossRef]

77. Jagger, S.; Sperling, E.; Inwood, H. What's growing on here? Garden-based pedagogy in a concrete jungle. *Environ. Educ. Res.* **2016**, *22*, 271–287. [CrossRef]

78. Randler, C. Teaching species identification—A prerequisite for leaning biodiversity and understanding ecology. *Eurasia J. Math. Sci. Technol. Educ.* **2008**, *4*, 223–231.

79. Morag, O.; Tal, T.; Rotem-Keren, T. Long-term educational programs in nature parks: Characteristics, outcomes and challenges. *IJESE* **2013**, *8*, 427–449.

80. Morag, O.; Tal, T. Assessing Learning in the Outdoors with the Field Trip in Natural Environments (FiNE) Framework. *IJESE* **2012**, *34*, 745–777. [CrossRef]

81. Lindemann-Matthies, P. Investigating Nature on the Way to School: Responses to an educational programme by teachers and their pupils. *IJESE* **2006**, *28*, 895–918. [CrossRef]

82. Roesch, F.; Nerb, J.; Riess, W. Promoting experimental problem-solving ability in sixth-grade students through problem-oriented teaching of ecology: Findings of an intervention study in a complex domain. *IJESE* **2015**, *37*, 577–598. [CrossRef]

83. Tal, T. Pre-service teachers' reflections on awareness and knowledge following active learning in environmental education. *IRGEE* **2010**, *19*, 263–276. [CrossRef]

84. Fägerstam, E.; Blom, J. Learning biology and mathematics outdoors: Effects and attitudes in a Swedish high school context. *J. Adventure Educ. Outdoor Learn.* **2013**, *13*, 56–75. [CrossRef]

85. Magntorn, O.; Hellden, G. Reading nature from a "bottom-up" perspective. *JBE* **2007**, *41*, 68–75. [CrossRef]

86. Barth, M.; Fisher, D.; Michelsen, G.; Nemnich, C.; Rode, H. Tackling the knowledge—Action gap in sustainable consumption: Insights from a participatory school programme. *JESD* **2012**, *6*, 301–312. [CrossRef]

87. Stevenson, K.T.; Peterson, M.N.; Carrier, S.J.; Strnad, L.R.; Bondell, H.D.; Kirby-Hathaway, T.; Moore, S.E. Role of Significant Life Experiences in Building Environmental Knowledge and Behavior among Middle School Students. *JEE* **2014**, *45*, 163–177. [CrossRef]

88. Tal, T.; Morag, O. Reflective Practice as a Means for Preparing to Teach Outdoors in an Ecological Garden. *JSTE* **2009**, *20*, 245–262. [CrossRef]

89. Weiland, I.S.; Morrison, J.A. The integration of environmental education into two elementary preservice science methods courses: A content-based and a method-based approach. *JSTE* **2013**, *24*, 1023–1047. [CrossRef]

90. Hendrix, R.; Eick, C.; Shannon, D. The integration of creative drama in an inquiry-based elementary program: The effect on student attitude and conceptual learning. *JSTE* **2012**, *23*, 823–846. [CrossRef]

91. Sadler, T.D. Promoting discourse and argumentation in science teacher education. *JSTE* **2006**, *17*, 323–346. [CrossRef]

92. Van Zee, E.H.; Roberts, D. Making science teaching and learning visible through web-based "snapshots of practice". *JSTE* **2006**, *17*, 367–388. [CrossRef]

93. Meng, Q. Study on the Case Teaching Method and the Sustainable Development Education for the Inner Mongol Colleges. *JSD* **2009**, *2*, 65–70. [CrossRef]

94. Alexandar, R.; Poyya moli, G. The Effectiveness of Environmental Education for Sustainable Development Based on Active Teaching and Learning at High School Leve—A Case Study from Puducherry and Cuddalore Regions, India. *JSE*, 25 December 2014. Available online: http://www.jsedimensions.org/wordpress/content/the-effectiveness-of-environmental-education-for-sustainable-development-based-on-active-teaching-and-learning-at-high-school-level-a-case-study-from-puducherry-and-cuddalore-regions-india_2014_12/ (accessed on 27 May 2016).

95. Vanhear, J.; Pace, P.J. Integrating knowledge, feelings and action: Using Vee Heuristics and concept mapping in education for sustainable development. *JTEFS* **2008**, *10*, 42–55. [CrossRef]

96. Lehesvuori, S.; Ratinen, I.; Kulhomäki, O.; Lappi, J.; Viiri, J. Enriching primary student teachers' conceptions about science teaching: Towards dialogic inquiry-based teaching. *Nord. Stud. Sci. Educ.* **2011**, *7*, 140–159.

97. Snaddon, J.L.; Turner, E.C.; Foster, W.A. Children's Perceptions of Rainforest Biodiversity: Which Animals Have the Lion's Share of Environmental Awareness? *PLoS ONE* **2008**, *3*, e2579. [CrossRef] [PubMed]

98. Spahiu, M.H.; Lindemann-Matthies, P. Effect of a Toolkit and a One-Day Teacher Education Workshop on ESD Teaching Content and Methods—A Study from Kosovo. *Sustainability* **2015**, *7*, 8051–8066. [CrossRef]

99. Mayring, P. Qualitative Content Analysis. *FQS* **2000**, *1*, 20. Available online: http://www.qualitative-research.net/index.php/fqs/article/view/1089 (accessed on 29 October 2016).

100. Tashakkori, A.; Teddlie, C. (Eds.) *Handbook of Mixed Methods in Social & Behavioral Research*; SAGE Publications: Thousand Oaks, CA, USA, 2010.

101. Elo, S.; Kyngäs, H. The qualitative content analysis process. *JAN* **2008**, *62*, 107–115. [CrossRef] [PubMed]

102. Creswell, J.W. *Qualitative Inquiry and Research Design—Choosing among Five Approaches*, 3rd ed.; SAGE Publications: Thousand Oaks, CA, USA, 2013; pp. 97–101.

103. Karami, M.; Pakmehr, H.; Aghili, A. Another view to importance of teaching methods in curriculum: collaborative learning and students' critical thinking disposition. *Procedia Soc. Behav. Sci.* **2012**, *46*, 3266–3270. [CrossRef]

104. Prince, M.J.; Felder, R.M. Inductive teaching and learning methods: Definitions, comparisons and research basis. *J. Eng. Educ.* **2006**, *95*, 123–138. [CrossRef]

105. Eisner, E.W. *Educational objectives—Help or hindrance? In The Curriculum Studies Reader*, 2nd ed.; Flinders, D.T., Thornton, S.T., Eds.; Routledge: New York, NY, USA, 2004; pp. 85–91.

106. Grant, R. A claim for the case method in the teaching of geography. *JGHE* **1997**, *21*, 171–185. [CrossRef]

107. Cooper, J.L.; MacGregor, J.; Smith, K.A.; Robinson, P. Implementing small-group Instruction: Insights from successful practitioners. *NDTL* **2000**, *81*, 63–76. [CrossRef]

108. Kern, E.; Carpenter, J. Effect of field activities on student learning. *JGE* **1986**, *34*, 180–183. [CrossRef]

109. Duschl, R.A. Science education in three-part harmony: Balancing conceptual, epistemic, and social learning goals. *RRE* **2008**, *32*, 268–291. [CrossRef]

110. Osborne, J. Arguing to learn in science: The role of collaborative, critical discourse. *Science* **2010**, *328*, 463–466. [CrossRef] [PubMed]

111. Sampson, V.; Clark, D. The impact of collaboration on the outcomes of scientific argumentation. *Sci. Educ.* **2008**, *93*, 448–484. [CrossRef]

112. Driver, R.; Newton, P.; Osborne, J. Establishing the norms of scientific argumentation in classrooms. *Sci. Educ.* **2000**, *84*, 287–312. [CrossRef]

113. Kiili, C. Online Reading as an Individual and Social Practice. Ph.D. Thesis, University of Jyväskylä, Jyväskylä, Finland, 2012.

114. Turner, J.E.; Husman, J.; Schallert, D.L. The importance of students' goals in their emotional experience of academic failure: Investigating the precursors and consequences of shame. *Educ. Psychol.* **2002**, *37*, 79–89. [CrossRef]

115. Gruenewald, D.A. Foundations of place: A multidisciplinary framework for place-conscious education. *AERJ* **2003**, *40*, 619–654. [CrossRef]

116. Strife, S. Reflecting on Environmental Education: Where Is Our Place in the Green Movement? *JEE* **2010**, *41*, 179–191. [CrossRef]

117. Simpson, E.J. *The Classification of Educational Objectives: Psychomotor Domain*; University of Illinois Press: Urban, IL, USA, 1972.

118. Bloom, B.S. *Taxonomy of Educational Objectives, Handbook I: The Cognitive Domain*; David McKay Co. Inc.: New York, NY, USA, 1956.

119. Uusikylä, K.; Atjonen, P. *Didaktiikan Perusteet [Introduction to Didactics]*, 4th ed.; SanomaPro: Helsinki, Finland, 2007.

120. Krathwohl, D.R.; Bloom, B.S.; Masia, B.B. *Taxonomy of Educational Objectives. Handbook II: Affective Domain*; McKay: New York, NY, USA, 1964.

121. Kearney, P. Affective learning scale. In *Communication Research Measures: A Sourcebook*; Rubin, R.P., Palmgreen, P., Sypher, H.E., Eds.; The Guilford Press: New York, USA, 1994; pp. 81–85, 238–241.

122. Rodriguez, J.; Plax, T.G.; Kearney, P. Clarifying the relationship between teacher nonverbal immediacy and student cognitive learning: Affective learning as the central causal mediator. *Commun. Educ.* **1996**, *45*, 293–305. [CrossRef]

123. Kärnä, P.; Hakonen, R.; Kuusela, J. Luonnontieteellinen osaaminen perusopetuksen 9. luokalla 2011. *Opetuksen Seurantaraportti* **2012**, *2*, 13–18.

124. Pekrun, R.; Goetz, T.; Titz, W.; Perry, R. Academic emotions in students' self-regulated learning and achievement: A program of qualitative and quantitative research. *Educ. Psychol.* **2002**, *37*, 91–105. [CrossRef]

125. Klopfer, L.E. The structure for the affective domain in relation to science education. In Proceedings of the the 46th Annual Meeting of the National Association for Research in Science Teaching, Detroit, MI, USA, 27 March 1973.

126. Johnson, D.W.; Johnson, R.T.; Smith, K.A. *Active Learning: Cooperation in the College Classroom*; Interaction Book Company: Edina, MN, USA, 1991; p. 153.

127. Turner, J.C.; Patrick, H. Motivational influences on student participation in classroom learning activities. *TC Rec.* **2004**, *106*, 1759–1785. [CrossRef]

128. Linnenbrink, E. The role of affect in student learning: A multi-dimensional approach to considering the interaction of affect, motivation and engagement. In *Emotion in Education*; Schutz, P.A., Pekrun, R., Eds.; Academic: Burlington, MA, USA, 2008; pp. 107–124.

129. Krathwohl, D. A revision of Bloom's taxonomy: An overview. *TIP* **2002**, *41*, 212–218. [CrossRef]

130. Vermunt, J.D. Process-oriented instruction in learning and thinking strategies. *Eur. J. Psychol. Educ.* **1995**, *10*, 325–349. [CrossRef]

131. Marso, R.N.; Pigge, F.L. Teachers' testing knowledge, skills and practises. In *Teacher Training in Measurement and Assessment Skills*; Wise, S.L., Ed.; Buros Institute of Mental Measurements, University of Nebraska-Lincoln: Lincoln, NE, USA, 1993; Available online: http://digitalcommons.unl.edu/cgi/viewcontent.cgi?article=1007&context=burosteachertraining (accessed on 25 November 2016).

132. Vermunt, J.D.; Verschaffel, L. Process-oriented teaching. In *New Learning*; Simons, R.J., van der Linden, J., Duffy, T., Eds.; Kluwer Academic: Dordrecht, The Netherlands, 2000; pp. 209–225.

133. Harlen, W.; Gipps, C.; Broadfoot, P.; Nuttall, D. Assessment and the improvement of education. *Curric. J.* **1992**, *3*, 215–230. [CrossRef]

134. Birenbaum, M. Assessment 2000: Towards a pluralistic approach to assessment. In *Alternatives in Assessment of Achievement, Learning Processes and Prior Knowledge*; Birenbaum, M., Dochy, F.J.R.C., Eds.; Kluwer: Boston, MA, USA, 1996; pp. 3–30.

135. Brown, G.; Bull, J.; Pendlebury, M. *Assessing Student Learning in Higher Education*; Routledge: London, UK, 1997.

136. Black, P.; Harrison, C.; Lee, C.; Marshall, B.; William, D. Working inside the Black Box: Assessment for learning in the classroom. *Phi Delta Kappan* **2004**, *86*, 9–21. [CrossRef]

137. Fuller, M.B.; Skidmore, S.T. An exploration of factors influencing institutional cultures of assessment. *IJER* **2014**, *65*, 9–21. [CrossRef]

138. Bryan, C.; Clegg, K. *Innovative Assessment in Higher Education*; Routledge: London, UK, 2006.

Article

An Internet-Based Medicine Education Intervention: Fourth Graders' Perspectives

Sirpa Kärkkäinen [1,*], Tuula Keinonen [1], Anu Hartikainen-Ahia [1], Kirsti Vainio [2] and Katri Hämeen-Anttila [3]

1   School of Applied Educational Science and Teacher Education, University of Eastern Finland, Yliopistokatu 2, 80100 Joensuu, Finland; tuula.keinonen@uef.fi (T.K.); anu.hartikainen@uef.fi (A.H.-A.)
2   Faculty of Health Sciences, School of Farmacy, University of Eastern Finland, Yliopistokatu 2, 80100 Joensuu, Finland; kirsti.vainio@uef.fi
3   Finnish Medicines Agency Fimea, Microkatu 1, 70210 Kuopio, Finland; katri.hameen-anttila@fimea.fi
*   Correspondence: sirpa.a.karkkainen@uef.fi; Tel.: +358-40-745-1301

Academic Editor: Eila Jeronen
Received: 28 September 2016; Accepted: 6 April 2017; Published: 11 April 2017

Abstract: Health education, which also includes medicine education, promotes social sustainability in society. Through the context of Internet-based intervention, this study reports on fourth graders' ($N = 51$, aged 10–11 years) perspectives on medicines, their use with common diseases and medicine-related information sources. The study was qualitative by nature. Data was collected in spring 2010, by audio recording students' group discussions during the study process and group interviews. After intervention, students were well aware of the proper use of medicines and how to find information both on medicines and health issues. The main challenge was finding websites that provide reliable and confidential information. The results of this study raise awareness of a concrete pedagogical approach to health education. The pedagogical approach conducted in the intervention could, to some extent, be transferred to any school setting. This study underlies the promotion of Internet-based health literacy and criteria, for evaluating online health information in the primary school context.

Keywords: medicine education; health education; internet-based education

1. Introduction

The Finnish education system, which incorporates the entire population, is a pillar of social and economic development. Education promotes responsibility, a sense of community, and respect for the rights and freedoms of the individual [1]. Thus, schools are also excellent places in which to promote the health and well-being of children and adolescents. Health education in schools should be developed in accordance with the requirements of three sustainable development aspects: environmental, socio-cultural and economical [2]. In order for social and cultural justice to be taken seriously, health and sustainability must mean equity and understanding between people and cultures, as well as peaceful, unprejudiced co-existence [2]. Health education that includes health knowledge, skills and values, is necessary to meet the challenges of schools both in the present and the future. This study focuses on medicine education which is a less-studied area of health education. The study, in the context of intervention, presents an Internet-based teaching method to promote medicine-related health literacy; it also examines fourth graders' perspectives on medicine use as well as promoting the search for information on diseases.

One of the central objectives of public health and the promotion of health is the worldwide development of health literacy. Health literacy is linked to health habits, health, the quality of life and differences in health [3]. Over the past decade, the interest and academic discourse dedicated to the concept of health literacy, has escalated enormously [4]. Without doubt, health literacy is an important and expanding topic in contemporary health care, health promotion, health education research and policy development. The probable reasons for health literacy becoming such a hot topic for researchers, health practitioners and educators alike, are essentially two-fold: first, the function of health literacy as an identified public health goal, added to the widely reported relationship of health literacy with behavior and measurable health parameters [5–8]; and second, the portrayal of health literacy as a direct outcome, the aim of health education as a school subject, as well as the outcome of health promotion practices exemplified through the whole school approach [9–12]. Generally, the increasing focus is not only on adult but also on adolescent health literacy [13].

Health literacy is defined as consisting of five core components: theoretical knowledge, practical knowledge, critical thinking, self-awareness, and citizenship. It is emphasized that the two last additional components are called for when the aim is to develop students' internal capacity to construct their own meanings regarding health topics. One of the main aims of health education in schools should be to foster students' ability to define their own beliefs, identity and social relations. Moreover, if it is desired that students should become responsible citizens acting in an ethically responsible way, competencies such as ethical reflection skills should be developed in schools. The development of certain health literacy components may demand specific kinds of learning conditions [12].

As health literacy is linked to health habits, health, quality of life and differences in health [14], poor health literacy is connected with an individual's inability to interpret health-related knowledge, such as the number of visits to the hospital and the incorrect use of medicines [15]. People with poor health literacy have difficulties in understanding diagnoses, are unable to follow instructions on how to take care of themselves as well as poorly benefitting from health care services [14–16].

Adolescents in Finland, as well as in Norway, Poland and Scotland, reported a high level of health-related symptoms; headache, backache, sleeping difficulties, with the intensity of most symptoms increasing with age [17]. Finnish parents reported that their children have a good health status, although approximately one-tenth had experienced some psychosomatic symptoms or long-term diseases [18]. Furthermore, Finland has a high rate of medicine use-related problems [19].

Limited attention has been given to the topic of adolescent health literacy, although (1) future health problems can be prevented by providing health knowledge and skills at an early age; (2) young people, especially those with chronic illnesses, at a younger age take an increasingly greater role in managing their health [20,21]; and (3) many important physical, behavioral, and sexual health issues arise prior to adulthood [22]. Educating children through school health programs is one of the means to develop the critical health literacy recommended in the goals of the EU.

Health literacy includes the skills needed to search for information on health issues, medicine use and diseases. Rational medicine use, the goal of medicine education, is defined as the right medicine taken in the right way at the right time for the right problem. The use of medicines is common to almost all adults and children [23–30], thus children are familiar with the most commonly used medicines and their use [31–37]. Children consider parents to be the most common source of information about medicines [23,34,35,38], other sources being the insert in the medicine package itself [23,39], physicians and nurses [23,35,38,39], and an increased use of the Internet [40].

Most individuals seek health information from the Internet [41]. Use of the Internet for this purpose by 50% of Europeans, has increased significantly in recent years [42]. Despite its advantages, the Internet is also a rich source of potentially alarming information about health and illness [43], especially disturbing for people who are already anxious about their health [44].

In the United Kingdom (UK) and the United States (USA), the Internet is the primary source of general information that adolescents use (11–19 years) and health information is generally regarded as being salient. Its saliency was increased through active searching and personalization. The perceived credibility of the Internet varies because expertise and reliability are sometimes difficult to determine; empathy can be facilitated through online communities but the individual can control disclosure. Internet sources combine positive traditional features of amateur and professional, personal and impersonal. Although it is unlikely to supplant the role of trusted peers and adults, the Internet has found an important place among adolescents' repertoire of health information sources. Adolescents are interested in finding information about a range of health topics, such as exercise, diet, sexual health, alcohol and drug misuse. Recognizing that Internet information may not be credible, some adolescents have developed strategies to test its reliability. Many also advocate the use of quality marks from well-known institutions. Here arises a hint of contradiction between adolescents' general perceptions of the Internet as a medium, and its specific use for health information [45].

The availability of reliable Internet material that provides high-quality information on mental health may assist young people in need of help to overcome barriers, and to improve awareness of the common symptoms related to mental problems [46]. Although there is significant variation in quality, at best, websites can also provide basic, evidence-based, self-help, and direct young people to sources of professional care [47]. The readability of online educational materials made available to patients also needs to be improved [48].

This research provides new information about Internet-based medicine education in the primary school context. Previous research has mainly focused both on the general aspects of how and why people use the Internet for health information purposes [49] as well as on the perceived credibility of online health information [43,45]. In this study, we are interested in students' perspectives on medicine education intervention, the focus being mainly on the theoretical knowledge about medicines, practical knowledge about the use of medicines, and critical thinking in searching for information on the Internet. The study is guided by the following research questions:

- What students perceive they have learned about medicines and their use?
- What students perceive they have learned about different diseases?
- How students perceive medicine-related Internet information sources?

2. Materials and Methods

2.1. Participants

This study involved a rural primary school in the eastern part of Finland. Three fourth grade classes participated in the study, totaling 51 students (ages 10 to 11 years). The medicine issues included in the research belong to the curriculum and the yearly schedule of the school, thus following their normal daily routines. Each class had their own teacher who was responsible for teaching during the intervention, modifying the case studies to suit the needs of their pupils. Three teachers and five researchers planned the intervention together.

2.2. Intervention

During the Internet-based intervention, students worked in small groups: seven groups in each class (three classes in all). Each group comprised of two or three students. Intervention embodied three phases; (a) the scenario; (b) the Internet-based inquiry; and (c) the compilation. In the scenario phase, each student group became familiarized with one case story; a fictitious person described his/her health problems or injuries and considered issues concerning the use of medicines (Table 1). The stories were aimed to promote the students' interest and motivation by connecting themes on disease and medical use, to a real-life context. The case stories concerned stomach ache, flu, accidents, migraine, snake bite, diabetes and asthma (Table 1). In the Internet-based inquiry phase, the students carried out structured inquiry tasks. From websites given to them in advance (Medicine education websites, the alternative medicine website, Terveyskirjasto website), they searched for information about the case person's symptoms and a possible cure. The aim was to develop students' theoretical and practical knowledge about medicines and diseases, as well as to develop students' critical thinking skills in relation to the use of Internet sources. In the last phase, the students presented to each other their own particular case, and the results and conclusions of their inquiry tasks. There was general discussion amongst the whole class about how to use medicines properly and the appropriate use of Internet sources.

The medicine education website is targeted at schoolteachers and it is designed to help them educate children about the proper use of medicines. As well as offering a lot of background information about the proper use of medicines and common childhood illnesses, it also includes assignments for different age groups of children, such as role-play about a visit to the pharmacy or a quiz about the proper use of medicines. The medicine education website is available in Finnish and in Swedish at www.laakekasvatus.fi. The idea of an alternative medicine website is offered as a general source of medical information and treatment, which also includes advertisements. The website 'Terveyskirjasto' (http://www.terveyskirjasto.fi/terveyskirjasto/tk.koti) comprises of 10,000 scientific articles about medicines, giving actual information about health and illnesses.

Table 1. Intervention case stories.

Case Story	Health Problems and Issues Concerning the Use of Medicine
Ville's stomach ache	Stomach ache (symptoms, disease and cure)
Veijo's case: How to get reliable information about flu?	Flu (symptoms, disease and cure)
Eetu's case: Once bitten, twice shy	Accidents: Hand wound and sprained ankle (symptoms and cure)
What is wrong with Sonja?	Headache: Migraine (symptoms, disease and cure)
A snake causes a woman serious symptoms	Snake bite (symptoms and cure)
What is wrong with Mikko?	Diabetes (symptoms, disease and cure)
Minna's story	Asthma (symptoms, disease and cure)

2.3. Data Collection

The main data was students' group interviews after the intervention and it was supplemented by audio recordings of students' group work during the study process. Semi-structured group interviews focused on the following themes: (1) medicines and medicine use; (2) disease under consideration; (3) medicine information sources; and (4) working within the intervention. One of the authors held audio-recorded group interviews with students in spring 2010, in a quiet, private room, during regular school hours; the interviews ranged in length from 20 to 35 min. The atmosphere established during the group interview was positive and relaxed and the interviewer tried to encourage students to admit any lack of understanding or anything else that might be unclear. The group interview began by students being asked in general about the medicine education intervention. Students were then asked to define medicine, explain what they had learnt about medicines and diseases, and how medicine information can be found. The interviewer also asked students to expand on particular points of issue. The order of the questions and topics was undefined and depended on the flow of discussion.

2.4. Data Analysis

Students' group discussions and group interviews were transcribed and checked for accuracy with the audio recording, and content analysis [50] was chosen for the analysis of students' descriptions throughout all the data. The answers were received to the following questions: What have the students learned about medicines and their use; what have the students learned about different diseases; and what are the students' perceptions of Internet-based intervention. Two researchers independently analyzed the data in order to create categories and sub-categories. Discussion followed as to whether or not the categories found were consistent. The analysis was quite convergent. An example of such categories and sub-categories can be found in Table 2, concerning what students learned about medicines and their use. A count was made of how many times each category was mentioned during the group interview. Data was analysed in the context of a particular setting and does not represent any absolute "truths" about students' perceptions of medicines, medicine use, diseases or searching for information [51–53].

Table 2. Students' descriptions of what they had learned about medicines.

Category	Number of Descriptions	Descriptions
		Use of Medicines
Adult permission	15	Medicines prescribed by a doctor may not be taken without adult approval (Boy 1) Children may take medicine with the permission of a physician or parents, or even children, of course take some Burana (ibuprofen) (Girl 4)
Medicine dosage	8	The prescription states a safe dosage, and if … (Boy 3) If you take more than the recommended dosage, then you get too much medicine; if you take too little, then you may not be cured (Boy 9)
Label/package instructions	9	In a way that is shown on the label (Girl 12) This means, if it reads e.g., one tablet per day for a specific age-group, then you should take only one; if you take more, then you may have a reaction (Boy 8) So, act according to the instructions on the packages (Boy 13)
Right time to take medicines	3	Take medicine at a certain time (Boy 2) You can take the medicine after a meal (Girl 1)
		Reason
For pain/feeling poorly	16	If you feel that you have headache or stomach ache, then you may take some 'off the shelf' medicine, or … (Girl 8) So if you are sick or allergic or you have a seizure or e.g., flu, then you may take (Girl 13)
Prescribed	6	I have a prescribed medicine, Burana (ibuprofen) (Boy 4)
When necessary	4	You should only take medicines when necessary (Girl 9)
For a health problem	3	If you have a very high fever, then you may take some kind of painkiller or something that lowers the fever, however, not just for only a slight headache (Girl 14)
		Storage
Medicine cabinet	3	In the medicine cabinet. And then there are some that need to be stored at a low temperature. Yes (Girl 7) And some must be locked in the medicine cabinet (Girl 11)
Out of access to children	2	So that small children cannot reach the medicine. (Girl 5)
		At What Age Can You Take Medicines without Parents' Consent
Fourth graders	4	Depends on the medicines. Some medicine for a fever or a cough, yes those can be taken, but if you have... (Boy 9) More serious symptoms (Girl 5) For example you are asthmatic and you get an asthma attack, then, if you don't know which medicines to take, you had better follow the advice of an adult (Boy 10) If your parents have shown you what medicines to take then you may use them, but if you're not sure, then it is not worth taking the risk (Girl 3)
4 year old age-limit	4	I think it was something up to 4 years old (Boy 14)
Ages from 8–12 years	3	You can take medicine I think that 8–12 is a suitable age and adults have their own medicines (Girl 14).
Total	80	

2.5. Ethical Issues

This study is part of a larger research project concerning medicine education, permission for which was granted by the Committee on Research Ethics, at the University of Eastern Finland. Students' views and participation was respected, therefore they had the right to drop out of the project at any stage of data collection. The interviewer highlighted the fact that participation was totally voluntary and during the interview the students could refuse to answer any question. Emphasis was placed on there being no right or wrong answers. The questions presented did not refer to personal illnesses or use of medicines.

3. Results

3.1. What Students Learned about Medicines and Their Use?

The students' group discussions about medicines were quite generalized. Almost everyone had used medicines such as painkillers and education on the careful use of medicine was highlighted. In the interview, students later described what they had learned during the medicine education intervention. Issues mostly mentioned were related to the use of medicines, the reason for using medicines, how to store them and who should use them. The descriptions could be classified into four categories: use, reason, storage and the suitable age for children to use medicines alone (Table 2). There were 80 descriptions in all.

Students explained that they had learned about different kinds of medicines. They described that if a cough continues, if one has a high fever, or if medicines do not help, then you should contact a physician. Students perceived that you should not take medicines prescribed for others and that it is important to know about the side effects. They spoke about *home care* in the following ways: domestic treatments do not require the presence of a physician, even though, if you visit a physician and ask what treatment can be done at home, he/she may be able to give certain instructions as to what to do.

Students knew the difference between over-the-counter medicines (OTC) and prescribed medicines:

It (OTC) is the kind of medicine you can take yourself. (Boy 21)

Prescribed medicines are those you can't buy without a prescription given by a physician. (Girl 19)

3.2. Students' Descriptions Regarding What They Had Learned about Different Diseases

Stomach-ache was perceived to be due to constipation, the runs, or appendicitis, and medicines should not then be used. Particularly highlighted was the importance of washing hands in order to avoid and prevent droplet infection. Students had acquired a lot of general information about flu, discussing the symptoms and home care for it. They were also able to name some commercial medicines. Flu was considered in a more detailed way after intervention. The difference between flu and influenza was also explained; students mentioned how best to avoid flu. They suggested keeping a distance from people who are sick, washing hands and taking care of your own health. There was very little discussion about First Aid during group discussions and the interview, but students recognized the need for First aid knowledge and highlighted the fact that accidents can be prevented in a number of ways. Students wanted to learn more about First Aid skills either at school or during their free time.

3.2.1. Migraine

At the beginning of the first lesson, students knew that migraine may cause a seizure, nausea, razor-like light formations, and that bright lights should be avoided. Later, they understood that video games and special movie effects might also worsen the situation. They had the impression that taking paracetamol is acceptable but ibuprofen should be avoided, even though both medicines may be used for migraine. Environmental aspects were mentioned in association with treating migraine; they suggested a dark, quiet place, with no bright lights, also mentioning such health aspects as sleeping and eating regularly. It was interesting to note that one of the students had searched for information on migraines at home, and had gathered a lot of facts on the subject.

3.2.2. Snakebite

Initially, students knew asnakebite to be dangerous but were not able to offer any form of treatment in such a situation. Furthermore, they thought that a typical reaction to a snake bite is increased sweating and nausea. The group discussed what should have been done to avoid getting bitten, suggesting that a First Aid kit and the use of rubber boots would have been a good preventative measure. During the group interview, the students were able to explain the symptoms and the First Aid required, in more detail. When a snake bites a person on the leg, the leg swells, the person is nauseous, the location of the bite is tender, bright red, and exhibits two small holes. You should then administer the tablet contained in the First Aid package for snakebites, the leg must be propped up and the patient should not be lifted. Finally, students suggested calling an ambulance, adding that snakebites can be avoided by stomping on the ground, watching where you walk and by wearing rubber boots.

3.2.3. Diabetes

At the beginning of the first lesson, students did not express any perceptions about the cause of diabetes. They described symptoms of weight loss, increased thirstiness, and a more frequent need to go to the bathroom. Later, they stated that you have to visit a doctor regularly, that the person needs insulin, which is injected either into the hand, stomach, or some other part of the body. Symptoms can be avoided by ensuring a sufficient amount of exercise and eating healthily.

3.2.4. Asthma

At the beginning of the first lesson, students had a very narrow comprehension of issues related to asthma, mentioning only that cold air is harmful and that it is worsened by the use of tobacco. A symptom of asthma is coughing and during an asthma attack, you need to breathe the medicine through an inhaler. After intervention, they were able to discuss more widely the different issues related to asthma and highlighted that asthma is a common, long-term disease among children. Environmental pollutants (dust, smoke) as well as the quality of outdoor air, were mentioned as being factors that may affect the severity of asthma. The students also knew that ibuprofen may worsen an asthma attack. Later, they broadened their perceptions of the symptoms, mentioning a prolonged cough and difficulty in breathing during an attack. They knew that prescription medicines such as Ventoline (salbutamol) are needed to combat asthma, but also spoke about OTC-medicines, First Aid and home care. According to students, 'you should remain calm' in order to control the symptoms.

3.3. Students' Perceptions about Searching for Information on Diseases

At the beginning of the first lesson, students considered that sources of reliable information could be acquired from a doctor, hospital, pharmacy and the Internet. However, the students also mentioned their doubts as to whether the Internet is completely reliable. After intervention, the information sources for diseases mentioned were Iltalehti (a Finnish afternoon tabloid), Google, the Internet, doctors, books, TV, pharmacy, parents, mothers, nurses, packages and labels.

Students perceived the medicine education site as being safe, contrary to Wikipedia, which can be modified by anyone. The same doubt applied to the alternative medicine website. Two students described the reliable website in the following way:

There was...the first site (Medicine education website) from which it was easy to find all the information. When you went to the website, there was a title and subtitles that you could use to read the symptoms. These were clearly written and there were no difficult words. (Boy 1)

The writer's name always appeared at the bottom of the paper, it was the name of the doctor at the end (website Terveysirjasto). (Boy 21)

The Terveyskirjasto website gave names of the experts, but the text included many concepts which were not easy to understand. Conversely, students considered that the texts on the Medicine Education website were fluent, logical and clear. They found that the information was easy to find and the links were good. Students would have wished for more subtitles.

3.4. Students' Perceptions of Internet-Based Intervention

Students were asked, during the interview, about their perceptions of the medicine education intervention. They acknowledged its role in learning, its significance, and how they felt about it. Students described learning about medicines, medicine use e.g., future knowledge of what medicines to take. Students perceived that medicine education is useful and necessary:

It is rather good that school provides opportunities for medicine education and there could be more of these lessons; they are quite useful. (Girl 2)

Everybody needs medicine education, learning to use medicines in the correct way. (Girl 14)

Students perceived medicine education studies as enjoyable, very nice or quite nice. They also perceived the topic as interesting. In conclusion, students perceived Internet-based medicine education as being important; it was a different, nice way to study a previously unfamiliar issue.

This was much nicer than working in normal lessons, because in this way you learned more important issues. (Girl 20)

It was interesting; this information is of use in your free time too, and then in the higher grades these issues will probably be easier to understand when they are revised. (Boy 3)

Some of the students perceived that it would be better to study medicines in the sixth grade. They considered medicine education to be difficult.

Some issues were difficult to understand, it was difficult to search for information and ponder on it yourself. (Girl 7)

The theoretical framework and main results are shown in Figure 1. Medicine education as a part of health education promotes social sustainability and health in society. Health literacy in the context of Internet-based medicine education intervention entails rational medicine use and awareness of reliable information.

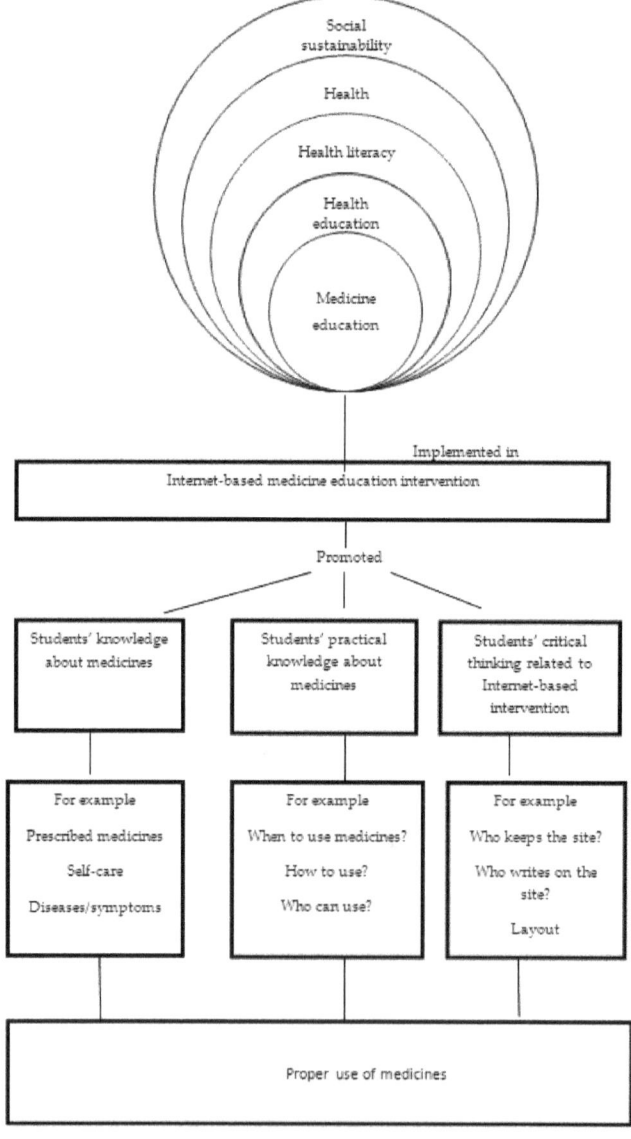

Figure 1. The theoretical framework and main results about the Internet-based medicine education intervention.

4. Discussion

This study examined fourth graders' perspectives on medicine issues in the context of the education intervention that was aimed at developing student health literacy and the further promotion of their health habits, health and quality of life, thus contributing towards solving the challenges of national and international health [1–11]. Self-awareness and citizenship were not considered, even though they are also essential components of health literacy [12].

Students' theoretical and practical knowledge about medicines and diseases was seen in their descriptions, which are in line with main processes in healthcare [14,15]: keeping healthy, detecting health problems, diagnosing diseases and treating diseases. Fourth graders were able to understand the causes of diseases, symptoms, treatment and prevention. Students especially described common illnesses; in moderation, they highlighted chronic illness, its symptoms and treatment, mentioning their own experiences, symptoms and treatments, as well as that of their friends or schoolmates. It seemed that the desire to take a greater role in managing their health was developing [20–22].

Students' perspectives on medicines and their use, was similar to that seen in previous studies in Finland [26,27,30]. Fourth graders' perspectives included the view that as well as the benefits, medication always includes risks such as the side effects. They knew that, generally, adult permission is needed; that the amount of medicine given must be accurate; that medicines should be used according to the instructions on the label/package and administered at the right time for pain or sickness. Fourth graders considered that in some cases, at least children of their own age could use medicines without the permission of adults, which is in line with international results of medicine use among adolescents [23–25,31,34,36,37]. As previous studies have also shown [29,30], students pointed out that medicines should be stored in a medicine cabinet, out of the reach of young children. The rational use of medicines and safe medicine storage decrease health risks and healthcare costs, thus being an important aspect of sustainability.

Searching for Internet-based information about diseases and their care was practiced according to the structured tasks. In the initial discussions, students pondered that reliable information could be acquired from doctors, from a hospital and from a pharmacy, as has been found in previous studies [23,34,35,38,39]. Unlike previous studies [23,26,34,35,38] fourth graders did not point out the role of parents, teachers or patient inserts as being an information source. During the group discussions after intervention, they mentioned packages and labels, showing an understanding of the rational use of medicines. Still, students did not consider schoolteachers to be a source of medicine information.

The students appropriately evaluated different websites; they were able to identify reliable sites and argue their perceptions. The students learned to evaluate the reliability of health information sources, even though this could be sometimes difficult to determine, and they recognized that Internet information might not be credible. Strategies were developed to test reliability. There were signs that fourth graders' general perceptions differed about the Internet as a medium and its specific use for health information. We would hope that high-quality health information from reliable websites, would aid in overcoming barriers for young people seeking help, and would improve awareness of common symptoms related to health problems. Students were able to find evidence-based self-help on the Internet, and they identified that there is significant variation in the quality of sources, as previous studies have shown [41,46]. Fourth graders expressed the need for improvement in the readability of online health educational material and considered that already at their age, medicine education is needed.

However, generalization of our findings is clearly limited, because conclusions based on our findings, are directional and transferable mainly in the Finnish settings. Due to its sample size, this study is limited, but the group interviews provided students with the opportunity to talk about the rational use of medicines. The objective was to understand fourth graders' perceptions rather than make generalizations. The Internet-based medicine education intervention was conducted in accordance with the age and developmental level of the students, and thus supports the healthy growth of children.

5. Conclusions

Research findings support previous national and international studies and show that this kind of Internet-based medicine education intervention and its research is important in the school context. The medicine education website, was found to develop students' conceptual awareness of diseases and awaken student values related to sustainable development, such as the prevention of diseases.

The results of this study show the importance of developing the content of Internet-based medicine education and education for sustainable development. This should focus especially on taking responsibility and seeking out critical information. The Internet-based medicine education intervention motivated and activated students. They discussed and complemented each other's thoughts and words and encouraged them to examine Internet-based health material. However, we acknowledge that Internet-based information replaces neither professional help nor the role of parents and teachers.

The prevalence of chronic diseases such as asthma and diabetes is obviously part of a student's everyday life. The need for knowledge concerning First Aid is also apparent. Students' prior knowledge of symptoms, what causes them and the treatment for diseases was quite relevant, but during the intervention this knowledge was deepened further. It is possible to say that this Internet-based medicine education intervention helped students understand health as a physical and social capability. Important skills were also developed relating to the acquisition and application of information, implying that the achievement of a level of knowledge and skills actually improves personal health.

This study suggests that fourth graders need well-structured tasks when searching for information on the Internet, addressing the possibility of them becoming distracted and straying too far from the actual task. Educational material on the Internet needs to be structured in the same way in order to support student inquiries. Furthermore, in health education, media literacy and health literacy should be developed side by side, improving students' skills and enabling them to use the Internet in their learning. Health literacy supports the understanding that prevention and health promotion are essential for improving sustainable development at the local, regional and national level.

Author Contributions: Sirpa Kärkkäinen is responsible author. She has participated in writing the article, planning the research and interventions, data collection and analysis; Tuula Keinonen has participated in writing the article, planning the research, data collection and analysis; Anu Hartikainen-Ahia has participated in planning the research and interventions as well as in writing the article; Kirsti Vainio has participated in planning the research and writing the article; Katri Hämeen-Anttila has participated in planning the research and writing the article.

Conflicts of Interest: The authors declare no conflict of interest.

1.   The Finnish National Board of Education. National Core Curriculum for Basic Education (NFBE). 2004. Available online: www.oph.fi/english (accessed on 29 October 2016).
2.   Jeronen, E.; Kaikkonen, M.; Lindh, A. Health education in the perspective of sustainable development in teacher education. In *Forum on Global Responsibility in Research and Education—Practices in Partnerships and Daily Activities*; Tapola, H., Suntioinen, S., Karjalainen, K., Eds.; University of Eastern Finland: Joensuu, Finland, 2010; pp. 13–21.
3.   World Health Organization. *Health Promotion Glossary*; WHO: Geneva, Switzerland, 1998. Available online: http://www.who.int/healthpromotion/about/HPR%20Glossary%201998.pdf (accessed on 13 March 2017).
4.   Paasche-Orlow, M.K.; Wolf, M.S. The causal pathways linking health literacy to health outcomes. *Am. J. Health Behav.* **2007**, *1*, 19–26. [CrossRef]
5.   De Walt, D.A.; Berkman, N.D.; Sheridan, S.S.; Lohr, K.N.; Pignone, M.P. Literacy and Health Outcomes. A systematic Review of the Literature. *J. Gen. Intern. Med.* **2004**, *19*, 1228–1239. [CrossRef] [PubMed]
6.   Institute of Medicine (IOM). Available online: http://www.nationalacademies.org/hmd/Reports/2004/Health-Literacy-A-Prescription-to-End-Confusion.aspx (accessed on 29 October 2016).
7.   Sanders, L.M.; Shaw, J.S.; Guez, G.; Baur, C.; Rudd, R. Health literacy and child health promotion: Implications for research, clinical care and public policy. *Pediatrics* **2009**, *4*, 306–314. [CrossRef] [PubMed]

8. Nutbeam, D. Defining and measuring health literacy: What can we learn from literacy studies? *IJPHS* **2009**, *54*, 303–305. [CrossRef] [PubMed]

9. Nutbeam, D. Health outcomes and health promotion: Defining success in health promotion. *Health Promot. J. Aust.* **1996**, *6*, 58–60.

10. Nutbeam, D. Health literacy as a public health goal: A challenge for contemporary health education and communication strategies into the 21st century. *Health Promot. Int.* **2000**, *15*, 259–267. [CrossRef]

11. St Leger, L. Schools health literacy and public health: Possibilities and challenges. *Health Promot. Int.* **2011**, *16*, 197–205. [CrossRef]

12. Paakkari, L.; Paakkari, O. Health literacy as a learning outcome in schools. *Health Educ.* **2012**, *112*, 133–152. [CrossRef]

13. Diamond, C.; Saintonge, S.; August, P.; Azrack, A. The development of Building Wellness, a youth health literacy program. *J. Health Commun.* **2011**, *16*, 103–118. [CrossRef] [PubMed]

14. Sun, X.; Shi, Y.; Zeng, Q.; Wang, Y.; Du, W.; Wei, N.; Xie, R.; Chang, C. Determinants of health literacy and health behaviour regarding infectious respiratory diseases: A pathway model. *BMC Publ. Health* **2013**, *22*, 261. [CrossRef]

15. Bergman, B.; Neuhauser, D.; Provost, L. Five main processes in healthcare: A citizen perspective. *BMJ Qual. Saf.* **2011**, *20*, 41–42. [CrossRef] [PubMed]

16. Cho, Y.L.; Lee, S.Y.; Arozullah, A.M.; Cittenden, K.S. Effects of health literacy on health status and health service utilization amongst the elderly. *Soc. Sci. Med.* **2008**, *66*, 1809–1816. [CrossRef] [PubMed]

17. Haugland, S.; Wold, B.; Stevenson, J.; Aaroe, L.E.; Woynarowska, B. Subjective health complaints in adolescence: A cross-national comparison of prevalence and dimensionality. *Eur. J. Publ. Health* **2001**, *11*, 4–10. [CrossRef]

18. Siponen, S.M.; Ahonen, R.S.; Savolainen, P.H.; Hämeen-Anttila, K. Children's health and parental socioeconomic factors: A population-based survey in Finland. *BMC Publ. Health* **2011**, *9*, 457. [CrossRef] [PubMed]

19. Lindell-Osuaqwu, L.; Sepponen, K.; Farooqui, S.; Kokki, H.; Hämeen-Anttila, K.; Vainio, K. Parental reporting of adverse drug events and other drug-related problems in children in Finland. *Eur. J. Clin. Pharmacol.* **2013**, *69*, 985–994. [CrossRef] [PubMed]

20. Hoffman, S.; Marsiglia, F.F.; Nevarez, L.; Porta, M. Health literacy among youth in Guatemala City. *Soc. Work Publ. Health* **2016**, *32*, 30–37. [CrossRef] [PubMed]

21. Manganello, J.A. Health literacy and adolescents: A framework and agenda for future research. *Health Educ. Res.* **2008**, *23*, 840–847. [CrossRef] [PubMed]

22. Greenberg, M.T.; Lippold, M.A. Promoting healthy outcomes among youth with multiple risks: Innovative approaches. *Annu. Rev. Publ. Health* **2013**, *34*, 253–270. [CrossRef] [PubMed]

23. Chambers, C.T.; Reid, G.J.; McGrath, P.J.; Finley, G.A. Self-administration of over-the-counter medication for pain among adolescents. *Arch. Pediatr. Adolesc. Med.* **1997**, *151*, 449–455. [CrossRef] [PubMed]

24. Dengler, R.; Roberts, H. Adolescents' use of prescribed drugs and over-the-counter preparations. *J. Public Health Med.* **2003**, *18*, 437–442. [CrossRef]

25. Hansen, E.H.; Holstein, B.E.; Due, P. International survey of self-reported medicine use among adolescents. *Ann. Pharmacother.* **2003**, *37*, 361–366. [CrossRef] [PubMed]

26. Ylinen, S.; Hämeen-Anttila, K.; Sepponen, K.; Lindblad, A.K.; Ahonen, R. The use of prescription medicines and self-medication among children—A population-based study in Finland. *Pharmacoepidemiol. Drug Saf.* **2010**, *19*, 1000–1008. [CrossRef] [PubMed]

27. Hämeen-Anttila, K.; Lindell-Osuagwu, L.; Sepponen, K.; Vainio, K.; Halonen, P.; Ahonen, R. Factors associated with medicine use among Finnish children under 12 years. *Pharmacoepidemiol. Drug Saf.* **2010**, *19*, 400–407. [PubMed]

28. Siponen, S.; Ahonen, R.; Kettis, A.; Hämeen-Anttila, K. Complementary or alternative? Patterns of complementary and alternative medicine (CAM) use among Finnish children. *Eur. J. Clin. Pharmacol.* **2012**, *68*, 1639–1645. [CrossRef] [PubMed]

29. Sanz, E.; Bush, P.; Garcia, M. Medicines at home: The contents of medicine cabinets in eight countries. In *Children, Medicines and Culture*; Bush, P.J., Trakas, D.J., Sanz, E.J., Wirsing, R.L., Vaskilampi, T., Prout, A., Eds.; Pharmaceutical Products Press: New York, NY, USA, 1997; pp. 77–105.

30. Hokkanen, J.; Elorinne, A.L.; Vainio, K.; Keinonen, T. Medicine case study highlights the problems of Finnish households in medicine consumption practices. *Probl. Educ. Century* **2016**, *71*, 31–43.
31. Sanz, E.J. Concordance and children's use of medicines. *BMJ* **2003**, *327*, 858–860. [CrossRef] [PubMed]
32. Gagliardi, A.; Jadad, A.R. Examination of instruments used to rate quality of health information on the Internet: Chronicle of a voyage with an unclear destination. *BMJ* **2002**, *324*, 569–573. [CrossRef] [PubMed]
33. Vaskilampi, T.; Kalpio, O.; Ahonen, R.; Hallia, O. Finnish study on medicine use, health behaviour and perceptions of medicines and health care. In *Childhood and Medicine Use in a Cross-Cultural Perspective: A European Concerted Action*; Trakas, D.J., Sanz, E., Eds.; European Commission: Luxembourg, 1996; pp. 191–219.
34. Menacker, F.; Aramburuzabala, P.; Minian, N.; Bush, P.; Bibace, R. Children and medicines: What do they want to know and how do they want to learn. *J. Small Anim. Prac.* **1999**, *16*, 38–52.
35. Hämeen-Anttila, K.; Juvonen, M.; Ahonen, R.; Bush, P.; Airaksinen, M. How well can children understand medicine related topics? *Probl. Educ. Century* **2006**, *60*, 171–178. [CrossRef] [PubMed]
36. Bush, P.; Joshi, M. Towards a universal curriculum for teaching children about medicines. In Proceedings of the Federation Internationale Pharmaceutique World Congress, Nice, France, 31 August–5 September 2002.
37. Almarsdóttir, A.; Hartzema, A.; Bush, P.; Simpson, K.; Zimmer, C. Children's Attitudes and Beliefs about Illness and Medicines: A Triangulation of Open-ended and Semi-structured Interviews. *J. Small Anim. Prac.* **1997**, *14*, 26–41.
38. Bozoni, K.; Kalmanti, M.; Koukouli, S. Perception and knowledge of medicines of primary schoolchildren: The influence of age and socioeconomic status. *Eur. J. Pediatr.* **2006**, *165*, 42–49. [CrossRef] [PubMed]
39. Stoelben, S.; Krappweis, J.; Rossler, G.; Kirch, W. Adolescents' drug use and drug knowledge. *Eur. J. Pediatr.* **2000**, *159*, 608–614. [CrossRef] [PubMed]
40. Westerlund, M.; Brånstad, J.-O.; Westerlund, T. Medicine-taking behavior and drug-related problems in adolescents of a Swedish high school. *Pharm. World Sci.* **2008**, *30*, 243–250. [CrossRef] [PubMed]
41. Huby, K.; Swallow, V.; Smith, T.; Carolan, I. Children and young people's views on access to a web-based applications to support personal management of long-term conditions: A qualitative study. *Child Care Health Dev.* **2016**, *43*, 126–132. [CrossRef] [PubMed]
42. European Commission. Managing Health Data (2016). Available online: https://ec.europa.eu/digital-single-market/en/managing-health-data (accessed on 29 October 2016).
43. Faith, J.; Thorburn, S.; Sinky, T. Exploring healthcare experiences among online interactive weight loss forum users. *Comput. Hum. Behav.* **2016**, *57*, 326–333. [CrossRef]
44. Singh, K.; Brown, R. Health-related Internet habits and health anxiety in university students. *Anxiety Stress Coping* **2014**, *5*, 542–554. [CrossRef] [PubMed]
45. Gray, N.J.; Klien, J.; Noyce, P.; Sesselberg, T.; Cantrill, J. Health information-seeking behaviour in adolescence: The place of the Internet. *Soc. Sci. Med.* **2005**, *60*, 1467–1478. [CrossRef] [PubMed]
46. Richards, C.; Hughes, J. 2016 The use of technology to support young people with mental health issues in schools. In *Mental Health and Wellbeing through Schools: The Way Forward*; Shute, R.H., Ed.; Routledge: London, UK, 2016; p. 230.
47. Reavley, N.J.; Jorm, A.F. The quality of mental disorder information websites. A review. *Patient Educ. Couns.* **2011**, *85*, 16–25. [CrossRef] [PubMed]
48. Hutchinson, N.; Baird, GL.; Garg, M. Examining the reading level of internet medical information for common internal medical diagnoses. *Am. J. Med.* **2016**, *129*, 637–639. [CrossRef] [PubMed]
49. Eysenbach, G.; Kohler, C. How do consumers search for and appraise health information on the world wide web? Qualitative study using focus groups, usability tests, and in-depth interviews. *BMJ* **2002**, *324*, 573–577. [CrossRef] [PubMed]
50. Roth, W.-M. *Doing Qualitative Research. Praxis of Methods*; Sense Publishers: Rotterdam, The Netherlands, 2005; pp. 78–98.
51. Gomm, R.; Hammersley, M.; Foster, P. *Case Study Method*; Sage Publishers: London, UK, 2000; pp. 111–113.

52. Lincoln, Y.S.; Guba, E.G. *Naturalistic Inquiry*; Sage Publications: Newbury Park, CA, USA, 1985; pp. 125–130.
53. Stake, R.E. Case studies. In *Handbook of Qualitative Research*, 2nd ed.; Denzin, N.K., Lincoln, Y.S., Eds.; Sage Publications: Thousand Oaks, CA, USA, 2000; pp. 435–455.

Article

Multimodal Languaging as a Pedagogical Model—A Case Study of the Concept of Division in School Mathematics

Jorma Joutsenlahti * and Pirjo Kulju

School of Education, University of Tampere, Tampere 33100, Finland; pirjo.kulju@uta.fi
* Correspondence: jorma.joutsenlahti@uta.fi; Tel.: +358-505-439-197

Academic Editor: Eila Jeronen
Received: 31 October 2016; Accepted: 28 December 2016; Published: 4 January 2017

Abstract: The purpose of this study is to present a multimodal languaging model for mathematics education. The model consists of mathematical symbolic language, a pictorial language, and a natural language. By applying this model, the objective was to study how 4th grade pupils ($N = 21$) understand the concept of division. The data was collected over six hours of teaching sessions, during which the pupils expressed their mathematical thinking mainly by writing and drawing. Their productions, as well as questionnaire after the process, were analyzed qualitatively. The results show that, in expressing the mathematical problem in verbal form, most of the students saw it as a division into parts. It was evident from the pupils' texts and drawings that the mathematical expression of subtraction could be interpreted in three different ways. It was found that the pupils enjoyed using writing in the solution of word problems, and it is suggested that the use of different modes in expressing mathematical thinking may both strengthen the learning of mathematical concepts and support the evaluation of learning.

Keywords: multiliteracy; languaging; division; mathematics; education

1. Introduction

Traditionally, there has been a strong emphasis on the use of symbolic mathematical language in representing mathematics. This has, however, been found to be a limiting factor in expressing mathematical thinking in learning processes [1–3]. The aim of this article is to present a multimodal languaging model, in which the ways to express mathematical thinking are expanded beyond mathematic symbolic language. A second objective is to observe how 4th grade pupils understand the concept of division based on this model.

Different ways of expressing thinking and making meaning form the underlying theoretical basis for this study. Theoretically, the multimodal languaging model is related to multiliteracy, a concept referring to various modes in the current communications environment [4]. The present model includes three types of semiotic systems of meaning-making: a symbolic mathematical language, a natural language, and a pictorial language [2,5]. It has been suggested that the use of different semiotic systems such as these supports the development of conceptual knowledge [6,7]. Furthermore, it has been recommended that, in a national assessment of learning outcomes [8], languaging should be an integral to the pedagogical method in learning mathematics.

In our earlier paper [9], we published the outline of our pedagogical model and preliminary results in Finnish from the point of view of integrating school subjects. In this paper, we will link the multimodal languaging model to a multiliteracies framework, present new data, and further discuss the concept of division based on the data.

2. The Theoretical Framework

2.1. Multiliteracy

The multimodal languaging model is connected to a multiliteracies framework. The basic principles of multiliteracy were set out in the manifesto of the New London Group (NLG) [10]. Since then, multiliteracies has become a key concept in describing the changes in the current textual world, in which the written mode can be complemented by, or even replaced by, other modes [4,11].

In research, multiliteracies is usually framed by semiotics, which emphasizes the "semiotic resource" as a potential key term in meaning-making [12]. Sociocultural approaches also seem to be inherent in multiliteracy [12]. These aspects reflect two of the "multis" inherent in multiliteracies, as stated by Kalantzis and Cope [4]. First of all, the variety of modes provides more options for meaning-making; secondly, a text may vary enormously, depending on social context such as different cultural settings, gender identity, or the subject matter [4].

Multimodal resources in school mathematics have been highlighted in several studies (e.g., O'Halloran [13]). The aspect of social diversity of multiliteracies in the context of mathematics is also acknowledged, for example, by Takeuchi [14], who studied English language learners (ELLs) in mathematics practices in an urban Canadian classroom.

The present multimodal languaging model intentionally takes advantage of different modes in making meaning. The underlying idea is that, if the pupils are obliged to use different modes in their expression, they gain a greater understanding of the topic. Thus, the students in this study wrote and drew while performing mathematical tasks. Culturally, our study is in the context of school mathematics in Finland: the study combines the international symbolic mathematical language with other ways of meaning-making. Students' productions must therefore be interpreted from this cultural point of view.

The multiliteracies approach has only recently been incorporated into the Finnish core curriculum [15] as one of the transversal competencies. It is defined as follows [15] (p. 33): "the competence to interpret, produce and make a value judgement across a variety of different texts, which will help the pupils to understand diverse modes of cultural communication and to build their personal identity."

We can see this idea, for example, in the objectives of instructions in mathematics for Grades 3–6 [15] (p. 398), for example: " . . . to encourage the pupil to present his or her conclusions and solutions to others through concrete tools, drawings, speech, and writing, also using information and communication technology."

It is to be noted that the theoretical concept of multiliteracies is rather complex. It is described as being a pedagogical approach, but in the Finnish curriculum is applied as a set of communication abilities [12,16]. However, there is an urgent need for research into the implementation of a multiliteracies approach in all school subjects by developing concrete yet theoretically relevant educational models.

2.2. Languaging of Mathematical Thinking

Traditionally, at least in Finnish mathematics education, pupils often work silently and independently in the mathematics classroom, and the solutions to mathematical problems are usually presented by mathematical symbols alone, without any clarifying text or drawing. Owing to this tradition, it is often difficult for mathematics teachers to follow how a pupil has thought through his/her solution to a mathematical problem. Has the pupil really understood the main idea of the solution?

The use of languaging breaks this tradition and serves as a means to express thinking in several different ways. It has been shown that writing and the use of natural language in the solutions of mathematical problems may in fact boost learning in mathematics, develop mathematical understanding, change the pupil's attitude towards mathematics for the better, and help the teacher's evaluation [17]. The use of natural language, both in the solution process of mathematical problems, and in formulating the presentation of the solutions, helps a pupil to organize her/his mathematical thinking for herself/himself and for the peer group [2,9,18]. In fact, it seems that the use of natural language and drawings helps most students in the solution process of mathematical problems not only at primary level, but also at higher levels of the education system [19].

At the primary school level, we have recognized three useful semiotic systems or "languages" of meaning-making in mathematical presentations (Figure 1). These semiotic systems are a mathematical symbolic language, a natural language, and a pictorial language [2,12,19]. In the school context, this means students are able to express their mathematical thinking either by using mathematical symbols (e.g., numbers, symbols), a natural language (mother tongue and/or second language), or pictures or other tangible devices [12,19]. The modes in using these are writing, speaking, and drawing.

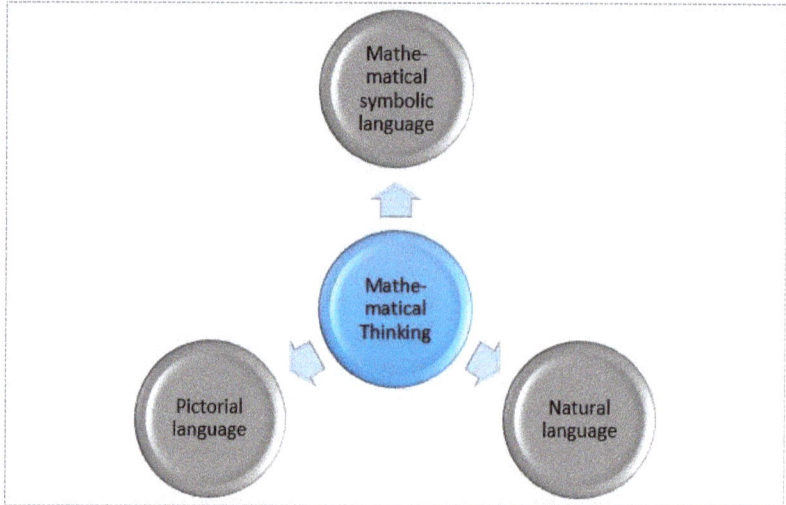

Figure 1. The three languages that can be used to express mathematical thinking [12,20].

Mathematical thinking is described as an information process monitored by one's metacognition [7]. The main purpose of using several semiotic systems in learning activities (e.g., in studying new mathematical concepts and doing exercises) is to develop the student's own meaning-making processes. We call this process "languaging", a concept that has been used in mathematics and in mother tongue didactics since the 1990s [21].

Languaging in mathematics refers to expressing one's mathematical thinking by different modes either orally (by natural language) or in writing (by natural language, mathematical symbolic language, or pictorial language) [12,20]. From a multiliteracies aspect, languaging can be seen as a multimodal approach to making meanings of mathematical concepts and procedures.

In addition to the meaning-making of concepts and procedures for a learner, multimodal languaging is also a tool for a teacher to evaluate how the learner has understood mathematics. In this study, we will use pupils' texts and drawings as a resource for semantic interpretations.

2.3. The Concept of Division in School Mathematics

In the Finnish National core curriculum for basic education, the objectives in division learning in Grades 3-6 are described as follows: "They learn division in cases of both quotition and partition. They practise division by number units. They utilise the properties of operations and the connections between them." [15] (p. 399).

Pupils are introduced to the concept of division after they have learned multiplication. The objective is that they should understand the connection between multiplication and division in Grade 3. In several studies, the concept of division is observed to be difficult to understand for pupils and even for prospective teachers [22], especially in word problems and in recognizing both of the aforementioned types of division. Typically, if we ask pupils to give an example of division, they describe it as being division into parts: e.g., "Mother had 24 cookies and she promised to divide them equally to me and my five friends. How many cookies did I get?" We could describe this as the primitive model of division [22]. In fact, the model of division by contents (e.g., "For how many children can mother divide packages of four cookies, if she has 24 cookies?") is understood by systemically teaching in upper grades [23].

3. The Division Research: Data Collection and Analysis

The use of different modes in mathematics was modeled and explored via a six-hour teaching process, which took place in the Training School of University of Tampere in 2012 in a 4th grade class of 21 pupils. All of the pupils were monolingual Finnish speakers. The process was planned and conducted in co-operation with the class teacher. After the teaching, we submitted a written questionnaire in order to evaluate the students' experiences and thoughts on the process. In this article, we concentrate on the following research questions:

1. How do the pupils interpret the concept of division?
2. How did the pupils experience the use of writing and drawing in learning mathematics?

The key idea in the teaching process and data collection was that the students were given a mathematical expression $(24/6-3)$, which was then the starting point for several different tasks. At first, the pupils were to invent a typical school word problem based on the given expression. This means that they had to construct verbal meanings and context for the numbers, division, and subtraction by themselves, in contrast to the usual ways of presenting mathematical problems. Then, the students were to solve their own invented mathematical word problem by using the multimodal languaging method: in this phase, they worked with a mathematical symbolic language, a natural language via writing, and a pictorial language by drawing. After this, they were to extend their own word problem into a story by planning and processing their stories as typically done in developing writing skills. The stories based on the mathematical word problem were eventually transformed into strip cartoon form in order to practice textual skills and to evaluate the student's mathematical thinking.

A qualitative content analysis was conducted on pupils' productions during the teaching process (word problems, written and drawn solutions, stories, and cartoons) and on the written answers to the questionnaire. Based on the productions, we were able to interpret what kind of meanings pupils constructed for the given mathematical expression. The process was successful, as nearly all of the pupils cooperated willingly during all the steps.

4. Results

4.1. How Do the Pupils Interpret the Concept of Division?

The use of multimodal languaging model in the process revealed the contexts into which abstract mathematical symbolic language was referring to in the student's thinking. Most of the students ($N = 21$) equated the contexts with food, e.g., cookies ($N = 9$), or animals, e.g., bunnies ($N = 6$).

Languaging through writing revealed how the students understood the mathematical concepts of division and subtraction. In the expression $24/6-3$, the key issue is what kind of meanings pupils gave to the subtraction "minus three." Interestingly, in the division into parts the subtraction was understood in two different ways: A: "minus three" from only one group ($N = 11$) or B: "minus three" from each of the six groups ($N = 8$) (Figure 2).

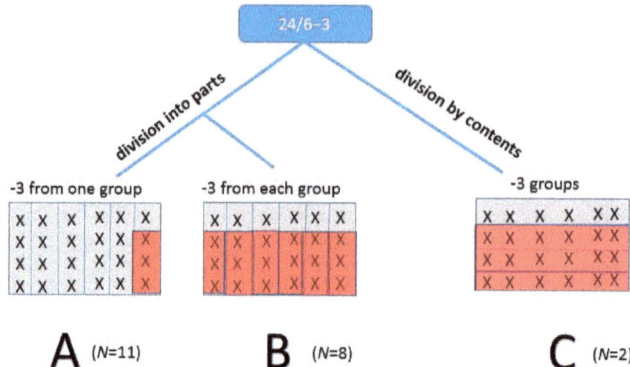

Figure 2. The ways the pupils (*N* = 21) interpreted the concept of division and subtraction in the expression *24/6–3* (modified from Joutsenlahti et al. [12]).

Against our expectations, we found two cases where the pupils had constructed division by contents. The two pupils had problems in formulating the word problem correctly to the end, but the main idea of the division by contents was properly presented (see Table 1, Case C). In the next two tables and in Figure 3, we show how three pupils constructed the word problem, its solution, and the whole story in the cartoons. In Table 1, we have taken three examples of the word problems in which division is needed for their solution.

Table 1. Word problem examples of divisions and subtractions (Types A, B, and C from Figure 1).

Type of Division	An Example
A	"In the tree there were 24 apples. Aku, Santeri, Miina, Liisa, Kaisa and Laura divided them. After that Kaisa gave to her mother 3 apples. How many apples did Kaisa get?" (Pupil 1)
B	"Emma divided 24 cookies to her six friends. Emma's sister took 3 cookies from each friend. How many cookies did each friend get?" (Pupil 2)
C	"Samppa had 24 ice hockey sticks. His task was to divide them into groups of six sticks." Three groups were left in the storage. How many groups of six sticks were taken to the training hall?" (This example is a combination of several pupils: First two sentences are from Pupil 3 and the rest of the problem from others)

In the second phase, pupils constructed solutions to their word problem firstly via natural language, and secondly via pictorial language (Table 2). The solutions by natural language were like little stories, which also contained mathematical symbolic language. The original handmade drawings were completed as shown in Table 2 (drawn by computer). Only Pupil 3 of the three pupils had problems in logically making a solution and cartoons. Pupil 3 had made the beginning of the solution of the word problem correctly, but the rest of the solution was insufficient. We present here only the correct parts of the example of Model C.

Table 2. Pupils' word problem solutions of divisions and subtractions by natural and pictorial language (Types A, B, and C from Figure 1). The solutions via pictorial language are based on pupils' drawings.

Type of Division	The Solution by Natural and Pictorial Language
A	"Kaisa got at first 24/6 = 4 (apples). When Kaisa came home she gave three apples to the mother 4 − 3 = 1. Kaisa got one apple." (Pupil 1). 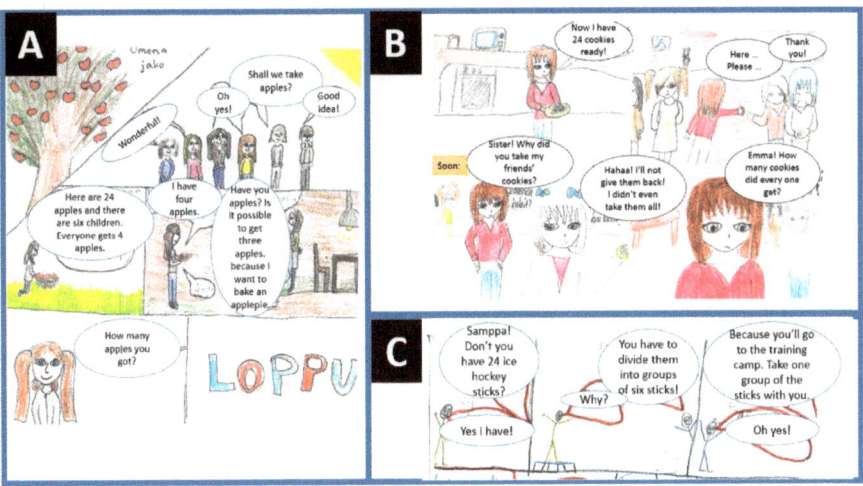
B	"24/6 = 4, 4 – 3 = 1. The cookies were divided and everyone got four (cookies). The sister takes from everyone else three cookies. Every girl got only one cookie." (Pupil 2).
C	"24/6 − 3 = 1. Samppa divides the ice hockey stics into six groups. He left three groups in the storage and took one group including four ice hockey sticks to the training camp." (Two sentences from Pupil 3 and the rest of the solution from others).

At the end, pupils drew cartoons in which they told the whole story: the word problem and its solution (Figure 3). Pupil 1 drew the cartoon about how Kaisa divided 24 apples, Pupil 2 drew the cartoon about how Emma divided 24 cookies (Case B in Figure 1), and Pupil 3 drew the cartoon about how Samppa divided 24 ice hockey sticks (Case C in Figure 1). The last cartoon, C, is not complete, because there were some misunderstandings at the end of the solution.

Figure 3. Three examples of pupils' cartoons (Models A, B, and C from Figure 1). The speech bubbles have been translated from Finnish to English.

All the pupils in the study succeeded in drawing logical cartoons from their word problem. All three pupils created a reliable context in their word problem (Table 1) and in their cartoons

(Figure 3) for the mathematical expression. The division into parts and the subtraction have acquired real meanings in the pupil's own cartoons from their point of views.

4.2. How Did the Pupils Experience the Use of Writing and Drawing in Mathematics Learning?

After the teaching process, we asked the pupils how they had experienced the multimodal approach in mathematics learning by a questionnaire. The results are shown in Tables 3–5. Most of the pupils liked writing the word problem and constructing a larger story about it. An interesting detail in Table 3 is that almost all of the girls liked writing the most, whereas most of the boys liked drawing cartoons. A mind map was needed in the planning of the story; that part of the study is omitted from this article. Mind map making develops analytical thinking.

Table 3. The most agreeable part in the project from the pupils' points of view (*N* = 21).

	Girls	Boys
Drawing cartoons	1	6
Writing word problem and story	11	1
Making mind map for a story	0	2

The pupils were asked whether they thought that writing (the use of natural language) supported the solution making for word problems. Almost all of the pupils thought that writing supported it (Table 4). The result is interesting, because writing was not favored by the boys.

Table 4. Do you think that writing (natural language) supports the solutions of word problems? (*N* = 21).

Answer	Girls	Boys
Yes	12	6
No	0	2
No answer	0	1

The pupils also provided their opinions as to why writing is important or not in the solving process. By content analysis, four main themes were found, which are presented in Table 5 with text examples.

Table 5. Examples of pupils' opinions on the importance of using natural language in solutions of word problems.

Theme	Examples
Better understanding	"I understand better how I have solved the problem." (5 pupils)
Easier to construct the solution	"It is easier to solve the problem when you can write." (5 pupils)
Checking of the answer	"You can justify from the written text that you have solved it correctly" (2 pupils)
Mother tongue learning (writing)	"You learn at same time mathematics and mother tongue" (1 pupil)

5. Discussion

The pedagogical model described in this paper is an example of using multimodal ways of meaning-making in school mathematics. The intentional use of multimodal languaging model revealed the meanings pupils made for the mathematical symbolic language and concepts (here, division and subtraction) and served in interpreting their thinking. These various types of ways to express one's thinking serve also as a way for the teacher to evaluate the students' understanding of the concepts.

Despite the unfamiliarity of the task, every pupil in the class managed to produce a proper word problem, solutions by natural language, and a pictorial language for the problem and the cartoons. The most typical interpretation of division was division into parts (Figure 1). From the point of view of the pupils, writing was seen as useful for a better understanding of the solution, and for constructing the solution more easily (Tables 4 and 5). A similar result has also been observed in the languaging surveys of university mathematics teaching. The girls liked writing more than the boys, and the boys liked drawing more than the girls (Table 3). Boys having problems in writing are seen on a wider scale in Finland; national Finnish assessments of learning outcomes at the end of comprehensive school have shown that boys are significantly worse than girls in writing [24]. There were no differences in the data between how pupils made solutions via natural or pictorial languages: all pupils could do both of them mainly correctly. All pupils were able to draw cartoons, presenting both the problem and its solution.

We suggest that the broadened ways of expressing mathematical thinking may help those who struggle with mathematics and for whom mathematical symbolic language as such is difficult to comprehend. The use of writing and drawing in problem solving may also strengthen the learning of mathematical concepts, as the use of different modes leads to organizing one's mathematical thinking. In this study, all of the pupils were monolingual Finnish speakers; however, the use of multimodality may also support, for example, L2 learners for whom the pictorial language may serve as a way to understand mathematical concepts.

The use of different modes in learning mathematics could easily be extended to the use of, for example, videos. The use of various modes and even digital technology would connect the symbolic mathematical language to more familiar ways of meaning-making for young students. In a broader sense, these kinds of educational applications are closely related to a multiliteracies approach and serve as a way to understand the various ways of making meaning in todays textual environment.

A few limitations of this study are to be mentioned. First of all, the data was collected in a specific educational context (monolingual Finnish classroom); secondly, the sample size is small, as is common in case studies. Nevertheless, the data showed potential in developing the multimodal languaging model, as it served to express thinking.

The multiliteracies framework with multimodality brings new insights into school mathematics. Further research is needed into how the intentional use of different modes serves in learning specific concepts, such as multiplication, or in multilingual classrooms.

Acknowledgments: We would like to thank class teacher Marja Tuomi for co-operation and for providing her class for this study.

Author Contributions: Both authors contributed to the development of this paper. Jorma Joutsenlahti and Pirjo Kulju concieved and designed the data collection. Jorma Joutsenlahti analysed the data regarding the concept of division. Both authors participated to the writing of this paper.

Conflicts of Interest: The authors declare no conflict of interest.

References

1. Bauersfeld, H. Language games in the mathematics classroom: Their function and their effects. In *The Emergence of Mathematical Meaning: Interaction in Classroom Cultures*; Cobb, P., Bauersfeld, H., Eds.; Erlbaum: Hillsdale, NJ, USA, 1995; pp. 271–294.
2. Joutsenlahti, J. Kielentäminen matematiikan opiskelussa. In *Opettaja, Asiantuntijuus ja Yhteiskunta. Ainedidaktinen Symposium 7.2.2003*; Turun yliopiston kasvatustieteiden tiedekunnan julkaisuja B: 72; Virta, A., Marttila, O., Eds.; Turun Opettajankoulutuslaitos: Turku, Finland, 2003; pp. 188–196. (In Finnish)
3. Lemke, J. Mathematics in the Middle: Measure, Picture, Gesture, Sign, and Word. In *Educational Perspectives on Mathematics as Semiosis: From Thinking to Interpreting to Knowing*; Anderson, M., Saenz-Ludlow, A., Zellweger, S., Cifarelli, V., Eds.; Legas Publishing: Ottawa, ON, Canada, 2002; pp. 215–234. (In Finnish)
4. Kalantzis, M.; Cope, B. *Literacies*; Cambridge University Press: Cambridge, UK, 2012.
5. Joutsenlahti, J.; Kulju, P. Kieliteoreettinen lähestymistapa koulumatematiikan sanallisiin tehtäviin ja niiden kielennettyihin ratkaisuihin. In *Toisensa Kohtaavat Ainedidaktiikat*; Tampereen yliopiston opettajankoulutuslaitoksen julkaisuja A31; Ropo, E., Silfverberg, H., Soini, T., Eds.; Tampereen Yliopisto: Tampere, Finland, 2010; pp. 66–77. (In Finnish)

6. Solano-Flore, G. Function and form in research on language and mathematics education. In *Language and Mathematics Education*; Moschkovich, J.N., Ed.; IAP-Information Age: Charlotte, NC, USA, 2010; pp. 113–149.

7. Joutsenlahti, J. *Lukiolaisen Tehtäväorientoituneen Matemaattisen Ajattelun Piirteitä: 1990-luvun Pitkän Matematiikan Opiskelijoiden Matemaattisen Osaamisen ja Uskomusten Ilmentämänä*; Acta Universitatis Tamperensis 1061; Tampereen Yliopisto: Tampere, Finland, 2005. (In Finnish)

8. Metsämuuronen, J. (Ed.) *Perusopetuksen Matematiikan Oppimistulosten Pitkittäisarviointi Vuosina 2005–2012*; Koulutuksen seurantaraportti 2013: 4; Edita Prima Oy: Helsinki, Finland, 2013. (In Finnish)

9. Joutsenlahti, J.; Kulju, P.; Tuomi, M. Matemaattisen lausekkeen kontekstualisointi sanalliseksi tehtäväksi ja tarinaksi. Opetuskokeilu kirjoittamisen hyödyntämisestä matematiikan opiskelussa. In *Ainedidaktinen Tutkimus Koulutuspoliittisen Päätöksenteon Perustana*; Ainedidaktisia tutkimuksia 4; Tainio, L., Juuti, K., Routarinne, S., Eds.; Suomen Ainedidaktinen Tutkimusseura ry: Helsinki, Finland, 2012; pp. 107–122. (In Finnish)

10. New London Group. A pedagogy of multiliteracies: Designing social futures. *Harv. Educ. Rev.* **1996**, *66*, 60–92.

11. Kress, G. *Literacy in the New Media Age*; Routledge: London, UK, 2003.

12. Kulju, P.; Kupiainen, R.; Wiseman, A.; Jyrkiäinen, A.; Koskinen-Sinisalo, K.-L.; Mäkinen, M. A Review of Multiliteracies in Primary Classrooms. **2016**, submitted for publication.

13. O'Halloran, K. *Mathematical Discourse: Language, Symbolism and Visual Images*; Continuum: London, UK, 2005.

14. Takeuchi, M. The Situated Multiliteracies Approach to Classroom Participation: English Language Learners' Participation in Classroom Mathematics Practices. *J. Lang. Identity Educ.* **2015**, *14*, 159–178. [CrossRef]

15. Opetushallitus. Finnish Core Curriculum for Basic Education 2014. Available online: http://www.oph.fi/ops2016/perusteet (accessed on 31 October 2016).

16. Palsa, L.; Ruokamo, H. Behind the concepts of multiliteracies and media literacy in the renewed Finnish core curriculum: A systematic literature review of peer-reviewed research. *Seminar. net-Int. J. Media Technol. Lifelong Learn.* **2015**, *11*, 101–119.

17. Morgan, C. The place of pupil writing in learning, teaching and assessing mathematics. In *Issues in Mathematics Teaching*; Gates, P., Ed.; Routledge: London, UK, 2001; pp. 232–244.

18. Chronaki, A.; Christiansen, I. Challenging perspectives on mathematics classroom communication: From representations to context, interactions, and politics. In *Challenging Perspectives on Mathematics Classroom Communication*; Chronaki, A., Christiansen, I., Eds.; IAP-Information Age: Greenwich, CO, USA, 2005; pp. 3–48.

19. Joutsenlahti, J.; Ali-Löytty, S.; Pohjolainen, S. Developing Learning and Teaching in Engineering Mathematics with and without Technology. Available online: http://www.sefi.be/conference-2016/papers/Mathematics_and_Engineering_Education/joutsenlahti-developing-learning-and-teaching-in-engineering-mathematics-with-and-without-technology-153_a.pdf (accessed on 31 October 2016).

20. Joutsenlahti, J.; Kulju, P. Kielentäminen matematiikan ja äidinkielen opetuksen kehittämisessä. In *Monilukutaito Kaikki Kaikessa*; Kaartinen, T., Ed.; Tampereen Yliopiston Normaalikoulu: Tampere, Finland, 2015; pp. 57–76. (In Finnish)

21. Joutsenlahti, J.; Rättyä, K. Kielentämisen käsite ainedidaktisissa tutkimuksissa. In *Rajaton Tulevaisuus: Kohti Kokonaisvaltaista Oppimista: Ainedidaktiikan Symposium Jyväskylässä 13-14.2.2014*; Suomen ainedidaktisen tutkimusseuran julkaisuja 8; Kauppinen, M., Rautiainen, M., Tarnanen, M., Eds.; Suomen Ainedidaktinen Tutkimusseura ry: Helsinki, Finland, 2015; pp. 45–62. (In Finnish)

22. Simon, M.A. Prospective elementary teachers' knowledge of division. *J. Res. Math. Educ.* **1993**, *24*, 233–254. [CrossRef]

23. Fischbein, E.; Deri, M.; Nello, M.; Marino, M. The role of implisit models in solving verbal problems in multiplication and division. *J. Res. Math. Educ.* **1985**, *16*, 3–17. [CrossRef]

24. Harjunen, E.; Rautpuro, J. *Kielenkäytön Ajattelua ja Ajattelun Kielentämistä. Äidinkielen ja Kirjallisuuden Oppimistulokset Perusopetuksen Päättövaiheessa 2014: Keskiössä Kielentuntemus ja Kirjoittaminen*; Kansallinen Koulutuksen Arviointikeskus: Helsinki, Finland, 2015. (In Finnish)

Article

Investigating the Effectiveness of Group Work in Mathematics

Anastasia Sofroniou * and Konstantinos Poutos

School of Computing and Engineering, University of West London, St. Mary's Road, London W5 5RF, UK;
Konstantinos.Poutos@uwl.ac.uk
* Correspondence: Anastasia.Sofroniou@uwl.ac.uk; Tel.: +44-208-231-2068

Academic Editor: Eila Jeronen
Received: 23 June 2016; Accepted: 12 August 2016; Published: 1 September 2016

Abstract: Group work permits students to develop a range of critical thinking, analytical and communication skills; effective team work; appreciation and respect for other views, techniques and problem-solving methods, all of which promote active learning and enhance student learning. This paper presents an evaluation of employing the didactic and pedagogical customs of group work in mathematics with the aim of improving student performance as well as exploring students' perceptions of working in groups. The evaluation of group work was carried out during tutorial time with first year civil engineering students undertaking a mathematics module in their second semester. The aim was to investigate whether group work learning can help students gain a deeper understanding of the module content, develop improved critical and analytical thinking skills and see if this method of pedagogy can produce higher performance levels. The group work sessions were conducted over four weeks whilst studying the topic of integration. Evaluation surveys were collected at the end of the intervention along with an investigation into the examination results from the end of semester examinations. In order to derive plausible and reasonable conclusions, these examination results were compared with an analogous cohort of first year mathematics students, also studying integration in their engineering-based degree. The investigation into the effectiveness of group work showed interesting and encouraging positive outcomes, supported by a combination of qualitative and quantitative analysis.

Keywords: group work; enhancing mathematical learning; collaborative and cooperative learning

1. Introduction

This paper evaluates the effectiveness of implementing group work in mathematics, in terms of student performance and students' perceptions of this didactic form of learning during tutorial sessions. Mathematics educators are always striving to improve learner performance and achievements in the field of mathematics. The issues of learning problems in mathematics and the lack of metacognitive awareness of mathematical thinking and problem-solving skills [1] still seem to persist, and despite differences amongst educators on an effective learning methodology, it can be suggested that there is at least a concurrence with respect to the reduced level of accomplishment amongst learners in mathematics [2].

In the mid-1980s there was a reform movement in mathematics education as a reaction to dissatisfaction with conventional teaching approaches [3]. Specific reports recommending the restructuring of mathematical delivery [4] marked the need for modifications in teaching methodology. The National Council of Teachers of Mathematics [5] endorses the use of increasingly intensive and effective instructional interventions for students learning mathematics, suggesting that these can be used during tutorial sessions as well. Employing multiple models and ways of structuring topics can present rich adaptions of mathematics content to effectively support student's needs [5].

Educators must therefore be encouraged to present active learning activities so that students can construct knowledge, and one way to accomplish this is to familiarise students with group work [4,6].

The current delivery of lectures often finds university students learning mathematics through conservative behaviouristic methods [1], leaving them to be passive and dependent on their lecturers [7]. Modern, enhanced taught mathematics focuses on a constructivist approach, asking students to face new challenges with prior knowledge and to absorb and adopt new information, thus allowing them to form their own significant interpretation and meaningful understanding of the taught material [8].

Without denying the importance of traditional mathematical lecturing, and acknowledging that, in a competitive academic environment, students are more often rewarded for individual effort, this study aims to reinforce and add to the current research literature on group work, though with a particular emphasis on the field of mathematics at a higher educational level. This would allow once-skeptical educators who have perceived group work as ineffective and problematic in this subject area to recognise and appreciate the value and benefits of also assigning group work to their students [9]. More explicitly, the research question posed is the following: can group work be considered an effective method of learning for the subject of mathematics, and can it enhance the student learning experience at a higher educational level? This study investigates the effectiveness of group work in university-level mathematics, a higher-level application perhaps slightly lacking in research output, by examining any improved student performance upon adoption of group work interaction as well as examining student perceptions of working in groups. In addition, the study considers whether group work learning can deepen student understanding of the module content and aid them in developing higher critical and thinking skills.

This paper begins with a brief literature review documenting the adoption of group work in education, particularly those relating directly to mathematics. Collaborative and cooperative group work are highlighted, including a description of the main shortcomings and benefits experienced by the practitioner. The paper continues with the methodology used to carry out the evaluation of the effectiveness of group work in mathematics during tutorial sessions. The findings from the investigation are then discussed and analysed using both qualitative and quantitative techniques. Finally, some concluding remarks and possible future assessments are presented.

2. Literature Review

Group work is centered upon the constructivism model of learning [10–13]. According to the report from the National Council of Teachers of Mathematics [4,5], it is said that group work in mathematical education plays an essential role in students' question acquisition and in criticising constructively [14], all leading to productive and beneficial outcomes in student learning.

The number of research studies carried out over recent years has increased noticeably in the field of mathematics at the primary and secondary school levels [15]. Substantial research within the mathematics education sector indicates that employing small groups for various activities and exercises does lead to constructive and beneficial outcomes for student learning.

From a review by Webb [16,17] concerning studies investigating peer interaction and achievement in small scale groups, various compatible outcomes were achieved. Conveying a clarification or simplification of an idea, solution or method to another group member was positively related to achievement, whereas experiencing non-responsive feedback from a group member, specifically no feedback or feedback that was irrelevant to what one has said or done, was characterised by a negative relation to achievement [16,17]. Webb's review also interestingly revealed that group work was most useful when students were taught how to work in groups and how to present, provide and accept assistance. This received aid was most fruitful and functional when it was in the form of detailed explanations and then applied by the student to the existing task or to a different task. Slavin's research showed positive effects from group work on cross-ethnic relations and enhancing student achievement [18]. Yackel, Cobb and Wood found that small-scale group work problem-solving followed by whole class dialogue generated many learning opportunities that do not usually occur in a conservative tutorial or class, comprising opportunities for collaborative discussion and resolution of contrasting viewpoints [19].

Over the past years, many studies have been conducted in order to investigate how effective competitive, individualistic, and cooperative group work methodologies are in endorsing and encouraging productivity and achievement [20,21]. Acknowledging these studies and using meta-analysis to study achievement in cooperative learning, the results showed that the average student learning through cooperative approaches performed at about two-thirds a standard deviation above the average student learning within a competitive (an effect size of 0.67) or individualistic (effect size equal to 0.64) structured lesson [22], prompting higher achievement levels when considering cooperative group work learning compared to competitive or individualistic learning strategies.

Group work plays a fundamental role both in cooperative and in collaborative learning methods, and has attracted significant research interest [21–29]. Studies demonstrate that these pedagogical customs of group work do produce higher achievement and more positive relationships amongst students, compared to competitive or individualistic experiences.

Research suggests that collaborative learning has quickly turned into a strong promoter of group work in educational institutions at all levels [24]. In collaborative learning, participants brainstorm, share information and work, tackle the same problem together continuously within their groups and learn from each other so their combined collaborative achievement surpasses the simple sum of individual contributions [29]. As Damon and Phelps clearly state, this is structurally different from cooperative learning, which refers to discrete practices and concepts such as specific role assignments in a group and goal related liability of both members and the group, so that each student is responsible for the entire concluding result [23]. Curtis discusses that cooperative learning mostly deals with tasks that are divisible into more or less independent subtasks, where cooperating parties work in parallel to process individual subtasks in an autonomous, independent way [28] as opposed to collaborative learning where a shared solution to a problem is built simultaneously, collectively and in liaison with all members of the group.

Group collaboration can take a variety of forms and has been investigated in a broad range of contexts, including classroom-based learning [30], computer-based learning [31], web-based and e-learning [32]. What these collaborations, however, have in common is that two or more learners interact in a synchronous form to negotiate shared meaning and jointly and continuously solve problems [26].

Since learning mathematics can often be viewed as a lonely, individualistic or competitive matter, with students developing mathematical anxiety or avoidance, collaborative and cooperative learning through group work can address these problems and enhance students' progress and achievements [33].

Group work interaction helps all members learn concepts and problem solving strategies, improve self-confidence and overcome the fear of mistakes [6,14,34]. Mathematics does offer opportunities for creative thinking, exploring open ended questions, and posing intriguing problems, and group work can help to face these trials and difficult tasks that are well beyond the capacities of individual work at that developmental phase. Group work can also be a convenient and helpful tool to help develop a supportive attitude towards learning. In a study by Bernero, the students who struggled with mathematics continued to stress and strain about it and became discouraged with individual work, but improved both academically and socially when it came to group work, due to an increase in self-assurance [34].

Group work, however, can also sometimes lead to unsuccessful operation, mainly due to a lack of understanding of the important elements that arbitrate its effectiveness. Group efforts can be unproductive in many aspects. For instance, less capable members of the group can sometimes leave it to others to accomplish and conclude the group's exercises [35], whereas more capable student members might put in less effort to avoid doing all the work [35]. The amount of time spent explaining concepts can be positively correlated with the amount of time learning, so more capable members might learn a great deal by providing detailed explanations of the taught material to less able students struggling to comprehend as a captive audience [35].

The educator plays a vital role in the effective running of group work. During group work, the educator should act 'both as an academic expert and as a classroom manager' [20], be able to specify the academic objectives and aims of the lesson, make instructional decisions, and explain the task clearly defining the assignment goals [25]. There are different grading models available for assessing group work. Some assess the end product only, while others assess both the process and the final outcome. The grading can be conducted entirely by the educators or by the students using a form of peer assessment. The benefits of peer assessment for student learning have been well documented [36,37]. Another option is for the educator to award an overall mark for the end product where each individual group member has a scaled grade according to their level of contribution as determined by their peers or lecturer, ensuring that all grading must align with the learning outcomes for the module [38].

3. Methodology

This investigation was carried out during tutorial time to first year Civil Engineering students, undertaking a Mathematics module in their second semester. The group work sessions were conducted over four weeks to the whole class, whilst studying the specific topic of Integration. The remaining tutorial sessions of the second semester involved practical exercises in the outstanding chapters of the syllabus, with students attempting these in an individualistic manner. Previous experience has led to the opinion that students find Integration the most challenging and difficult to understand topic within the whole syllabus. As a result, selecting this chapter seemed to be suitable in order to demonstrate the potential effectiveness of group work in enhancing the students learning experience. The tutorial sessions had a steady attendance of 23 students, of which 4 were female. None of the students surveyed had been in a group work environment in Mathematics before, but have had this form of learning experience in their other modules. All the students who attended agreed to participate in this research.

3.1. Group Work Setup

Group work was conducted whilst studying the Integration chapter, over four weeks during one hour tutorial sessions which ran twice per week, and the following material relating to Integration was covered:

- Week 1: Integration by Substitution;
- Week 2: Integration by Parts;
- Week 3: Integration using Partial Fraction decomposition;
- Week 4: Applications of Integration in the Civil Engineering field.

For this investigation, the educator provided a vital role in the effective running of group work in mathematics. The lecturer was able to specify the academic objectives and aims of the session, make instructional decisions (such as size group, how long groups should stay together, student assignment roles) and clarify the task clearly defining the assignment goals.

Students were paired up in groups, making sure that each group consisted of a mixture of calibers of students, in other words, weaker and stronger students were arranged to work together, but never a group consisting solely of weak students. The problems that the students had to tackle in their group work were based on the theory taught in lecture, and were either provided by the lecturer or set by the actual group members. The latter was a more complex challenge for the students, as they had to think and produce, within their groups, suitable and workable problems that were then given to other fellow groups for them to tackle. The group work interaction was at times collaborative but also cooperative in nature, with students tackling and working together on the same problem or on specific role assignments.

For instance, students were asked in their respective groups to consider a curve of their choice, which had to consist of a product of functions, be able to plot it on a Cartesian plane either manually or employing graphical software tools, and then, by applying the integration techniques learnt during the lectures, the remaining task was to determine the area of the region bounded by the curve and the axis or by the curve and straight lines of their choice. In this problem, each group member was assigned a role to fulfill, working cooperatively, but simultaneously each student was responsible for the concluding solution.

During the intervention, the role of each group member was observed by the lecturer, making sure that there was sufficient collaboration and cooperation and that each student contributed equally to the final outcome. The educator provided guidance and support during group work activities, observed the group interaction and student engagement, gave hints or clarifications, provided encouragement, drew members into the discussion, behaved in a friendly and constructive manner, managed to balance too much or too little assistance and intervened when necessary in a facilitative way in order to enable successful completion of the task by the group.

Upon completion of the problems, the results were handed back to the team which had posed the task initially, or simply to another fellow group, in order to mark and provide appropriate feedback to their peers. In this way, not only were students deepening their understanding of the theory with the help of their classmates, but they were also learning to communicate, to deliberate, to assess and to improve their mistakes accordingly.

In order to investigate the effectiveness of group work in mathematics, a more detailed and substantial quantitative approach was employed using two sets of level 4 classes, where all students had engineering-based backgrounds. For clarification purposes, the cohort which was engaged in group work shall be referred to as the *Experimental class* and the other class which had no group work involvement during the semester shall be considered as the *Control class*. To benefit from accurate and feasible conclusions on the effectiveness of group work, an indirect approach was accomplished by comparing these two classes. More specifically, in the Experimental class, only the teaching and learning on Integration was delivered in the form of group work during tutorial time, whereas the remaining syllabus was covered under normal learning arrangements. The control class, which consisted of 16 students, had their teaching and learning experience delivered under normal traditional arrangements throughout the whole semester.

3.2. Data Collection

A questionnaire (see Appendix A) was administered on the experience of group work during the sessions, as well as an investigation into the exam results from the end of semester examinations. Students were invited to participate in the study, which was voluntary due to ethical considerations and involved completion of questionnaires, observations of collaborative activity with hand written observations made by the educator. The survey was administered only to the Experimental class, with all 23 students completing the questionnaires. Some questions required opinionated handwritten replies and the rest of the responses were sought on 3-point Likert scales ranging from "Disagree" to "Agree".

At the end of the semester, with the aid of the outputs of the final exams, the performance of the students in the Integration questions was compared with the analogous performance of the students in the rest of the assessed questions (Integration vs. Rest of examinable questions). This difference in performance between the questions in the Experimental class was additionally later then compared with the corresponding difference in performance of the students in the Control Class.

The Integration questions within the end of year examinations for each cohort, the Experimental and the Control Class, had a different percentage weighting, specifically 60% of the exam from the Experimental Class had Integration questions assigned to it, whereas the examination for the Control Class had 50% of Integration examinable material. When regarding the performance of students in Integration questions compared to their performance of the rest of the assessed questions, this weighting was taken into consideration. Thus, not only was the student's performance on the integration topic assessed relative to the rest of the syllabus for the class with group work learning, but also a comparison was made with the analogous performance of students not experiencing group work from another cohort, the control class. Hence, any difference in the level of difficulty of the

Integration questions with respect to the rest of the questions in the exam and any dissimilarities in the academic capabilities and strengths of the students of the two cohorts were taken into account in the analysis.

In this context the authors employed, as a tool to measure the effectiveness of group work, the ratio of student performance on integration questions relative to their performance in the remaining questions, and from here on after this ratio shall be considered as the performance ratio. This performance ratio shall be used as an indicator to evaluate the effectiveness of group working. The authors suggest that this ratio be calculated by examining the quotient of student's performance in individual integration questions over the remaining exam questions respectively.

$$Performance\ ratio = \frac{Total\ \%marks\ from\ Integration\ questions}{Total\ \%marks\ from\ the\ Rest\ of\ the\ questions\ in\ the\ exam}$$

For example, in the Experimental Class, a randomly selected student managed to accumulate 44 out of the 60 marks that relate to the Integration topic, hence approximately 73.3% ((44/60) × 100) was the total percentage of allocated marks from the Integration questions. 16 out of the 40 marks were received for the remaining questions, hence 40% ((16/40) × 100) was the total percentage of successful marks from the rest of the questions in the exam. Applying the suggested performance indicator, the performance ratio for this specific student was 1.83 (73.3%/40%).

It must be noted for elucidation purposes that a performance ratio value greater than 1.0 indicates that a student performed better in the integration section of the exam compared to the rest of the questions in the exam paper, due to the value of the numerator of the performance ratio quotient being greater than the denominator value.

4. Results and Discussion

4.1. Qualitative Analysis: Discussion of the Findings from the Questionnaire Survey

The evaluation survey filled in by all students of the Experimental class is the main source of feedback examined as the qualitative analysis section of this project. The results of the first three questions of the survey, which required individual comments of opinion, have been summarised and grouped in a thematic way by considering the response frequency, and depicted as Figure 1.

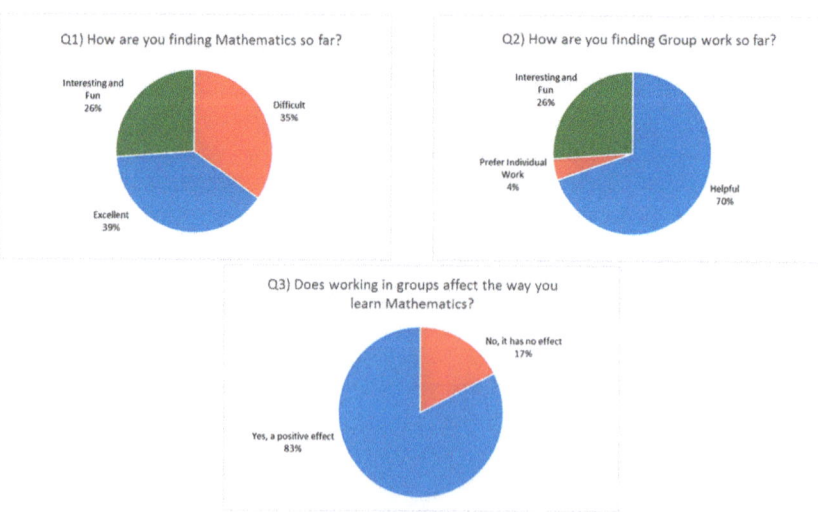

Figure 1. Student responses to Q1–3 of the Questionnaire (see Appendix A).

From these responses, it is deduced that in general students perceive mathematics as a difficult, challenging and yet rewarding subject, with all students agreeing that their group work experience in this hard module has been helpful and enjoyable. More detailed individual comments are that group work was found to be constructive, deepening the student's understanding of Integration. The majority of the participants believe that working in groups positively affected the way they learn mathematics and allowed them to develop their critical thinking and analytical skills. Acknowledging that group work allows for collaboration between classmates, it strengthened their confidence in the subject, and it served as another learning approach to reinforce their mathematical knowledge.

As part of the opinioned responses, a couple of students did mention a few possible foreseeable drawbacks of working in groups, namely that it can slow down the lesson and that this form of learning can be nonproductive if only one member of the group does all the work.

Figure 2 is a bar chart showing students responses about their perception of what contributes to the effectiveness of teaching mathematics. More than 86% of the students believed that teaching mathematics is more effective when it builds on previous knowledge, when it creates connections between topics and most importantly when it uses group work as a didactic approach. More than three quarters of the responses also referred to encouraging reasoning rather than simply getting an answer as another effective teaching strategy for mathematics.

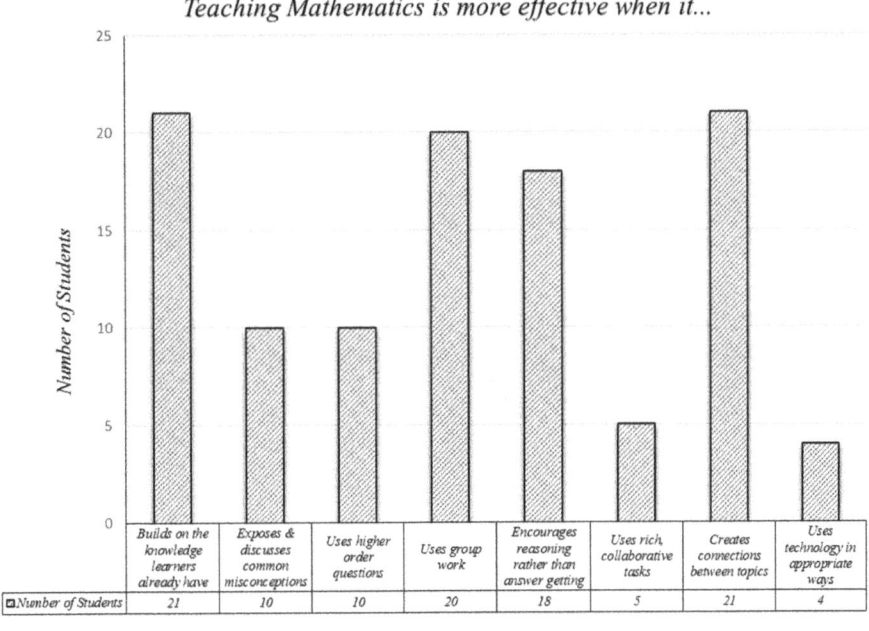

Figure 2. Diagram showing the number of students responding to the different options for effectiveness of Question 4 in the questionnaire.

An unexpected outcome of this specific question is that only a few students (4 out of the 23 students) consider teaching mathematics to be more effective when it uses technology. In this era, with the current advancements in technology, it can only be assumed that students would perhaps expect or demand the teaching delivery to be more updated and in compliance with the changing technological improvements. However, based upon these responses, it seems that students do not consider it necessary for mathematics to conform to a more technological method of delivering effective teaching.

Figure 3 depicts using a bar chart, an analysis of the Likert scale data of the questionnaire. The significant conclusions here are that the majority of students agree that they learn from working as a group, believe that group work is a good idea, enjoyed taking part in group work and think that all group members were given an equal opportunity to contribute to the final outcome of the group activity.

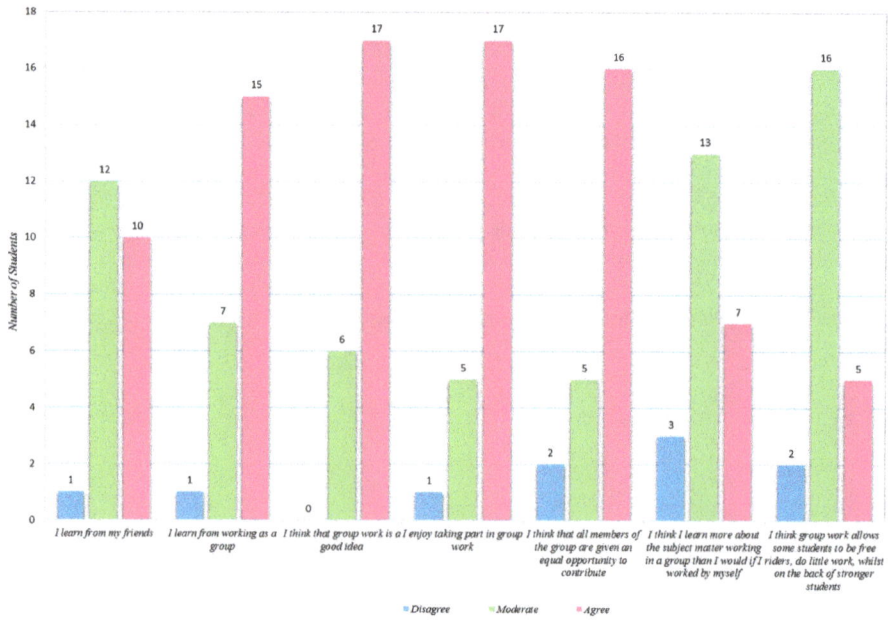

Figure 3. Bar chart showing the number of students responding to the Likert scale questions in the questionnaire.

Most students also seem to be indifferent to the issue that group work allows some students to be free riders, or that they learn more by being in a group as opposed to working individually. Additionally, taking into account the educators' views of group work for this intervention, it can be assumed that group work becomes useful for social reasons as well as the positive effects on learning mathematics. It was noted that learning within groups helped to improve students' attitude towards mathematics and allowed the struggling students to get over their anxiety about the subject. Moreover, this way of learning seemed to be more fun and enjoyable for learners assisting them to learn through discussion instead of memorisation during mathematics lessons.

4.2. Quantitative Analysis: Findings from the Data Retrieved from the End-of-Year Examinations

The end-of-year mathematics examination results for the respective semesters were retrieved and outputs were gathered in order to extrapolate interesting and valuable conclusions for this research study. To determine whether group work was effective in the learning of mathematics, the main objective of the investigation, it was necessary to be able to produce an empirical indicator to aid in this analysis. Examining each student's performance ratio (refer to section 3.2 to recall how this ratio was individually calculated) in both the Experimental and the Control classes, the following average performance ratios were derived, approximated to three decimal places:

Average Performance Ratio for the Experimental Class (with group work) $= 1.807$

Average Performance Ratio for the Control Class (no group work) $= 0.863$

These average performance ratios show that students working in groups performed better in the integration-related questions compared to the class which did not have any group work arrangements. The data analysis indicates that when students worked in groups their performance in the integration related questions improved by around 109% ($\frac{(1.807-0.863)}{0.863} \times 100 = 109.4\%$) compared to the performance of the students that attended a normal class environment.

Figure 4 below illustrates the performance ratio of the students that attended the experimental class (blue) against this of the students that attended the control class (red). The ratios present the individual students' performances and are displayed in increasing performance value. It must be noted that as the cohort numbers of these classes were different, specifically 23 students for the experimental class and 16 for the control class, the upper and lower end values of the performance ratios have been truncated in order to provide a more realizable, feasible and longitudinal comparison.

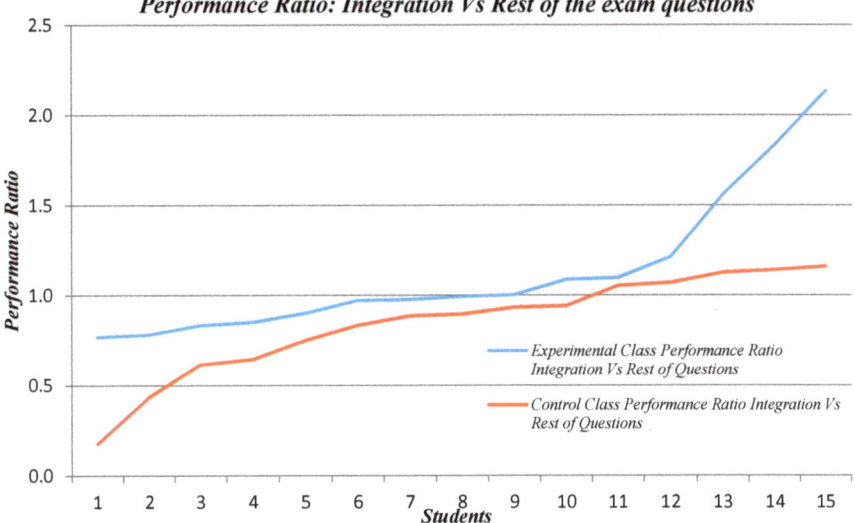

Figure 4. Experimental and Control class performance ratios of Integration questions compared to the rest of the examinable questions against the respective number of students.

The analysis of these results indicate that, throughout the spectrum, the performance ratio values of students learning integration in the experimental class were always higher than those of the students of the control class, as can be seen by the blue line always having an upward trend above the red line. Hence, this figure clearly portrays and supports the benefits of group work on the topic of integration.

Figure 5 below presents the percentage of students that performed better in the Integration topic compared to the rest of the questions in the exam for each class. Recall that a performance ratio greater than 1.0 indicates a better performance in the integration section of the exam. The results show that when students worked in groups 47.8% of the class achieved better marks in Integration (11 out of the 23 performance ratios were greater than the value 1) whilst only 37.5% of the students performed better in integration when working in normal class arrangements (6 out of the 16 students). These percentages also highlight the efficiency of group work in teaching mathematics.

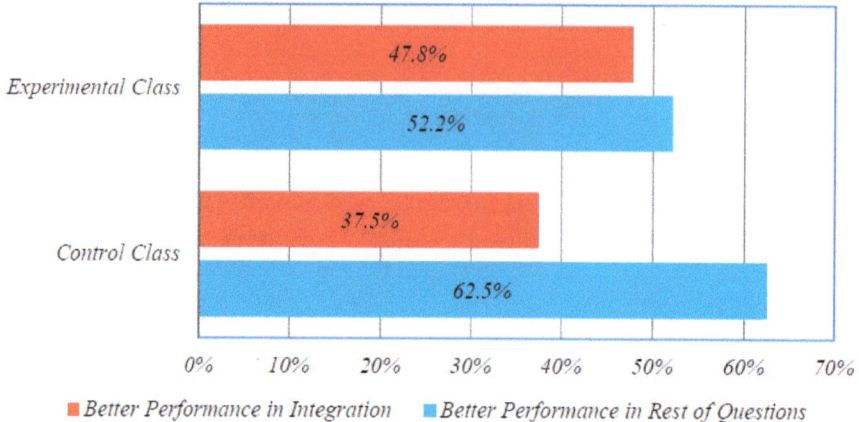

Figure 5. Percentage of students performing better in Integration questions vs. the rest of the exam questions for both the Experimental and Control class.

Figure 6 presents the average result achieved by students in integration questions with respect to the different range of overall performance in the exam. Students were clustered in performance categories over 20% intervals. Students were arranged in these categories in order to assess group work effectiveness for the different academic strength levels of the students.

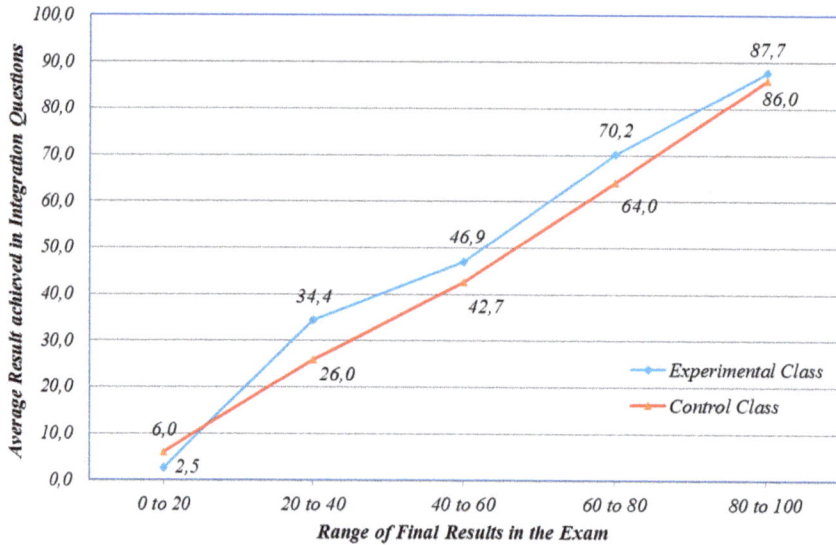

Figure 6. The average result (%) achieved by students in integration questions with respect to the different range of overall performance in the exam for both the Experimental and Control class.

The results illustrate the beneficial effect of group work for almost all student categories. For example, students achieving a final result between 60% and 80% in their exam presented an average mark of 70.2% in the integration section when working in groups. In the Control class this percentage corresponded to 64%. This trend was similar throughout the performance categories and emphasises the effectiveness of group work in mathematics for this study.

By now placing the emphasis on an important aspect of this project, the size of the effect on the performance of students using group work in mathematics, the so called "effect size" promotes a more scientific approach to accumulate this knowledge. Effect size is simply a way of quantifying the effectiveness of a particular intervention, relative to some comparison. It allows the researcher to move beyond the simplistic 'does it work or not?' to the far more sophisticated, 'How well does it work?' The effect size (*d-index*) is therefore an important tool in reporting and interpreting effectiveness, and for this study, it is defined as the difference in the average performance ratio of the experimental class relative to the control class, divided by the average of the two class standard deviations, pooled standard deviation [39].

Based on the data gathered from the examination of the Experimental and Control classes, an analysis of this goal based on the average performance ratio of each class on the topic of integration was accomplished and the results are listed in the table below

Statistical Measure	Output
Experimental Class Average Performance Ratio Mean:	1.807
Control Class Average Performance Ratio Mean:	0.863
Experimental Class Standard Deviation:	4.431
Control Class Standard Deviation:	0.281
Experimental Class Size:	23
Control Class Size:	16
Pooled Standard Deviation:	3.140
d-index (Effect Size):	0.301
Variance of d-index:	0.113
Margin of Error:	0.659
Lower Confidence Limit:	−0.358
Upper Confidence Limit:	0.960

The analysis deduced an effect size of 0.3, meaning that the performance of the average student in the experimental class is 0.3 standard deviations above the average student in the control class and hence exceeds the scores of 62% of the control class (see Interpretations of effect size table in [39]). In other words, based on the data gathered from the examination scripts for these two classes, with this effect size value, this analysis quantifiably shows and supports previously stated deductions that group work in mathematics does moderately improve students' performance.

If an effect size is calculated from a very large sample, it is likely to be more accurate than one calculated from a small sample. This margin for error can be quantified using the idea of a confidence interval. Due to the small sample size of this study, this error analysis shall also be employed so as to provide more substantial results.

To calculate a 95% confidence interval for an effect size, a formula given by Hedges and Olkin is used [40]. The results emanating from the detailed investigation of the performance ratios for the two types of classes show that the standard error of the effect size is $SE[0.3] = 0.336$ with the margin of error being $1.96 SE[d] = 1.96 \times 0.336 = 0.659$. Hence, the 95% confidence interval is $[-0.36, 0.96]$. This can be interpreted as meaning that the true effect size of student's performance due to group work on the topic of Integration is very likely (95% confident) to lie between -0.36 and 0.96.

5. Conclusions

This study set out to evaluate the effectiveness of implementing group work in a university-level mathematics module, in terms of student performance and students' perceptions of this didactic form of learning. Observing the group interaction and the group's solutions, it is possible to say that group work learning helped to deepen students' understanding of the material, a conclusion that is also reflected in the final examination results prompting higher performance levels for the class which underwent group work learning on the specific topic of Integration.

The educator taking part in this intervention further observed that students did attempt to be critical and developed their analytical thinking skills whilst working in a group. Struggling students that once became discouraged with individual work experienced reduced strain and felt less stress when tackling a mathematical problem whilst collaborating with fellow group members. Perhaps this increase in self-esteem and greater social competence could in the long run, also contribute to a more positive attitude towards the university experience. Moreover, it was observed that students found themselves discussing the importance of different proposed solutions, searching for applicable problems, and surpassing their capacities for individual work at that developmental stage.

In addition, the findings discussed in the previous section do relate to similar experiences described in literature by educators who have adopted group work techniques in their own practice. Specifically, Tarmizi and Bayata [1] found that collaborative problem-based learning in a group environment did have a significant influence on student performance, and Kocak et al. [14] observed that students who study mathematics in a group are encouraged to discuss and learn to be more attentive in class, resulting in better understanding mathematics instead of memorizing the relevant information and proofs. Edwards and Jones [27] describe the perspectives of secondary school students who have had considerable experience with collaborative small group work in mathematics and D'Souza and Wood [33] describe tertiary students' views and opinions of group work based on in-depth interviews, though both studies allow for only a descriptive qualitative approach to support their results. Thus, building and scientifically expanding upon previous studies and literature, both the qualitative and quantitative analysis in this paper provide encouraging and positive reflections on group work in mathematics at a tertiary context level, reinforcing the effectiveness of this didactic method. Adapting this method of learning at the university level but also in a subject that students always find challenging and a subtopic that students always struggle with (an extrapolation from educator's teaching experience) has led to findings in this study that are significant and can complement the existing literature on this evergreen method of learning.

While the outcomes of this study are positive and endorse the benefits of group work, one possible limitation of this study was the relatively small sample size of both the experimental and control classes. In view of this, one possible improvement would be to consider larger control and experimental class sizes as well as extending the duration and period of group work interaction. The authors invite researchers to investigate this in greater detail and possibly enhance the findings of this study so that they can be generalized to a broader context.

From a wider perspective, businesses and employers are continuously looking for employees who are able to work collaboratively on projects and to tackle and solve tasks as a team. Consequently, it is vital to be able to give students the practice and training to develop these skills by working in groups on a variety of problems and helping them see this teaching and learning method as a fun and enjoyable one, adding further that when students are motivated and inspired, their learning capabilities are usually enhanced.

It is important, however, to mention that the group work model is not necessarily the answer to all encountered pedagogical failing practices. The role of the educator is still key with regard to determining what is effective for one particular class or student and it is the educator's choice that is relevant to the approach which has the greatest influence based on personal experience with mathematical modules. The barriers for educators using group work in mathematics in tertiary education could be considered to be time management concerns, assessment issues and the impact of their experience and own knowledge.

Being reflective in one's teaching philosophy and always being enthusiastic to adapt teaching styles in order to accommodate the diverse backgrounds of students, their abilities and motivation levels are traits that will conceivably have the most impact in teaching mathematics effectively.

Author Contributions: Both authors contributed to the development of this paper. Anastasia Sofroniou gathered all the data information, analysed results and prepared the first draft of the paper. Konstantinos Poutos added to the analysis of the results and verified the calculations. Anastasia Sofroniou revised the text of the manuscript.

Conflicts of Interest: The authors declare no conflict of interest.

Appendix A

Student Questionnaire

Please answer the following questions with as much honesty and detail as possible. Your responses are anonymous. It is important to give your true feelings as it will have the best impact on your future learning.

(1) How are you finding mathematics so far?

(2) How are you finding working in groups so far in this subject?

(3) Does working in groups affect the way you learn mathematics?

Views on the Subject of Mathematics

Please circle the response most appropriate to your thoughts and feelings.

	Disagree	Moderate	Agree
(4) I learn from my friends.	1	2	3
(5) I learn from working as a group.	1	2	3
(6) I think that group work is a good idea.	1	2	3
(7) I enjoy taking part in group work.	1	2	3
(8) I think that all members of the group are given an equal opportunity to contribute.	1	2	3
(9) I think that I will learn more about the subject matter working in a group then I would if I worked by myself.	1	2	3
(10) I think group work allows some students to be free riders, do little work, whilst on the back of stronger students.	1	2	3

(11) Circle any of the below comments (as many as you wish), that in your opinion apply to the following sentence:

Teaching mathematics is more effective when it . . .

(a) builds on the knowledge learners already have

(b) exposes and discusses common misconceptions

(c) uses higher-order questions

(d) uses cooperative small group work

(e) encourages reasoning rather than 'answer getting'

(f) uses rich, collaborative tasks

(g) creates connections between topics

(h) uses technology in appropriate ways.

References

1. Tarmizi, R.A.; Bayata, S. Collaborative problem-based learning in mathematics: A cognitive load perspective. *Procedia Soc. Behav. Sci.* **2012**, *32*, 344–350. [CrossRef]
2. Ali, R.; Hukamdad; Akhter, A.; Khan, A. Effect of using problem solving method in teaching mathematics on the achievement of mathematics students. *Asian Soc. Sci.* **2010**, *6*, 67–72. [CrossRef]
3. The Education Alliance. Closing the Achievement Gap: Best Practices in Teaching Mathematics. The Education Alliance, 2006. Available online: www.educationalliance.org (accessed on 29 May 2015).
4. National Council of Teachers of Mathematics. *Curriculum and Evaluation Standards for School Mathematics*; National Council of Teachers of Mathematics: Reston, VA, USA, 1989.

5.   National Council of Teachers of Mathematics. *Intervention: A Position of the National Council of Teachers of Mathematics*; National Council of Teachers of Mathematics: Reston, VA, USA, 2011.

6.   Davidson, N. Small group cooperative learning in mathematics: A selective view of the research. In *Learning to Cooperate, Cooperating to Learn*; Slavin, R., Ed.; Plenum Press: New York, NY, USA, 1985; pp. 211–230.

7.   Wood, T.; Cobb, P.; Yackel, E. Change in Teaching Mathematics: A Case Study. *Am. Educ. Res. J.* **1991**, *28*, 587–616. [CrossRef]

8.   Amit, M.; Fried, M.N. Research, reform, and times of change. In *Handbook of International Research in Mathematics Education*; English, L.D., Ed.; Erlbaum: Mahwah, NJ, USA, 2002; pp. 355–381.

9.   Nardi, E.; Stewart, S. Is Mathematics T.I.R.E.D? A Profile of Quiet Disaffection in the Secondary Mathematics Classroom. *Br. Educ. Res. J.* **2003**, *29*, 345–367. [CrossRef]

10. Vygotsky, L.S. *Mind in Society: The Development of Higher Psychological Processes*; Harvard University Press: Cambridge, MA, USA, 1978.

11. Bruner, J. *Child's Talk: Learning to Use Language*; Norton: New York, NY, USA, 1983.

12. Bruner, J. *Actual Minds, Possible Worlds*; Harvard University Press: Cambridge, MA, USA, 1986.

13. Piaget, J. *The Construction of Reality in the Child*; Routledge: London, UK, 2013; Volume 82.

14. Kocak, Z.F.; Bozan, R.; Isik, O. The importance or group work in mathematics. *Procedia Soc. Behav. Sci.* **2009**, *1*, 2363–2365. [CrossRef]

15. Kilpatrick, J. A history of research in mathematics education. In *Handbook of Research on Mathematics Teaching and Learning*; Grouws, D.A., Ed.; Macmillan: New York, NY, USA, 1992; pp. 3–38.

16. Webb, N.M. Task-related verbal interaction and mathematics learning in small groups. *J. Res. Math. Educ.* **1991**, *22*, 366–389. [CrossRef]

17. Webb, N.M.; Troper, J.D.; Fall, R. Constructive activity and learning in collaborative small groups. *J. Educ. Psychol.* **1995**, *87*, 406–423. [CrossRef]

18. Slavin, R.E. Student team learning in mathematics. In *Cooperative Learning in Math: A Handbook for Teachers*; Davidson, N., Ed.; Addison-Wesley: Reading, MA, USA, 1990; pp. 69–102.

19. Yackel, E.; Cobb, P.; Wood, T. Small-group interactions as a source of learning opportunities in second-grade mathematics. *J. Res. Math. Educ.* **1991**, *22*, 390–408. [CrossRef]

20. Johnson, D.W.; Johnson, R.T. Social skills for successful group work. *Educ. Leadersh.* **1990**, *47*, 29–33.

21. Johnson, D.W.; Johnson, R.T.; Smith, K.A. Cooperative learning: Improving University Instruction by Basing Practice on Validated Theory. *J. Excell. Coll. Teach.* **2014**, *25*, 85–118.

22. Johnson, D.W.; Johnson, R.T.; Smith, K.A. *Cooperative Learning: Increasing College Faculty Instructional Productivity*; ASHE-ERIC Report on Higher Education; The George Washington University: Washington, DC, USA, 1991.

23. Damon, W.; Phelps, E. Critical Distinctions among Three Approaches to Peer Education. *Int. J. Educ. Res.* **1989**, *13*, 9–19. [CrossRef]

24. Gamson, Z.F. Collaborative Learning comes of age. *Change* **1994**, *65*, 44–49. [CrossRef]

25. Smith, K.A. Cooperative learning: Making "group work" work. In *Active Learning: Lessons from Practice and Emerging Issues. New Directions for Teaching and Learning*; Bonwell, C., Sutherlund, T., Eds.; Jossey-Bass: San Francisco, CA, USA, 1996; Volume 67, pp. 71–82.

26. Dillenbourg, P. Introduction: What do you mean by collaborative learning? In *Collaborative Learning—Cognitive and Computational Approaches*; Dillenbourg, P., Ed.; Pergamon: Amsterdam, The Netherlands, 1999; pp. 1–19.

27. Edwards, J.; Jones, K. Students' Views of Learning Mathematics in Collaborative Small Groups. In Proceedings of the 23rd Conference of the International Group for the Psychology of Mathematics Education, Haifa, Israel, 25–30 July 1999; Zaslavsky, O., Ed.; 1999; Volume 2, pp. 281–288.

28. Curtis, D.D. Exploring Collaborative Online Learning. *J. Asynchron. Learn. Netw.* **2001**, *5*, 21–34.

29. Kanev, K.; Kimura, S.; Orr, T. A framework for Collaborative Learning in Dynamic Group Environments. *Int. J. Distance Educ. Technol.* **2009**, *7*, 58–77. [CrossRef]

30. Berg, K.F. Scripted cooperation in high school mathematics: Peer interaction ad achievement. Presented at the Annual Meeting of the American Educational Research Association, New Orleans, LA, USA, 4–8 April 1994.

31. Scardamalia, M.; Bereiter, C. Higher levels of agency for children in knowledge building: A challenge for the design of new knowledge media. *J. Learn. Sci.* **1991**, *1*, 37–68. [CrossRef]

32. Hron, A.; Friedrich, H.F. A review of Web based collaborative learning: Factors beyond Technology. *J. Comput. Assist. Learn.* **2003**, *19*, 70–79. [CrossRef]

33. D'Souza, S.; Wood, L. Tertiary students' views about group work in mathematics. In Proceedings of the Educational Research, Risks and Dilemmas—New Zealand Association for Research in Education (NZARE) and Australian Association for Research in Education (AARE) Joint Conference, The University of Auckland, Auckland, New Zealand, 29 November–3 December 2003; Available online: http://www.aare.edu.au/03pap/dso03154.pdf (accessed on 7 June 2016).

34. Bernero, J. *Motivating Students in Math Using Cooperative Learning*; ERIC Document reproduction Service No. ED 446 999; ERIC: Washington, DC, USA, 2000.

35. Kerr, N.; Bruun, S. The Dispensability of Member Effort and Group Motivation Losses: Free-Rider Effects. *J. Pers. Soc. Psychol.* **1983**, *44*, 78–94. [CrossRef]

36. Stefani, L.A.J. Peer, self and tutor assessment: Relative reliabilities. *Stud. High. Educ.* **1994**, *19*, 69–75. [CrossRef]

37. Falchikov, N. Peer feedback marking: Developing peer assessment. *Innov. Educ. Teach. Int.* **1995**, *32*, 175–187. [CrossRef]

38. Fry, H.; Ketteridge, S.; Marshall, S. *A Handbook for Teaching and Learning in Higher Education*, 3rd ed.; Routledge: New York, NY, USA, 2009.

39. Cohen, J. *Statistical Power Analysis for the Behavioural Science*; Academic Press: New York, NY, USA, 1969.

40. Hedges, L.; Olkin, I. *Statistical Methods for Meta-Analysis*; Academic Press: New York, NY, USA, 1985.

Article

Reconceptualizing Scientific Literacy: The Role of Students' Epistemological Profiles

Rodrigo Drumond Vieira [1,*], Viviane Florentino de Melo [1], Lucy Avraamidou [2] and João Avelar Lobato [3]

[1] Department of Society, Education and Knowledge, Faculty of Education, Fluminense Federal University, rua Prof. Marcos Valdemar de Freitas Reis, s/n, Bloco D, Campus do Gragoatá, Niterói – RJ, 24210 201, Brazil; melovivi2211@hotmail.com

[2] Institute for Science Education and Communication, University of Groningen, Nijenborgh 9, 9747 AG Groningen, The Netherlands; l.avraamidou@rug.nl

[3] Cooper & Sacks, Research Lead, 52 Coopers close, E1 4BB. London, UK; joao.lobato@cantab.net

* Correspondence: rodrumond@gmail.com; Tel.: +55-21-3619-2776

Academic Editor: Eila Jeronen
Received: 2 August 2016; Accepted: 30 March 2017; Published: 13 April 2017

Abstract: In this theoretical article we construct an argument for a pedagogical perspective based on the notion of epistemological profiles for scientific literacy for primary and secondary education. Concurrently, we offer a discussion of the implications of this proposal to the preparation of teachers and the development of their pedagogical skills. Underlining cultural practices in the construction, communication and validation of knowledge—called epistemic practices which are informed by an ideological perspective on science, are implied in the notion of epistemological profiles in the context of science teaching, particularly physics. Using the concept of *mass* in the context of science education, we discuss how different ideological perspectives on science reflect distinct aspects of reality. Thus, in this paper we propose an 'order' and 'direction' to scientific literacy and education in science, emphasizing the construction of a clear empirical perspective for primary school and a rationalistic ideological perspective for secondary school. We complement our argument with resources from activity theory and discourse studies, alongside a discussion of issues and challenges. In concluding this paper, we point out that such proposal requires a change in the classroom teaching culture.

Keywords: science education; epistemological profile; ideological perspective on science; model for learning; philosophy models; culture; activity theory; discourse

---

1. Introduction

The field of science education acknowledges the importance of scientific literacy for effective citizenship and conscious actions in today's world [1–3]. The concept of scientific literacy was first introduced by Hurd [4] in 1958 and has been used in the literature for more than 50 years [5]. According to Hurd [4] science and technology are the most prominent characteristics of the modern world, which suggests that scientific literacy is a requirement for contemporary citizenship.

While a goal for education in science, scientific literacy is still a polysemous term, as its definitions do not necessarily converge. Also, the methods on how scientific literacy can be acquired still lack convergence, as we can see from inspections of the situation of many countries that use the term in their official documents, but in practice such a literacy is still not a reality in these cases. In paper we raise the following question: *is there no consensus about what scientific literacy is or how it can be achieved* [2,6]?

As Roberts [7] argued, there is no scientific literacy (SL) if students do not know any subject content:

"there is no consensus about the meaning, or even the parts, of SL—with one exception: everyone agrees that students can't be scientifically literate if they don't know any subject matter. The literature contains many expressions of frustrations about the implications of the lack of consensus for research and practice" [7] (p. 13).

In his review of SL, DeBoer [8] expresses the following:

"instead of defining SL in terms of specifically prescribed learning outcomes, SL should be conceptualized broadly enough for local school districts and individual classroom teachers to pursue the goals that are most suitable for their particular situations" [8] (p. 582).

McEneaney [9] argues that there is no consensus in defining the specifics of SL. She describes it as a "worldwide catcher" in terms of a "scientific literacy approach" that, in her view, enjoys worldwide attention as a science education goal. In her analysis she provides examples from curricular statements, textbooks, and assessments materials in a variety of countries.

Despite such issues in defining SL and how to acquire it, the National Science Educational Standards [10] consider scientific literacy necessary for all students. In this case, it is related to equity and excellence, so science in schools must be available to all students, regardless age, sex, cultural background, and so on. Also, The Standards defines levels of understanding and abilities that all should develop.

According to The Standards: "Excellence in science education embodies the ideal that all students can achieve understanding of science if they are given the opportunities. Students will achieve the outcomes at different rates, some sooner than others. But all should have opportunities in the form of multiple experiences over several years to develop the understanding associated with the Standards." Our point of interest is the problem of the time-scale and its implications for life in society. If all students should acquire such competences, they inevitably will acquire at different times along life, which makes the work of teachers even more difficult. However, as studies have showed even teachers in many countries, including Brazil, are not scientific literate. Given this issue, the question then becomes one of, *how can we expect that students to be scientific literate if their teachers are not?*

Also, SL can be considered as the domain of methods and language of science. From this perspective, a student is SL if she/he is capable of serial, compare, contrast, deduce, induce, communicate, associate and interpret variables and so on. Of course, these procedures are part of the work of scientists, but they are not capable, alone, to assure if a person or a group of people are scientific literate, even because the definition for SL still weak in these cases, and lack of a structure that gives meaning to levels of SL, what, in our vision, needs to be more compatible with the reality of schools and the work of teachers.

In order to address this problem, it is necessary to ensure that teachers themselves are scientific literate and this is a problem in many countries in which teachers lack interesting in teaching due to low pay, bad teaching conditions, lack of students motivation and interest, among others [11–13]. Aligned with this problem, there is the definition problem: *what exactly does it mean to be scientific literate?* Such a question lead us again to the problem of demarcation, cleared posed by Roberts [7] and mentioned above. Furthermore, is SL possible in basic education or even in fundamental education?

Another trend in SL is the socio-scientific approach [14,15] and eco-reflective approach [16] which are used for framing the responsibility of individuals towards global sustainability. However, these approaches carry a strong sense of enforcement given that in order to critically debate, one needs to have a strong understanding of the scientific subject. Lee, Sohn & No [17] have shown that the socio-scientific debates still show that students awareness of contemporary world problems are weak and they are not pro-active in solving and discussing these problems.

In this paper, we argue that the socio-scientific approach provides a means for SL, but much work has to be done to integrate socio-scientific discussions in the curriculum. In this sense, we consider we need a model for scientific literacy that encompass such convergence areas at the same time avoid some of the mentioned problems.

Other issues related to this discussion are the logical operations students take when they are considered scientific literate [18,19]. The operations the authors describe are embodied in the daily interactions among people and in our vision they are not capable, alone, to distinguish if one is or is not SL, We consider that SL could be more than that in any given group or society. That is, SL encompasses it but in some sense it is much more than the domain of these operations (induction, deduction, analogy, causality, definition, consistency, and so on). As Piaget [20] proposed, humans pass for well-defined stages of development and this shall not be confused with SL, which, in turn, can take advantage of these stages to promote the literacy. Therefore, one would argue that an individual can "deduce" from naive realism, as well "deduce" from empiricist, and "deduce" from rationalistic perspectives and so on, and this makes the whole difference for the type of literacy we are proposing in this article and for life in society as a whole. We will explain such perspective in details further.

At this point, we briefly present a synthesis of the discussion: on the one hand, scientific literacy is a goal and a condition to be achieved. On the other hand, there is no consensus about the meaning of scientific literacy and how it can be achieved in the teaching of science (for contrasts see Holbrook & Rannikmae [21]). The incoherence is clear. It is important to have a theoretically based and established definition of literacy that incorporates the cultural practices of the students and, at the same time, the work of teachers.

It is important to note that we conceptualize culture as the historical process of accumulation and transmission of knowledge, meanings, values, rituals, expectations and norms, which are distributed in the systems of activities of a society [22]. We share the idea that culture began jointly with the emergence of discursive practices among humans, which enabled the construction and transmission to each new generation of the achievements of the previous ones. Furthermore, the culture is constantly changing given the urges of creation of new motives to constantly new human needs [23] emergent from the daily human-machine-environment interactions; science, by its turns, is the privileged form of knowledge to overcome the difficulties that arise from such rapid evolvement of technology-society-environment dimensions [24].

Building upon these theoretical perspectives, in this article we propose a theoretical alternative to the understanding of scientific literacy derived from the notion of *epistemological profile* proposed by Bachelard [25] and resources from *activity theory* [22,23,26] and *discourse studies* (sociolinguistics and textual linguistics).

2. The Notion of Epistemological Profile

Bachelard [25] proposes the notion of epistemological profile to conceptualize different forms individuals understand and deal with reality. The epistemological profile consists of "zones", called 'philosophies' and 'levels' by Bachelard. They range from the most common in the daily culture, like animism and naive realism, to empiricism, which is related to techniques of measurement with instruments, and rationalism, made of abstract models and concepts that impose an order of theoretical causality in the comprehension of reality. Each "zone" is epistemologically and ontologically characterized. Each 'zone' is different and a new zone cannot be achieved by adding knowledge but by ruptures, as Bachelard explains.

Bachelard uses as an example different ways of conceptualizing the definition of mass from his own epistemological profile. He proposes an auto-analysis of his profile for conceptualizing mass. Different "zones" interact, such as naive realism, empiricism, Newtonian rationalism, complete rationalism and discursive rationalism (dialectical). We will call these "zones" as "ideological perspectives on science" as we will explain further.

While our proposal does not encompass all "zones" available in the culture of basic education, we will comment all presented by Bachelard to clarify the notion of epistemological profile. Like Bachelard, we will use the concept of mass to exemplify his proposal. We will explain Bachelard's perspective and enrich it with perspectives from the field of education.

For the naive realism, mass is something large, with volume, something that becomes quantity if it is large enough. Most people work under this perspective when they think and talk about mass. This is the common sense that guides previous concepts of students, as documented in works on conceptual change [27–36]. The culture of daily life operates in the construction of such "zone". Cultural differences imply differences in the comprehension and usage of the same concept or idea. Despite the differences, this "zone" is characterized by immediatism in the construction of affirmations, visual appreciation, inconsistent usage of fragmented theories—non-systematic and locals—and an almost complete lack of generalization.

The next "zone" (ideological perspective on science according to our usage) in Bachelard's evolutionary line is the empiricism, characterized by certain measurement standards and techniques. Bachelard's evolutionary line coincides with the historical line of science, in which the "zones" posteriorly developed are located at the right of the epistemological profile, establishing a hierarchy of philosophies. The transition to this new zone of the profile overcomes epistemological obstacles from the previous zone, the naive realism. The transition presupposes the abandonment of the sensitive immediatism of naive realism and follows systematization and use of controlled techniques and methods of comparison, mediated by instruments that presuppose usage orientated by theories and ideas, even when those theories are unknown to the individuals operating them. Mass is understood here as something that can be measured and connected to an instrumental objectivity: mass can be compared to other mass using scales calibrated in a systematic standard. The prototypical image of this "zone" is the work of technicians making measurements according to certain standards and using available techniques to make such measurements even when technicians themselves do not know the theories that constitute, orientate and give meaning and purpose to the instruments and techniques.

The "zone" of rationalism derives from works in science that culminated with the first rationalist synthesis in science: Isaac Newton's classical mechanics. Individuals under rationalism use abstract models, rational and generals, to understand and explain the world. An example is the expression F=ma, which relates mass, force and acceleration in an abstract and rational way. Each variable is discriminatory, formal and general as they can be any mass, any acceleration and any force, regardless how the variables were measured or obtained. The knowledge of one variable is immediately deduced from the knowledge of the other two. Rationalism creates a formal and apodictic order of the world. The variables are understood and structured as a rational relation and only acquire full meaning in this relation. Synthesis and generality are characteristics of rationalism which is also aligned with knowledge of theories that give meaning to entities and exercises of the constant conceptual thought (action and thoughts mediated by concepts).

The founding of the constant $\pi = 3.14$, is another instance of how rationalism operates. In the case, 'π' (Pi) is the inclination of the straight line of a graph of the diameter vs. perimeter of a circumference, which is given by the tangent of the angle of both cathetus. As this constant number (Pi) was modeled to be achieved, it reveals the nature of rationalism, which is the usage of elements of nature and their relation through formal mathematics expressions, which imposes an order of causality and then provides previsions and more control to humans in the world. Thus, with rationalism, humans come to control more and more nature.

The next step in the hierarchical scale of the epistemological profile is the complete rationalism, in which mass is a complex function of velocity. The mass of a body can increase and decrease according to its speed. The notion of mass acquires an internal functional structure. This is the realm of relativistic mechanics, which inaugurated the complete rationalism. Einstein questioned: (1) the problem of non-invariance in Maxwell's equations of electromagnetism when submitted to Galileo's transformation, leading to the questioning of the principle of relativity; (2) the asymmetry in the explanation of electromagnetic phenomena when analyzed under different inertial references. Based on the knowledge available at the time, Einstein decided that the principle of relativity could be extended to electromagnetism, which turned out to be correct, and in this case the transformations of Galileo and Newtonian mechanics would not be correct in certain circumstances, requiring the modifications established by the theory of relativity. In this new perspective, light becomes constant and independent of the framework used to measure it, time and space are not absolute anymore, and the mass of a body becomes a complex function of velocity. It is important to observe that the theory of relativity derived from the clash between theories from the mechanics and electromagnetism, inaugurating the complete rationalism in the epistemological profile hierarchy.

Bachelard proposes a last philosophy or "zone": the discursive or dialectical rationalism. The status of this philosophy derives from the notions of dialectics and discourse, in which the object is not determined once and for all but it is instead constructed in the discursive and dialectical relations humankind creates and (re)creates continually, marking historical and ideological phases in the various levels discourse and counter-discourse operate.

Based on the knowledge he had at his time, Bachelard raises the possibility of asking: 'can mass be negative?'. The individual answers: 'why not?'. This is a dialectical step that looks for an entirely new concept, detached from common reality. Bachelard takes as an example Dirac's mechanics, in which the propagation determines what is propagated. Bachelard says about the concept of mass:

> Calculation yields up this notion to us along with the others, the magnetic and electric moments, the spins, respecting to the very end the fundamental syncretism which is so characteristic of complete rationalism. But now comes the surprise, now comes the discovery. At the end of the calculation, the notion of mass is delivered up to us strangely dialectized. One mass was all we needed. Calculation gives us two, two masses for a single object. One of these masses sums up perfectly everything that was known about mass in the four antecedent philosophies: naive realism, clear empiricism, Newtonian rationalism, full Einsteinian rationalism. But the other mass, the dialectic of the first, is a negative mass. That is a concept which cannot be assimilated at all in the four antecedent philosophies. (Bachelard [25], p. 29)

In this quotation, Bachelard [25] (p. 30) proposes that reality is preceded by "realization" (the equations and calculations). In his own words "Thus, realization takes precedence over reality. By so doing it demotes reality".

It is important to emphasize that each philosophy (according to Bachelard's usage) establishes itself in relation to underlying cultural practices. These cultural practices create possibilities that might reinforce or hinder the construction of the philosophy at stake. Discursive practices in the classroom should reflect different aspects of scientific culture, encompassing knowledge, procedures, attitudes, meta-knowledge and the scientists' discursive practices of construction and validation of knowledge, which are based on the dominant scientific paradigm, as mentioned by Kuhn [37]. We can say that each "zone" or philosophy in the epistemological profile is constituted by multiple paradigms, we just have to remember the case of rationalism, which encompasses the paradigms of classical mechanics and electromagnetism.

The knowledge of the philosophies of the epistemological profile related to sciences can inform and contribute to consistent discursive and practical changes in the work of teaching professionals. The new discursive practices and the classroom culture need to be aligned with a "zone" of the epistemological profile that will be centered on the construction and strengthening of the teacher's knowledge. The requirements for the formation of teaching professionals in this proposal are new but feasible. However, a dialogue between the tradition and the vanguard in the science education is vital to inform and move it forward.

Having presented the notion of epistemological profile, in the next section we offer a discussion of how this perspective provides an alternative for the understanding of scientific literacy.

3. Scientific Literacy and Epistemological Profile

As discussed earlier, scientific literacy can be understood as the strengthening and construction of new zones in the epistemological profile of individuals based on practices and knowledge of science.

Such practices are cultural. Therefore, it does not make sense to talk about an acting zone without relating it to the cultural and discursive practice that constructs and validates it.

The naive realism is both the result and component of practices kept between individuals in a certain culture. Those practices are always presented in the daily interactions between individuals sharing meanings when they act and talk. This is the zone in the epistemological profile that most people have in common and the education in science needs to take into consideration modes of acting and knowledge related to this zone of the epistemological profile. The naive realism mediates the type of knowledge students usually bring to science classes. Research on students' previous conceptions and conceptual change have documented the nature and operational mode of the naive realism in the conceptualization of acceleration, force, heat, optics, electrical circuits, chemical balance, among others [27–35] .Teachers are again central. They must be able to operate within the naive realism and aim at overcoming it. Teachers need to master at some level the language of their students and the implicit assumptions to be overcame by the construction of a scientific zone in the epistemological profile of their students.

It is neither desirable nor possible to eliminate this mode of producing and reproducing knowledge. Put in another way, it is not possible to eliminate the subtract of that zone in the epistemological profile, which are cultural practices uniting most people and allowing them to undertake daily discursive exchanges aimed at giving meaning to immediate and apparent experience, even though when they have no scientific basis.

Primary school students are curious but have not yet developed abstract thinking completely, which will be done in adolescence [20,38,39]. Individuals are born under certain biological circumstances and this is framed, as Vygotsky circle as shown, by the culture and speech of adults surrounding them. The main problem to be posed is: How to cross both perspectives to develop personalities akin to a better world and to themselves? Under this circumstance, this level of basic education can counteract naive realism brought by students to clear empiricism brought by teachers, in which students gradually come to realize, recognize and operate under control variables and the technique and domain of standard procedures. In such perspective, students compare, classify and put in order the empirical reality. The procedures are constructed and repeated. In turn, the measurement and comparison become more precise, and also become the axis of this practice, through which the students can explore the natural world, realizing empirical correlation between the entities and measures, recognizing patterns and elaborating a certain degree of the empirical reality. In this process, the material tools acquire a central importance. They allow the classification and identification of measures and relations, which in turn allows the measurement of those relations and contribute as means for the students actions.

In that level, it is clearly possible to use some rationalist concepts to explain the theoretical causality of certain phenomena measured and realized empirically. What is in question is the priority: in that level priority is given to the construction of the empiricism, making it, for the students, clear and distinct from naive realism. The construction of a new zone in the epistemological profile of the students would be a goal in the scientific literacy of primary students.

The establishment of correlations, the comparison, the measurement, the identification of empirical patterns and the technique are means of action of an individual that acts under the clear empiricism and should, therefore, be privileged in the practice of teaching science education at primary level. Natural sciences offer several modes to achieve that objective, from the use of control variables to the measurement and establishment of correlations, such as the relations between a shadow in relation to the position of bulkhead of the object and light source.

The construction of that also presupposes a discussion and teaching of questions related to science, technology, environment [2,3,40,41] as well as the exercise of argumentation as a scientific practice in the establishment of statements empirically and theoretically based, and in the effective citizenship in today's democratic societies [42–44]. The construction benefits from those perspectives and at the same re-signify a new epistemological order distinct and more advanced than naive realism.

In secondary school, physiological, psychological, social and cultural aspects and the students' ability to abstract evolve quickly [20,38,39], allowing the construction and strengthening of rationalism, which contributes to the structuration and consistency of the evolving abstract thought. At this level, causality, the laws, theories and meta-knowledge are privileged. They are based on the construction of models used to understand empirical relations established at primary school. It is not a collection of knowledge, but the construction of a new epistemological order in the action and thought, based on conceptual, abstract and theoretical parameters.

The construction of the rationalism supports the development of the students' cognitive abstraction, becoming a requirement for action, thought, speech and rationalization of the world, in which ideas are based on other ideas and concepts are defined in a structured and organized conceptual net. The teaching of Newtonian mechanics clearly supports the construction and development of rationalism, and can be taken as a prototype theory of it. Concepts are defined by the type of relation they have with other concepts. Understanding and operating according to such logic is radically different from operating with the logic of naive realism, in which the epistemological obstacles need to be overcome and understood, supporting the acquisition of a larger understanding of zones of the epistemological profile that influence the students' actions.

Questions related to science, technology, society, environment, discussions of socio-scientific issues and the use of argumentation in effective citizenship [2,3,10,40–48] are suggested at primary school. At secondary school, such approach can be re-signified and elaborated again taking into consideration the rationalism that is being constructed and strengthened.

From this perspective, students are faced with questions and problems that require modeling, construction and synthesis of concepts, and abstraction. They in turn are the means to discuss, problematize and use of argumentation, making arguments widen in scope and in meaning. Reciprocally, the questions and problems benefit from argumentation, which enlarge their scope, generality and consistency.

4. A New Proposal for Reconceptualizing Scientific Literacy

In our proposal, scientific literacy develops within the creation and strengthening of 'zones', what we will call for the sake of clarity, "ideological perspectives on science" in the epistemological profile of the students, which will in turn make it possible for them to act and think scientifically. This identification is no accident and for a clearer definition of what we are calling "ideological perspectives on science", we will discuss some of the resemblances of the Aristotelian philosophy and modern Science, in such a way that both are synthesis of reality, and how they differ from each other on the basis that sustain their "zones" (ideological perspectives), which in turn will lead us to discuss the notion of epistemological profile.

4.1. Aristotelian Philosophy and Modern Science: Their Main Differences and Implications for the Notion of Epistemological Profile

Modern science resembles Aristotelian philosophy in using models to explain phenomena. The difference between these ideological perspectives of knowledge chronologically separated relies on the bases which sustain their models. In the case of the Aristotelian philosophy, by basing its statements on observations, immediately sensations and immediate impressions; in modern science, the models are based in other models, in experiences and observations, which are mediated by instruments, available technology and by the particular scientific community. Thus, this is a clear difference of "ideological perspectives" among these two models to explain reality. Both sustain on the real and have had the authority and the right to claim about it. The main difference between them and common sense resides in the antinomy: synthesis and syncretism/fragmentation and unsystematic.

Common sense is based on immediate impressions, like Aristotelian philosophy, but, unlike it, the common sense does not provide a model and synthesis of reality. In few words, the common sense knowledge is noticeable unsystematic and disperse, although it serves to construct localized explanations which are incorporated in the discursive memory of a culture or micro-culture, constituting and reproducing the common sense.

The notion of epistemological profile proposed by Bachelard [25] is useful to this discussion, as it clarifies the "ideological perspectives on science" behind the zones of the epistemological profile of individuals. For instance, the epistemological profile of a professional physicist generally covers various zones, as is the case for Newtonian mechanics, the relativity and quantum mechanics, just to stay in examples from physics. The transition among the zones of the profile does not happen by continuity, but by the overcoming of the epistemological obstacles. Thus, between the common sense and the Sciences there are epistemological obstacles that are not overcome simply by experience or accumulation of more information and quotidian thoughts. Science Education is decisively one via for the overcoming and for the construction of scientific zones in the students' epistemological profiles.

The zones of the epistemological profile are representations of the different ideological perspectives on science of knowledge that influence the individual who acts. These ideological perspectives encompass cultural practices in the classroom in the construction and validation of the new ways to deal to knowledge of content and in relation to meta-knowledge, that is, knowledge about other forms of knowledge (for example, knowledge about the nature and history of science [49–53]). Additionally, as Carvalho [54] have suggested, it is also necessary to create conditions for the development of the students' conceptual, procedural and attitudinal dimensions and their understanding of Science, Technology, Society, Environment and socio-scientific issues [55–58].

The conceptual dimension is related to the learning of a given field; the procedural dimension has to do with doing well established operations (procedures) to accomplish a determined goal of an action. Finally, the attitudinal refers to the feelings, beliefs and values held about an object that may be the enterprise of science, school science, the impact of science on society or scientists themselves [59]. In addition, of course, these three types of dimensions are interrelated since a type of attitude can evoke a set of procedural dimensions (operations), which in turn can affect the learning outcomes of a given subject.

Individuals need to be careful and sensitive to global issues, respect each other and take responsibility for their actions to solve current problems [40,60]. And this encompass the three related dimensions: attitudinal, procedural and subject matter (conceptual), what in turn, are (re)conceptualized in terms of the ideological perspective on science at stake of the epistemological profile of the interactors.

In our view, these outcomes would be difficult to achieve with individuals discussing under different ideological perspectives of the epistemological profile, because they will not enter in agreement since the basis that sustain their knowledge bases are epistemologically different. We consider the epistemological profile approach is a fruitful mean to join people together of different backgrounds in conversations with the same dominant ideological perspective on science, which enable them to have "fruitful debates", as instance, about socio-scientific issues in terms of SL with the support of the teacher, who mobilizes the perspectives underpinning the discussions.

4.2. Middle Point

The knowledge of the ideological perspectives of the epistemological profile related to sciences can inform and contribute to consistent discursive and practical changes in the work of teaching professionals. The new discursive practices and the classroom culture need to be aligned with a knowledge of such perspectives that will be centered on the construction and strengthening of the teacher's.

However, the question is how students and teachers can acquire such skills? It does not rests only on acquire competency in using one or another concept in typified assessment activities, but mainly of the student be able to act and operate according to determined ideological perspectives on science in problem-situations, and know how to evaluate the product of his/her actions in terms of the mobilized ideological perspective; in our case, we are interested in science—that is—the ideological perspectives on science.

From this perspective, the learning of sciences acquires a fundamental importance, since it presupposes the passage from common sense to new ideological perspectives—that of sciences (more general, theoretical and systematized than the common sense). In this passage (i.e., along the teaching and learning) the students move forward and backward between the ideological perspectives, mobilizing different concepts depending of the situational demands, including as a way to deal and understand the particular demands posed by teaching. Thus, the classrooms are privileged spaces to students gradually acquire resourcefulness with ideological perspectives distinct from the common sense, mainly the scientific ones. This, however, leads us to a demarcation problem: what is scientific?

The sciences have common assumptions, such the empirical nature, the rationality principle and the mediation of knowledge by models, instruments and theories. The methods, approaches and theories used, however, varies between the sciences and among fields of the same science, depending of the scientific community, the problems of study, the counter positions erased and active, of the accepted argumentations, of the available techniques and of the cultural-historical collection of its time. One central process for the individual to domain the paradigms, theories and methods of one determined scientific field is his/her acculturation in this field.

From this point of view, the gradually acculturation of the students in the epistemic practices in the classroom can bring them opportunities to collectively develop competency in talk, write, read and produce science [61]. One important step in this process is the understanding by the student that science is a privileged form to understand and possess knowledge of the world. In appropriating and producing science the student gradually acquire competence in talk and think under scientific perspectives. Regarding the epistemic practices, Sandoval [62] poses a clear definition on learning:

> [in the model of cognitive apprenticeship] learning science entails the appropriation of discipline-specific modes of discourse and action. These ways of talking, thinking, and acting include often tacit epistemological commitments, commitments to the kinds of questions worth asking, the kinds of answers worth having, and acceptable methods for making them. Developing an apprentice-oriented science pedagogy thus requires an epistemic focus, an effort to understand how knowledge is made within a discipline.

Our position is that learning science does not have to do only with "equip", but mostly in "empowering" intellectually the students with scientific resources of our era and history. The demand this conception of teaching and learning implies is urge, however, in Brazil there is a lack of teachers in their specific areas of teaching, more specifically in science. In the physics teaching, unfortunately this index is alarming. It is necessary to overcome the older problems of teacher education [63] and advance, in the teacher education and continue education, the modeling of the practices, what presupposes reflections and dialogue among universities, schools, government and community attended.

This perspective implies changes and investments in the teacher education programs. It is essential to inform the understanding of teachers about science and its value to the contemporary citizen. The visions of science of teachers and students needs to be questioned and widen, aiming to an approach that implies the introduction of the processes of science into the classroom, and the development of the conceptual, procedural and attitudinal skills of the students.

According to Kelly [61], discursive and ethnographic investigations of the epistemic practices of daily life in the classroom evince how science is "performed" moment-by-moment in these scenarios by students and teachers. Such an analytical approach studies how the epistemic practices of classrooms offer possibilities and constraints to what counts as science, who can participate and how science is accomplished among the members of the group.

Kelly [61] claims that the focus on epistemic practices situates the learning of science in social contexts and insert a new set of demands to research. The analysis should include the multiple actors, the modes how roles of the individuals are established, the norms and expectations, the mediators' artifacts and the local histories of sociocultural practices.

According to the author, the discursive investigations of the epistemic practices in the classroom benefit of more widen analysis, which include the school, the media, university, parents, and cultural practices of daily life of the students. The crossing of these perspectives informs the research and the practice and propitiates opportunities to more critically analysis by the part of researches, students and teachers.

The study of discourse is a strong theoretical and analytical perspective to deal with issues and demands of science education for democracy, well-being and consequent decision makings. Under this perceptive, we will discuss in the next sections the perspective of activity theory and cross this perspective with resources from the discourse studies and of the epistemological profile, and then discuss their contributions to inform and widen the problem developed until this point.

5. Activity Theory and Discourse Studies

Activity theory has its roots in soviet psychology in the beginning of the 20th century. Such a theory emerged from the shared works of Vygotsky, Luria and Leont'ev, and it was systematized and articulated by Alexei Leont'ev [23,26]. The historical, dialectical and material components of human development based on a Marxist ideology had a great influence in the formulation of activity theory. According to this perspective, cognition and human development are interrelated to practical activities, which provide structure and content to individuals' inner activities.

The development and continuity of the human activity systems succeeds at the light of processes of acculturation created by society, in which individuals appropriate of knowledge historically accumulated by previous generations [22]. This phenomenon implies mediation, the use of instruments (both material and ideal), rules, division of labor, situated identities and, evidently, discourse. These processes are constitutive of, and constituted by, the structure of human activity. In this structure, the level of action emerged with the division of labor among humans engaged in social activities. This is a conscious level and regards what must be done which not necessarily converge directly to the motive of the collective activity. We will explain this point of view.

According to Leont'ev [23,26] and validated by the academic community [22], any human activity can be analyzed by means of its structure in levels, each one representing an authentic and particular reality: Activity, action, and operation. Each level has its own characteristics and objects and will be discussed. We begin by the activity level.

5.1. Activity: Originated in a Need/Motive

Human activity has origins in a need, whether biological or cultural. The needs are the departure point to an activity beginning, but alone they cannot give them a start and orientation. It only happens when the need meets one determined object (ideal or material) that can satisfy it, and this object is called the motive of one's activity, Leont'ev call this process an "objectification of a need", which is the "filling" of a need with content of the objective world.

We highlight that the motive is the "motor" for the development of all actions that unfold from the activity. As instance, we have in school activities, extra-school activities and leisure activities distinct motives that characterize and determine these activities.

We recognize that teachers must be capable to manage different motives for their classes, considering the curriculum, the teaching planning, feedbacks from students and contextualized clues from previous classes. This is an alternative perspective for teachers' motives approach, which generally are imposed mostly exclusively by the didactic textbook, inflicting one unique motive to all of their classes—seek uncritically the didactic textbook and, as a consequence, the deflation of the teaching activity and its image upon society

The discourse, and its domain by the part of teachers can offer opportunities for them to consciously domain and manage their motives according to contextualized clues they are able to recognize and understand from their classes. The students, by their turn, and usually, are not initially conscious of the class' motive. They are, actually, conscious of the object of their actions, constructed and transferred gradually and discursively to them by their teachers, as we will explain next.

5.2. Action: Related to the Satisfaction of a Conscious Goal

With the advent of the division of labor, for one single activity the individuals may appeal to different processes, obtaining different and partial results; the articulation of these processes may result in a common product that may satisfy one individual's need or a group of individuals. Leont'ev calls "actions" these processes, which are related to the individual's representations of a product or result, that is, a conscious goal. Thus, each action is oriented to a previous or emergent goal. This perspective is evident in the classroom, since in these learning spaces the teacher's didactic intentionality cannot lost sight of; his/her intentionality manages the students' actions and manages the discursive rhythm that is oriented to the motive (or the "main teacher's goal") for that class.

Again, the discursive perspective is crucial for teachers understand the conscious goals that must pass by ideological formations and negotiations of group of teachers that gradually transfer this responsibility to their students, making them the objective of their actions, which are related to various discursive components, as is the case for the linguistic-structural components, among them the discursive orientations (e.g., Vieira, Kelly & Nascimento [64]; Vieira & Kelly [65], as for narrations, explanations, argumentations, descriptions, injunctions, and dialogues). Such discursive orientations are derived from the notion of "sequence" from studies on textual linguistics [66,67], and are dominant modes of language structuring that transcend the phrasal level of analysis. Each discursive orientation can allow or restrict the satisfaction of a determined didactic goal. Thus, is evident how the discursive-linguistic-structural and activity theory work together to inform the teaching practice in the classroom. As instance, narrations, explanations and injunctions can help the satisfaction of more authoritative goals, while argumentation and dialogues are related to more open-ended goals.

Besides its intentional aspect (what must be done or obtained), every action also presents an operational aspect (how and by which means the goal can be satisfied). This operational aspect is determined by the material and symbolic conditions available to the goal satisfaction. These considerations lead us to the level of operation, which will be the next point to be discussed.

5.3. Operation, Related to Conditions and Methods

As we mentioned before, any action develops according to certain objective conditions, which determine the methods for accomplishment of the action. Leont'ev calls "operations" these methods.

Operations are usually unconscious and are subordinated to the goal of the action they contribute to realize. An individual may form operations through conscious processes. With time, they begin to structure more complex chain of actions, losing their intentional aspect, which is no longer recognized by the individual, but keeping their operational aspect, which becomes automated in the form of an operation. To execute an operation the individual needs to know how to make it and this is the reason why an operation is generally automatic, that is, without the need of intentional effort to be realized.

Again, the discursive perspective allows us to understand how operations help to establish patterns at the action level by means of what we have called "Discursive Didactic Procedures", which are the means arising from the conjunction of the teacher's propositions with convergent meanings (propositions are the less units of meaning of discourse, as can be found in Vieira, Kelly & Nascimento [64]; and Vieira & Kelly [65]). The delimitation of propositions, taking into account the cultural or micro-cultural character of the classroom, are established by sociolinguistics criteria [68], such as pauses, intonation, eye gaze, etc., and verbs of change (run, jump, etc.) which often co-varies and mark changes in the content and direction of the established discourse. This evinces the historical-cultural nature of the discursive perspective informed by activity theory.

Activity theory places the human being as an agent in the historical-cultural processes of knowledge, ideology and work. It is in the advent of division of labor that arises the fundamental differentiation of animal and human activities: the level of action. That is, this difference is born in the concerted relations between humans.

In a few words, the division and articulation of actions and activity were historically elaborated with the advent of division of labor concomitantly with the use, production and accumulation of material and symbolic instruments. Such a division of labor was mediated by, and constitutive of, language in labor activities, what enabled the negotiation and establishment of meanings, reassembling then the emergence of the culture as a discursive practice and the human consciousness as the product of the appropriation of the systems of meanings cultural-historically constructed and construed by humans.

6. Implications for Science Education in School Science Activities

As an example on how such perspectives can improve science education, in school science activities the students have the opportunities to learn in discursive dynamics in which a concept or subject may be initially a motive of the shared activity, with coordinated actions that may not be necessarily directed to the definition of the concept or subject, but helping in circumscribe and contextualizing it, and, as a consequence, passing to the conscious action of the students in another activity, until arrive to the level of the operation, assuming then the status of condition or method for the realization of other actions, and, finally, turning again the motive of a new shared activity, at this time with a meta-reflexive motive. Such a meta-reflexive activity presupposes the reflection of the students regarding the fields and limits of applicability of the concept, whether a concept of common sense, fragmented and with little generality, whether a concept under the paradigm of Newtonian mechanics, more general, systematized and rational. Metacognition serves as an important component to people as they encounter various problems that relate to personal, societal, and global issues [69].

This dynamic of the concept or subject in transiting between the motivational, the intentional and the conditional is afforded by the engagement of the students in the discursive practices in the classroom mediated and managed by the teacher (for a discourse perspective in science classrooms see Kelly [70]). In turn, the students begin to domain concepts and their fields of application, beginning to construct zones of their epistemological profile related to science, as instance, domain the ideological perspective of classic mechanics. It is important to stress that in the passage of the common sense to the scientific ideological perspectives there are epistemological ruptures that the individuals need to be conscious.

Furthermore, the implicit assumptions, so common in discursive activity [66], initially operate "naturally", but with the advance of these activities the implicit assumptions come to turn to explicit, even because of the results of the ideological power of explanations that the epistemological profiles have to offer. Also, the interplay of discursive implicit-explicit [66] affords the emergence of various constructions and interpretations performed by the individuals who interact in the considered group [70]. The control of the teacher over these interpretations passes precisely by his/her knowledge of the psychology of humans (activity theory), of the discourse features that constitutes the school activities, and finally, of the ideological aspects that give meanings to the science constructed and construed in the classroom. It is in this last step the epistemological profile approach acquires a fundamental function, since it is recognizable a new instance for the comprehension of scientific concepts and meanings that the automatization of teaching darkens.

We consider that the provided theoretical perspectives can inform the consciousness of the teachers about the structural, discursive and epistemological components of their activities, and of their students'. Our point of view is that the relation and interpretation the individuals have of their discursive memories present a qualitative change when they pass to have the "lens" and consciousness of the structure of their activities and that of their peers. As we mentioned earlier, such a lens articulates the motivational, intentional and circumstantial spheres of human activity and its appropriation by the individual, along the appropriation of discursive and ideological perspectives resulted by the uses and application of discourse analysis and of the epistemological profile approach produce new effects of sense regarding their memories, constructed in and by the discursive interactions. These changes influence the way the individual sees the world, how sees him or herself and how actively lives and act in the world, what can collaborate or no to a (re)production of a model of society.

7. Scientific Literacy and Epistemological Profile

As evident in the discussion so far, scientific literacy can be understood as the construction and strengthening of new ideological perspectives in the epistemological profile of individuals based on practices and knowledge of science. Such practices are cultural. Therefore, it would not be wise to offer a discussion about an acting ideological perspective without relating it to the cultural and discursive practice that constructs and validates it.

The naive realism is both the result and component of daily practices kept between individuals in a certain culture. Those practices are always presented in the daily interactions between individuals sharing meanings when they act and talk. This is the ideological perspective that most of people have in common and the education in science needs to take into consideration the modes of acting and knowledge related to this zone of the epistemological profile. The naive realism mediates the type of knowledge students usually bring to science classes. Teachers are again central. They must be able to operate within the naive realism and aim at overcoming it. Teachers need to master at some level the language of their students and the implicit assumptions to be overcome by the construction of a scientific ideological perspective.

It is neither desirable nor possible to eliminate this mode of producing and reproducing knowledge. Put in another way, it is not possible to eliminate the subtract of naive realism, which are cultural practices uniting most of people and allowing them to take daily discursive exchanges that give meaning to immediate and apparent experience, even though when they have no scientific basis.

Primary school students are curious but have not yet developed abstract thinking completely, which will be done in adolescence [20]. Under this circumstance, this level of education can counteract naive realism brought by students to clear empiricism, in which students gradually come to realize, recognize and operate under control variables and the technique and domain of standard procedures, thus acquiring familiarity with the natural world. In such perspective, students compare, classify and put in order the empirical reality. The procedures are constructed and repeated. In turn, the measurement and comparison become more precise, and also become the axis of this practice, through which the students can explore the natural world, realizing empirical correlations, recognizing patterns and elaborating a certain degree of the empirical reality. In this process, the material tools acquire a central importance. They allow the classification and identification of relations, which in turn allows the measurement of those relations and contribute as means for the students' actions.

In that level, it is clearly possible to use some rationalist concepts to explain the theoretical causality of certain phenomena measured and realized empirically. What is in question is the priority: in that level priority is given to the construction of the empiricist ideological perspective, making it, for the students, clear and distinct from naive realism. The construction of a new ideological perspective on science in the epistemological profile of the students would be a goal for the scientific literacy of primary students. Their control of the knowledge, procedures, attitudes and meta-knowledge related to this new ideological perspective, once added, orientates and restructure all these processes of knowledge in the action and operation in course.

The establishment of correlations, the comparison, the measurement, the pattern and the technique are means of action of an individual that acts under the ideological perspective of clear empiricism and should, therefore, be privileged in the practice of teaching science education at primary level. Natural sciences offer several modes to achieve that objective.

The construction of that ideological perspective also presupposes a discussion and teaching of questions related to science, technology, environment [1,10,45,46,71]. As well as the exercise of argumentation as a scientific practice in the establishment of statements empirically and theoretically based, and in the effective citizenship in today's democratic societies [43,44]. The construction of an empiricist ideological perspective benefits from those perspectives and at the same time re-signify a new epistemological order distinct and more advanced than naive realism.

In secondary school, physiological, psychological, social and cultural aspects and the students' ability to abstract evolve quickly [1,10,20,39,45,46,71] allowing the construction and strengthening of the rationalistic ideological perspective, which contributes to the structuration and consistency of the evolving abstract thought. At this level, causality, the laws, theories and meta-knowledge are privileged. They are based on the construction of models used to understand empirical relations established at primary school. It is not a collection of knowledge, but the construction of a new epistemological order in the action and thought, based on conceptual, abstract and theoretical parameters. At this stage the concepts are part of a net that weaves the web of a system, a conceptual system that can integrate and explain phenomena from different orders, making this ideological perspective highly general.

The construction of the rationalistic ideological perspective supports the development of the students' abstraction, becoming a requirement for action, thought, speech and rationalization of the world, in which ideas are based on other ideas and concepts are defined in a structured and organized epistemological net. In physics education, the teaching of Newtonian mechanics clearly supports the construction and development of this perspective, and can be taken as a prototype theory of the rationalistic ideological perspective on science.

8. Discussion and Final Remarks

Several reform documents report that students need to learn the practices and processes of science, including the understanding of the role of argumentation in the accomplishment of science [1,10,45,46,71,72]. Students are asked to engage in more active activities and investigations open to rational discussions, including the consideration and debate of socio-scientific issues and the learning about nature and history of science. There is a clear tendency in contemporary science education in promoting the learning of "science as argument" [73–75]. However, science teachers and future teachers still lack specific orientations about the new recommendations for the teaching of sciences. According to Duschl & Osborne [76] (p. 1), "An examination of recent policy reports [...] strongly suggest that classroom and school environments and teaching practices, for all intents and purposes, remain essentially unchanged during this 50 year period".

The problem of the preparation of teachers for science education in the 21st Century becomes even more complex in light of the theoretical perspectives recommended in this article. The point that we bring forward is: students should engage in argument, but argumentation should follow a set of paradigms in an epistemological and conceptual evolution, in which elaborating ideological perspectives on science support the improvement of discussion of fundamental and diverse issues, including socio-scientific ones [2,3,16,41,43].

Thus, this article proposes a perspective for scientific literacy based on epistemological profile that privileges the construction of the clear empiricism in the teaching of primary school and rationalism in secondary school. The proposal establishes a re-conceptualization of scientific literacy that provides means for ideological science paradigms evolving into a human being, at a certain moment and under certain conditions. The demand for ideological perspectives on science is given by the development of individuals in the activity systems of society, such as the complete rationalism (for those studying physics at university) or the strengthening and enlargement of ideological perspectives previously established, like the clear empiricism (for whose studying chemistry in a technical course, for example).

According to Wickman & Ostman [77] (p. 1):

> Research in science teaching is currently dominated by constructivism. This school of thought rests on the legacy of Piaget, and learning is seen a change of cognitive structures that interacts with the environment [78]. The central aim of this research has been to describe people's ideas about different concepts and phenomena and to explain "conceptual change" [79,80]. Originally it had an epistemological stance, where people's naive ideas about nature were compared with scientific theories or paradigms. [29,34]

In our proposal, we have not eliminated such a research trend, but instead it was integrated into a larger scope framework, in which the teachers consider and identify the ideological perspectives on science that the students have and show their inconsistency. By doing so, the students gradually, through adequate discursive practices in the classroom and other spaces of learning, construct and strengthen a new ideological perspective on science. It does not mean the students will abandon the previous one, as they will have a new option to understand and deal with reality. The consciousness individuals have of their profiles and their consciousness of contemporary questions and problems of their societies under a determined ideological perspective on science are other aspects privileged by teachers and need more clarification.

Such consciousness depends on the ideological perspective under which the reality is understood and reflected. Rationalism's understanding of reality or of a phenomenon is quite distinct from the naive realism. In this sense, as Lundqvist, Almvist & Östman [81] argued, a question is raised: "How often do we as teachers or students act as a direct result of an epistemological belief in a philosophical sense?" The differences have implications for life in society and effective citizenship aimed at the well-being of the individual and society at large. It also encompasses mutual respect and a deeper consciousness and engagement in the physical and social reality that constitutes the "subtract" of activities and personalities of human beings.

Several questions regarding the difficulty to implement our proposal may arise. For example, we can immediately recognize the distance between the satisfaction of the proposal and the reality of science teaching, in which students finish secondary school without knowing basic scientific concepts. They also have reading and writing challenges and do not present even a minimum empiricist zone in their epistemological profile. Unfortunately, this is the reality of most schools in which students finish basic education almost totally under the domain of the naive realism, not having, therefore, an informed and deep understanding of fundamentals questions about contemporary issues. Such perspective unfortunately worsens what is already bad in the world and is reflected in the official documents of many countries, which aim to reverse this situation in the schools by means of a new science education approach [1,10,23,45,46,71,72].

Despite the difficulties, the proposal is justified by the suggestion of a "perspective" and, in a certain way, "a goal" for scientific literacy. The goal is still far from being full-filled but this does not eliminate its value as a goal and its contribution to the process of reformulation of science education where such reformulations are needed. Such a goal requires changes in today's culture in science classrooms and in the activity of the teachers. A better understanding of the structure and discourse of the students' activities and the structure of scientific ideological perspectives can inform the dialogue between researchers and teachers. Such a dialogue could provide new means for allowing discursive practices and the ideological perspectives on science to be constructed and strengthened in the classroom more coherent and consistent. Framed within these theoretical constructs, this article proposes a re-conceptualization of scientific literacy by placing at the heart of its account students' epistemological profiles.

Author Contributions: Rodrigo Drumond Vieira idealized the proposal with Viviane, wrote the text and added the references. Viviane Florentino de Melo idealized the proposal, wrote the text and added references. Lucy Avraamidou commented on the text and added references. João Lobato commented on the text and revised it.

Conflicts of Interest: The authors declare no conflict of interest.

References

1. National Research Council NRC. *A Framework for K-12 Science Education*; National Academies Press: Washington, DC, USA, 2012.
2. Santos, W.L.P. Educação científica na perspectiva de letramento como prática social: Funções, princípios e Desafios. *Rev. Bras. Educ.* **2007**, *12*, 474–492. [CrossRef]
3. Zeidler, D.L.; Sadler, T.D.; Simmons, M.L.; Howes, E.V. Beyond STS: A research-based framework for socioscientific issues education. *Sci. Educ.* **2005**, *89*, 357–377. [CrossRef]

4. Hurd, P.D. Science literacy: Its meaning for American schools. *Educ.Leadersh.* **1958**, *16*, 13–16.
5. Laugksch, R.C. Scientific literacy: A conceptual overview. *Sci. Educ.* **2000**, *84*, 71–94. [CrossRef]
6. Chassot, A. *Alfabetização Científica: Questões e Desafios Para a Educação*; Editora UNIJUÍ: Ijuí, Brazil, 2000.
7. Roberts, D. Scientific literacy/science literacy. In *Handbook of Research on Science Education*; Abell, S.K., Lederman, N.G., Eds.; Lawrence Erlbaum: Mahwah, NJ, USA, 2007; pp. 729–780.
8. DeBoer, G. Scientific literacy: Another look at its historical and contemporary meanings and its relationship to science education reform. *J. Res. Sci. Teach.* **2000**, *37*, 582–601. [CrossRef]
9. McEneaney, E. Elements of a Contemporary Primary School Science. In *Science in the Modern World Polity: Institutionalization and Globalization*; Drori, S.G., Ed.; Stanford University Press: Stanford, CA, USA, 2003; pp. 136–154.
10. National Research Council (NRC). *National Science Education Standards*; National Academy Press: Washington, DC, USA, 1996.
11. Chan, D.W. Emotional intelligence and components of burnout among Chinese secondary school teachers in Hong Kong. *Teach. Teach. Educ.* **2006**, *22*, 1042–1054. [CrossRef]
12. Kyriacou, C.; Sutcliffe, J. Teacher stress: Prevalence, sources and symptoms. *Br. J. Educ. Psychol.* **1978**, *48*, 159–167. [CrossRef] [PubMed]
13. Salanova, M.; Grau, M.; Martínez, I. Job demands and coping behaviour: The moderating role of Professional self-efficacy. *Psychol. Spain* **2006**, *10*, 1–7.
14. Boyes, E.; Skamp, K.; Stanistreet, M. Australian secondary students' views about global warming: Beliefs about actions, and willingness to act. *Res. Sci. Educ.* **2009**, *39*, 661–680. [CrossRef]
15. Mueller, M.P.; Zeidler, D.L. Moral-ethical character and science education: Ecojustice ethics through socioscientific issues (SSI). In *Cultural Studies and Environmentalism: The Confluence of Eco justice, Place-Based (Science) Education, and Indigenous Knowledge Systems*; Tippins, D., Mueller, M.P., van Eijck, M., Adams, J., Eds.; Springer: New York, NY, USA, 2010; pp. 105–128.
16. Sjostrom, J.; Eilks, I.; Zuin, V. Towards eco-reflexive science education: A critical reflection about educational implications of green chemistry. *Sci. Educ.* **2016**, *25*, 321–341. [CrossRef]
17. Lee, M.; Sohn, W.; No, U. *The Result from PISA 2006(RRE 2008-10)*; Korea Institute for Curriculum and Evaluation: Seoul, Korea, 2008.
18. Jimenez-Aleixandre, M.P.; Rodríguez, A.B.; Duschl, R.A. "Doing the lesson" or "doing science": Argument in high school genetics. *Sci. Educ.* **2000**, *84*, 757–792. [CrossRef]
19. Sasseron, L.H.; Carvalho, A.D. Almejando a alfabetização científica no ensino fundamental: A proposição e a procura de indicadores do processo. *Investigações em Ensino de Ciências* **2008**, *13*, 333–352.
20. Piaget, J. *The Language and thought of the Child*; Routledge & Regan Paul: London, UK, 1926.
21. Holbrook, J.; Rannikmae, M. The meaning of scientific literacy. *J. Environ. Sci. Educ.* **2009**, *4*, 275–288.
22. Engeström, Y. Activity theory and individual and social transformation. In *Perspectives on Activity Theory*; Engeström, Y., Miettinen, R., Punamaki, R.-L., Eds.; Cambridge University Press: Cambridge, UK, 1999; pp. 19–38.
23. Leont'ev, A.N. *Activity, Consciousness, and Personality*; Prentice-Hall: Englewood Cliffs, NJ, USA, 1978.
24. Sadler, T. Situating socio-scientific issues in classrooms as a means of achieving goals of science education. In *Socio-Scientific Issues in the Classroom: Teaching, Learning and Research*; Sadler, T., Ed.; Springer: Dordrecht, The Netherlands, 2011; pp. 1–9.
25. Bachelard, G. *The Philosophy of No*; The Orion Press: New York, NY, USA, 1968.
26. Leont'ev, A.N. *Problems of the Development of the Mind*; Progress Publishers: Moscow, Russia, 1981.
27. Aguiar, O., Jr. Mudanças conceituais (ou cognitivas) na educação em ciências: revisão crítica e novas direções para a pesquisa. *Ensaio Pesquisa em Educação em Ciências* **2001**, *3*, 1–25. [CrossRef]
28. Lee, G.; Byun, T. An explanation for the difficulty of leading conceptual change using a counterintuitive demonstration: The relationship between cognitive conflict and responses. *Res. Sci. Educ.* **2012**, *42*, 943–965. [CrossRef]
29. Posner, G.J.; Strike, K.A.; Hewson, P.W.; Gertzog, W.A. Accommodation of a scientific conception: Toward a theory of conceptual change. *Sci. Educ.* **1982**, *66*, 211–227. [CrossRef]
30. Gilbert, J.K.; Watts, D.M. Concepts, misconceptions and alternative conceptions: Changing perspectives in science education. *Stud. Sci. Educ.* **1983**, *10*, 61–98. [CrossRef]

31. Duit, R.; Treagust, D.F. Conceptual change: A powerful framework for improving science teaching and learning. *Int. J. Sci. Educ.* **2003**, *25*, 671–688. [CrossRef]
32. Baser, M. Effects of conceptual change and traditional confirmatory simulations on pre-service teachers' understanding of direct current circuits. *J. Sci. Educ. Technol.* **2006**, *15*, 367–381. [CrossRef]
33. Jaakkola, T.; Nurmi, S.; Veermans, K. A comparison of students' conceptual understanding of electric circuits in simulation only and simulation-laboratory contexts. *J. Res. Sci. Teach.* **2011**, *48*, 71–93. [CrossRef]
34. Vosniadou, S. Capturing and modelling the process of conceptual change. *Learn. Instr.* **1994**, *4*, 45–69. [CrossRef]
35. Clement, J. The role of explanatory models in teaching for conceptual change. In *International Handbook of Research on Conceptual Change*; Vosniadou, S., Ed.; Routledge: New York, NY, USA, 2008; pp. 417–452.
36. Villani, A. Conceptual Change in Science and Science Education. *Sci. Educ.* **1992**, *76*, 223–238. [CrossRef]
37. Kuhn, T.S. *The Structure of Scientific Revolutions*; University of Chicago Press: Chicago, IL, USA, 1962.
38. Eidt, N.M. *A Educação Escolar e a Relação Entre o Desenvolvimento do Pensamento e a Apropriação da Cultura: A Psicologia de A. N. Leontiev como Referência Nuclear de Análise*; Tese de Doutorado; Programa de Pós-Graduação em Educação Escolar; Universidade Estadual Paulista: Araraquara, Brazil, 2009.
39. Vygotsky, L.S.; Luria, A.R.; Leont'ev, A.N. *Linguagem, Desenvolvimento e Aprendizagem*, 10th ed.; Ícone: São Paulo, Brazil, 2006.
40. Berkowitz, M.W.; Simmons, P. Integrating science education and character education: The role of peer discussion. In *The Role of Moral Reasoning on Socioscientific Issues and Discourse in Science Education*; Zeidler, D.L., Ed.; Kluwer Academic Press: Dordrecht, The Netherlands, 2003.
41. Evagorou, M. *Preparing Elementary Pre-Service Teachers to Teach Socioscientific Argumentation: From Theory to Practice*; National Association for Research in Science Teaching (NARST): Chicago, IL, USA, 2015.
42. Erduran, S.; Kaya, E. Scientific argumentation and deliberative democracy: An incompatible mix in school science. *Theory Pract.* **2016**, *55*, 302–310. [CrossRef]
43. Jiménez-Aleixandre, M.P.; Erduran, S. Argumentation in science education: An overview. In *Argumentation in Science Education: Recent Developments and Future Directions*; Erduran, S., Jiménez-Aleixandre, M.P., Eds.; Springer: Dordrecht, The Netherlands, 2008; pp. 3–27.
44. Vieira, R.D.; Nascimento, S.S. *Argumentação no Ensino de Ciências: Tendências, Práticas e Metodologia de Análise*; Appris: Curitiba, Brazil, 2013.
45. American Association for the Advancement of Science (AAAS). *Benchmarks for Science Literacy: Project 2061*; Oxford University Press: New York, NY, USA, 1993.
46. Brasil. *Ministério da Educação. Secretaria de Educação Média e Tecnológica. PCN+ Ensino Médio: Orientações Educacionais Complementaresaos Parâmetros Curriculares Nacionais. Ciências da Natureza, Matemática e suas Tecnologias*; Brasília: MEC/Semtec: Brasília, 2002.
47. Sadler, T. Informal reasoning regarding socioscientific issues: A critical review of research. *J. Res. Sci. Teach.* **2004**, *41*, 513–536. [CrossRef]
48. Vieira, R.D.; Bernardo, J.R.R.; Evagorou, M.; Melo, V.F. Argumentation in Science Teacher Education: The simulated jury as a resource for teaching and learning. *Int. J. Sci. Educ.* **2015**, *37*, 1113–1139. [CrossRef]
49. Abd-El-Khalick, F.; BouJaoude, S. An exploratory study of the knowledge base for science teaching. *J. Res. Sci. Teach.* **1997**, *34*, 673–699. [CrossRef]
50. Akerson, V.; Masters, H.; Fouad, K. Using history of science to teacher nature of science to elementary students. *Sci. Educ.* **2015**, *24*, 1103–1140.
51. Lederman, N.G. Students' and teachers' conceptions of the nature of science: A review of the research. *J. Res. Sci. Teach.* **1992**, *29*, 331–359. [CrossRef]
52. Mellado, V. Preservice teachers' classroom practice and their conceptions of the nature of science. *Sci. Educ.* **1997**, *6*, 331–354. [CrossRef]
53. Cooter, R.; Pumfrey, S. Separate spheres and public places: Reflections on the history of science popularization and science in popular culture. *Hist. Sci.* **1994**, *32*, 237–267. [CrossRef]
54. Carvalho, A.M.P. *Os Estágios nos Cursos de Licenciatura*; Cengage Learning: São Paulo, Brazil, 2012.
55. Aikenhead, G.S. Border crossing: Culture, school science, assimilation of students. In *The Multiple Meanings of a School Subject: Essays on Science and the School Curriculum*; Roberts, D.A., Östman, L., Eds.; Teachers College Press: New York, NY, USA, 1996.

56. Baxter, G.; Sommerville, I. Socio-technical systems: From design methods to systems engineering. *Interact.Comput.* **2011**, *2*, 4–17. [CrossRef]
57. Ratcliffe, M.; Grace, M. *Science Education for Citizenship: Teaching Socio-Scientific Issues*; McGraw-Hill Education: London, UK, 2003.
58. Solomon, J.; Aikenhead, G.S. (Eds.) *STS Education: International Perspectives on Reform*; Teachers College Press: New York, NY, USA, 1994.
59. Osborne, J.; Simon, S.; Collins, S. Attitudes towards science: Are view of the literature and its implications. *Int. J. Sci. Educ.* **2003**, *25*, 1049–1079. [CrossRef]
60. Hodson, D. Time for action: Science education for an alternative future. *Int. J. Sci. Educ.* **2003**, *25*, 645–670. [CrossRef]
61. Kelly, G.J. Scientific literacy, Discourse and Epistemic Practices. In *Exploring the Landscape of Scientific Literacy*; Linder, C., Östaman, L., Roberts, D., Wickman, P.-O., Erickson, G., Mackinnon, A., Eds.; Routledge: New York, NY, USA, 2011; pp. 61–73.
62. Sandoval, W.A. Conceptual and epistemic aspects of students' scientific explanations. *J. Learn. Sci.* **2003**, *12*, 5–52. [CrossRef]
63. Diniz-Pereira, J.E. *Formação de Professores: Pesquisas, Representações e Poder*, 2nd ed.; Autêntica: Belo Horizonte, Brazil, 2006.
64. Vieira, R.D.; Kelly, G.J.; Nascimento, S.S. An activity theory-based analytic framework for the study of discourse in science classrooms. *Ensaio Pesquisa em Educacação em Ciências* **2012**, *14*, 13–46. [CrossRef]
65. Vieira, R.D.; Kelly, G.J. Multi-level discourse analysis in a physics teaching methods course from the psychological perspective of activity theory. *Int. J. Sci. Educ.* **2014**, *36*, 2694–2718. [CrossRef]
66. Adam, J.M. *A Lingüística Textual: Introdução à Análise Textual dos Discursos*; Cortez: São Paulo, Brazil, 2008.
67. Bronckart, J.P. *Atividade de Linguagem, Textose Discursos: Porum InteracionismoSociodiscursivo*; EDUC: São Paulo, Brazil, 1999.
68. Gumperz, J.J. *Discourse Strategies*; Cambridge University Press: Cambridge, UK, 1982.
69. Choi, K.; Lee, H.; Shin, N.; Kim, S.; Krajcik, J. Re-conceptualization of scientific literacy in South Korea for the 21st century. *J. Res. Sci. Teach.* **2011**, *48*, 670–697. [CrossRef]
70. Kelly, G.J. Discourse in science classrooms. In *Handbook of Research on Science Education*; Abell, S., Lederman, N., Eds.; Lawrence Erlbaum Associates: Mahwah, NJ, USA, 2007.
71. European Commission/EACEA/Eurydice. *Developing Key Competences at School in Europe: Challenges and Opportunities for Policy*; Eurydice Report; Publications Office of the European Union: Luxembourg, 2012.
72. Ministério da Educação, Secretaria de EducaçãoMédia e Tecnológica. *Parâmetros Curriculares Nacionais: Ensino Médio*; Ministério da Educação: Brasília, Brazil, 1999.
73. Kuhn, D. Science as argument: Implications for teaching and learning scientific thinking. *Sci. Educ.* **1993**, *77*, 319–337. [CrossRef]
74. Osborne, J. Arguing to learn in science: The role of collaborative, critical discourse. *Science* **2010**, *328*, 463–466. [CrossRef] [PubMed]
75. Zembal-Saul, C. Learning to teach elementary school science as argument. *Sci. Educ.* **2009**, *93*, 687–719. [CrossRef]
76. Duschl, R.A.; Osborne, J. Supporting and promoting argumentation discourse in science education. *Stud. Sci. Educ.* **2002**, *38*, 39–72. [CrossRef]
77. Wickmann, P.-O.; Ostman, L. Learning as discourse change: A sociocultural mechanism. *Sci. Educ.* **2002**, *86*, 601–623. [CrossRef]
78. Bliss, J. The relevance of Piaget to research into children's conceptions. In *Children's Informal Ideas in Science*; Black, P.J., Lucas, A.M., Eds.; Routledge: London, UK, 1993; pp. 20–44.
79. Driver, R.; Squires, A.; Rushworth, P.; Wood-Robinson, V. *Making Sense of Secondary Science: Research into Childrens Ideas*; Routledge: London, UK, 1994.

80. Pfundt, H.; Duit, R. *Students' Alternative Frameworks and Science Education*, 4th ed.; Institute for Science Education: Kiel, Germany, 1994.
81. Lundqvist, E.; Almqvist, J.; Östman, L. Epistemological norms and companion meanings in science classroom communication. *Sci. Educ.* **2009**, *93*, 859–874. [CrossRef]

Article

Relevancy of the Massive Open Online Course (MOOC) about Sustainable Energy for Adolescents

Maija Aksela [1,2,*], Xiaomeng Wu [3] and Julia Halonen [1,2]

1   The Unit of Chemistry Teacher Education, University of Helsinki, Helsinki 00100, Finland;
     julia.halonen@helsinki.fi
2   The LUMA Centre Finland, University of Helsinki, Helsinki 00100, Finland
3   Graduate School of Education, Peking University, Beijing 100871, China; wuxm@pku.edu.cn
*   Correspondence: maija.aksela@helsinki.fi; Tel.: +358-505-141-450

Academic Editor: Eila Jeronen
Received: 5 October 2016; Accepted: 23 November 2016; Published: 1 December 2016

Abstract: Sustainable energy is one of the biggest global challenges today. This paper discusses how we can promote adolescents' learning of sustainable energy with the help of an international massive open online course (MOOC). The aim of this case study is to understand: (i) What do the adolescents find relevant in the MOOC course about sustainable energy? and (ii) What are the opportunities and challenges of the MOOC for the adolescents to learn sustainable energy? In our study, 80 voluntary adolescents around the world, who were at least 15 year old, took part in two surveys. The themes of our MOOC course were, e.g., sustainable growth, solar power, wind power, biofuel production and smart power generation. This 38 work-hour, free of charge, online course includes an introduction video, interviews of specialists, lecture videos, reading materials of the newest research and multiple choice questions on the topics. Research data was classified by using content analysis. The study indicates that adolescents feel that both the MOOC course and sustainable energy as a subject are relevant to them. Their decision to take part in an online course was mostly influenced by individual relevance and partly influenced by both societal and vocational relevance, according to the relevancy theory used. The MOOC was experienced to be relevant for the three following reasons: (i) good content (e.g., energy production) and implementation of the course; (ii) the course makes it possible to study in a new way; and (iii) the course is personally useful. The characteristics of the MOOC, such as being available anywhere and anytime, free access, and online learning, bringing out a flexible, new way of learning and thus promoting Education for Sustainable Development (ESD) in the context of sustainable energy at school level around the world. This MOOC provided the school students with choice-based learning and expanded their learning opportunities in understanding sustainable energy. In the designing of MOOCs for studying sustainable energy, it is important to take the following things into consideration: (i) the balance between theory and practical examples; (ii) the support for interaction; and (iii) other support (e.g., technical and learning strategies) for students. Communication with other learners and getting feedback from teachers and tutors remain the vital challenges for the developers of MOOCs in the future.

Keywords: Education for Sustainable Development (ESD); sustainable energy; online learning; MOOC

---

1. Introduction

The promotion of Education for Sustainable Development (ESD) will be even more important in the future [1,2]. In particular, promoting the learning of sustainable energy is one of the central global contents of ESD at school levels. In addition to learning the topic, it may add to the student and his/her family's social knowledge about it and it may also help in bringing new students to the field [3].

Sustainable energy can be described as a production and using of energy that supports sustainable development. This kind of energy is renewable and is produced durably, both socially and economically. For example, solar energy, water-based production of energy, and the production of biofuels with the help of microbes are all called as renewable energies [4]. For our massive open online course (MOOC) about sustainable energy, the themes of sustainable growth, solar power, wind power, energy efficiency, energy, water and food, energy consumption, fusion energy, biofuel production, smart power generation and cities, towns and renewable energy were selected. One of the main aims was to increase the students' ability to critically follow the societal and technical discussions on sustainable energy.

In a meaningful teaching of sustainable energy, it would be important to take into consideration four strategic viewpoints: equality, flexibility, student orientability and creativity [5]. The themes about sustainable development such as sustainable energy should be dealt with holistically and in a student-oriented manner [2,5]. In particular, adolescents want to study natural science phenomena that they find interesting and socially essential, and they would like to deal with moral questions having to do with the phenomena. It has been proven that they would like it if the teaching contained more personal activity and included the effects of the professions in the fields of natural sciences and technology in solving challenges shared by the entire world [6]. Adolescents like to take into consideration also the social and ethical points of the topic in addition to the academic points [7,8]. In this research, international adolescents study sustainable energy with the help of an online course (MOOC) that has been produced communally. It has been designed exploiting previous information from earlier researches (see Section 4 for further information).

2. Promoting Sustainable Energy Learning through the MOOCs

Massive open online course (MOOC) is thought of as an innovative method both in the teaching and researching of sustainable energy [9]. According to Zhan et al. [9] MOOCs on sustainable energy can offer learning resources and opportunities for people to cultivate their awareness of global environmental protection, of a sense of sustainability, and also to learn about the ways in which universities teach sustainability-related knowledge in an open online environment. In earlier research discussions, forums and lecture videos were most frequently used as the pedagogical methods of the earlier MOOCs for university students [9].

Originally the term MOOC, coined by Dave Cormier, was used to represent the phenomenon of their course called "Connectivism and Connective Knowledge (CCK08)", which was facilitated by S. Downes and G. Siemens in 2008. The MOOC has been described as an online course with the option of free and open registration, a publicly-shared curriculum, and open-ended outcomes [10]. They characterized the MOOC as integrating social networking and as being an accessible online resource. The MOOCs were facilitated by leading practitioners in the fields of study, and significantly, they were built on the engagement of learners who self-organize their participation according to learning goals, prior knowledge and skills, and common interests [10]. In general, these kinds of MOOCs are based on connectivism and the social construction of knowledge. Therefore, they are called cMOOCs (Connectivist MOOCs).

Although the first MOOC was carried out in 2008, the interest in MOOCs at that time was quite limited among researchers and mainstream media [11,12]. In 2011, Stanford launched three MOOCs, including the "Introduction to Artificial Intelligence" ('CS221') course, for which about 160,000 learners were registered. In the beginning of 2012, the MOOC models made by companies Coursera, Udacity and edX, were launched by Stanford, MIT and Harvard. MOOC was hyped up as the revolution of high education by the media and, 2012 was named "The year of MOOC" [13]. Different to the original MOOC led by S. Downes and G. Siemens, the pedagogy of Stanford's MOOC was more instructivist and behaviorist [12,14]. In this kind of a MOOC, there were weekly recorded video lectures and quizzes with immediate feedback. Some courses consisted of assignments that were peer-reviewed. All of the courses had discussion forums that students could use for their own purposes, and in some courses, instructors directly encouraged students to use these forums, though none of the instructors had a strong presence on the forums [15]. These kinds of MOOCs were labeled xMOOCs, as used in this study.

From 2012 onwards, the number of MOOCs has increased rapidly. But the concept of the MOOC remains relatively poorly defined. Matthew Plourde's diagram illustrates that every letter in MOOC is negotiable. In this paper, we use the definition of MOOC developed by OpenupEd [16], in which MOOCs are "online courses designed for large numbers of participants, that can be accessed by anyone anywhere as long as they have an internet connection, are open to everyone without entry qualifications, and offer a full/complete course experience online for free". This definition is shared by many European partners and has some empirical data to support [17].

Although MOOCs, especially xMOOCs, have not led to the disruptive innovation of education portrayed by the media, it is a valuable low-cost supplement to formal education [18,19]. A survey from Duck University suggested that learners under the age of 18, learners over the age of 65, and learners who reported a lack of access to the course contents indicated that the MOOCs provided expanded opportunities to their current formal education and their present and future career experiences [20]. MOOCs can help in meeting the increasing demand for on-the-job continuous professional development as employment patterns and lifelong learning change [13,18]. For developing countries, MOOCs help to improve the information literacy of people [21]. In Finland, MOOCs have been found useful for learning programming at school level [22].

However, MOOCs also have to face many challenges in their teaching because of the massive amount of participants in one course. The completion rate of MOOCs is usually very low [18,23]. The motivational, emotional and intellectual commitments, and the skill profiles of MOOC learners, affect the development and use of MOOCs [24]. The assessment of the higher levels of learning remains a challenge for MOOCs [18].

3. The Relevancy of the MOOC Course about Sustainable Energy

In this case study, we are interested in how relevant the course participants experience a MOOC course on sustainable energy. The results of this MOOC course are examined from the point of view of relevance theory [25].

"Relevance" is a concept that is often used when talking about the teaching of natural sciences. Teaching should be relevant, but the concept does not have a specific meaning and it therefore has been used in many different ways across time and from speaker to speaker. In the beginning of the 20th century, teaching of natural sciences was relevant when it served the purposes of the state and companies, and it was meaningful from the point of view of the functioning of society. Later on, the general education in natural sciences and their meaning in daily life became important [25,26].

As a concept, relevance has been used in order to illustrate a student's interests [27,28], and to illustrate how meaningfully the phenomena of daily life appear from the point of view of individuals and society, for example: applying science and technology to social, economic, environment, and political questions through sustainable development [29,30]. Relevance has also been used to explain how well the students are able to perceive the significance of using daily life contexts in teaching [31–34]. And it has been used as a synonym for importance, usefulness and correspondence of needs [35,36].

Even though people have not always agreed on the meaning of the concept of relevance, the relevance in science learning has been studied quite a lot. The most well-known research project dealing with the relevance of scientific education has been the international ROSE (The Relevance of Science Education) project. In the ROSE project, the concept of relevance was thought of mostly as a synonym for motivation and interest, but the organizers of this research were given the possibility to define relevance in the way they preferred [37].

Because there was not a previous similar model for relevance, Stuckey et al. [25] have aimed at creating a similar model for the relevance of teaching natural sciences, which considers the previous notions. According to this model, the relevance of teaching can be evaluated in three different dimensions: individual, societal and vocational relevance. The usefulness of this model is also supported by the fact that also Van Aalsvoort [38] has previously described the concept of relevance similarly. In addition to these above-mentioned three dimensions, intrinsic and extrinsic relevance is often talked about, as well as whether or not learning is relevant right at this moment or only later in the future.

Stuckey et al. [25] presents a model in their article for evaluating the relevance of learning natural sciences. This model can be tangibly exploited in addition to research in planning teaching. Here we can observe that, as a concept, relevance is more comprehensive than just interest or significance. The principle of the model can be observed in Figure 1, below.

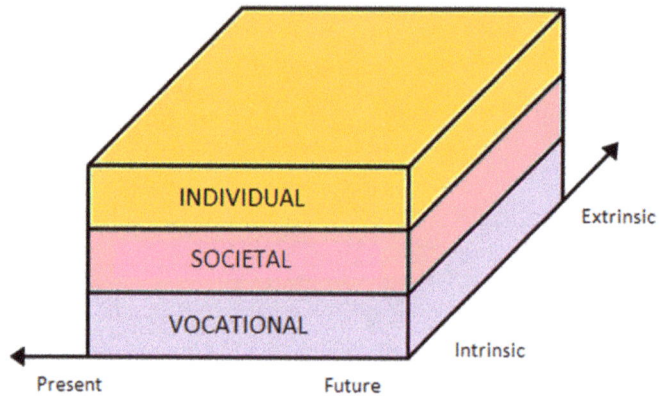

Figure 1. The dimensions of relevance [25].

In this model, individual relevance consists of, for example, subject matters that increase the student's interest or help the student to be successful in school and daily life. Things that can be considered to fit under societal relevance are, for example, those that help the learner act as a responsible member of society, to better understand the society around them and to be active in helping to develop the society. Vocational relevance consists of knowledge and skills that for example give a person the qualifications for a certain field or that bring support to the possible future profession. The present–future dimension in the model of relevance means that the thing being dealt with may be relevant to the learner either in the same exact moment or far in the future. Intrinsic relevance supports the student's interests and motivation, whereas extrinsic relevance is caused by the demands arranged by the surroundings.

It is briefly stated by Stuckey et al. [25] that the teaching of natural sciences becomes relevant training when teaching has positive effects on a student's life. Relevance, as a concept, should be available to the teachers and people who make the core curriculum, so that they can evaluate the relevancy of their lesson plans [39]. A model created on the basis of Stuckey et al.'s research has been created in order for the teachers to be able to actively analyze their lesson plans and perhaps edit these plans, so that teaching would be as relevant as possible from the students' point of view [25].

Stuckey et al. [25] have themselves used this model, created by them, in teacher training, where it has been used as a helping tool for reflecting on the aims for relevant education in natural sciences and as a tool for evaluating different teaching methods. Using this model in analyzing core curriculums makes it possible to find strengths and weaknesses, as well as the different levels of relevance in teaching [25].

4. The Aim and Content of the MOOC Course "Sustainable Energy"

A MOOC course, arranged for the first time, was organized by the University of Helsinki and in cooperation with the Aalto University and Technology Academy Finland (TAF). This course was held in autumn 2015. It was especially meant for over 15-year-olds all over the world who were interested in the subject. It was free of charge.

The goals of this MOOC course about sustainable energy are to:

- give a versatile glimpse into one of the biggest global challenges of today, sustainable energy;
- strengthen the students' skills on sustainable energy and its production based on the latest research and technology innovations;
- help to understand energy production in the future as a multidimensional entity;
- increase the students' ability to evaluate the choices connected to sustainable development in the daily life;
- promote Finnish knowledge of energy and future study possibilities, as well as the Millennium Technology Prize;
- inspire learning about mathematical subjects, natural sciences and branches of technology.

The teachers of this course were top-level researchers from a wide range of fields: there were lecturers from professors to doctoral students and from representatives from branches of science to representatives from commercial fields. Also, the themes chosen for this course dealt widely with sustainable development: from solar energy to nuclear energy (see details in Introduction). The themes dealt with the effects of renewable energy on the electrical network in the future and with increasing the effectiveness of using energy. This course aimed to bring forth both advantages and possible disadvantages for students. A more specific description of this course can be found here in the webpage: https://www.lumate.fi/event/millennium-youth-course-sustainable-energy/.

In order to be able to pass this course, the students would have to familiarize themselves with the specialists' interviews (videos), lecture videos (20 minutes each) and articles (the topics: Smart Power Generation and Cities, Towns and Renewable Energy) and then answer multiple-choice questions designed mostly by specialists. This course, implemented in the *Moodle* learning environment, was a 38 work-hour high school course, suitable for independent study, because it unifies the natural science entity in schools. Against a course diploma, a student could apply for a course performance from their school, a student could apply for a one study point marking of performance from the University of Helsinki, or they could apply for a study point also from our Open university. The subject of this course followed the new Finnish National Core Curriculum's (for high schools) theme: the necessity of a sustainable lifestyle.

An international MOOC course "Sustainable Energy in Education", a further training course for teachers, was implemented in the spring of 2016 on the basis of the research study of Sustainable Energy course.

5. Research Methods

There are two research questions in this case study:

(1) What do the adolescents find relevant in the MOOC course about sustainable energy?
(2) What are the opportunities and challenges of the MOOC for the adolescents to learn sustainable energy?

In this case study, 80 adolescents took part in research. Data for the first research question was collected in the beginning of this online course (the first task). A research form was compiled communally on the basis of relevance theory. Data for the second research question was collected at the end of the online course. In total there were two open questions about possibilities and challenges related to the second research question.

Data from the first research question was classified with the help of theory based content analysis [40]. All answers were divided into three classes: (i) individual relevance; (ii) societal relevance; and (iii) vocational relevance, according to the relevancy theory explained in Section 3. In addition, frequency of the answers for each class was calculated (see Table 1).

Table 1. The Relevancy of the Course.

Relevance Theory	The Answers of the Students	Frequency
Individual	• An interesting topic (26) • Wants to learn more about sustainable energy (24) • Interested in energy production (11) • Interested in natural sciences (11) • Course is in English (10) • Interested in sustainable energy (10) • Wants a coursemark (7) • An important topic (5) • Online course (5) • MOOC is cool • Useful information for the future • Might be helpful in the matriculation examination • Course was suggested by a teacher • To improve grade in physics • A challenging course • A flexible course • Wants to know about implementing courses in Finland • Wants to gain experience about the university life • Interested in learning in general	117
Societal	• Wants to make the world a better place • People should know more about sustainable energy	11
Vocational	• Wants to work with sustainable energy in the future • Wants to be a better teacher	4

Data from the second research question was classified using inductive content analysis [41]. Subclasses were formed first from the answers and then the upper classes were formed on the basis of the subclasses. First, all opportunities of the MOOC were coded and 12 codes were formed by a researcher, for example: (i) flexible learning (34 answers; e.g., an adolescent's answer: "could study anywhere and anytime"); (ii) interesting topic (25 answers; e.g., an adolescent's answer: "course topic was interesting"); (iii) good lectures (18 answers; e.g., "lectures were clear and well organized"). Then, they were classified into three categories by another researcher (see Table 2) and compared with earlier research.

Table 2. The opportunities of the MOOC during the course.

The Opportunities	An Example of the Answers	Frequency
Course design	- Course topic was interesting (24) - Lectures were clear and well organized (18) - Lecturers were great (11) - Videos were clear and re-watchable (9) - Quiz system was clear (8)	70
Providing a new way of learning: flexible learning and new learning strategies	- Could study anywhere and anytime (34) - Course was free and online (3)	37
Personal benefit: Learned lots of new things, learned English, encouraged towards learning about science and Finnish research	- Learned lots of new things (11) - Learned English (4) - Encourages children towards learning science (student teachers) (2) - Learn about Finnish research (2)	19

Secondly, all challenges of the MOOC were classified and nine codes were formed by a researcher, for example: (i) not enough interaction (16 answers; e.g., an adolescent's answer: "There was not enough interaction between students"); (ii) problems with technology (14 answers; e.g., an adolescent's answer: "there were some technical difficulties") and (iii) lecturers' skills in English (7 answers; e.g., an adolescent's answer: "lecturers should learn to speak English"). Then, they were classified into three categories by another researcher (see Table 3) and compared with earlier research.

Table 3. The challenges of the MOOC during the course.

Challenges	An Example of the Students' Answers	Frequency
Course design	- Lecturers should learn to speak better English (7) - Instructions were unclear (6) - Something other than questionnaires (5) - Wanted more practical examples (5) - Didn't like the reading tasks, they were too long (4)	27
Interaction	- There was not enough interaction between students - Would like to have feedback after every chapter	18
Learning support	- There were some technical difficulties - Would like to have some deadlines	17

The results of the case study have been confirmed by three researchers according to the research method [40,41]. The classifications of both data were checked, on the basis of the examples, by all the three researchers (two from the same research group and one from another research group), and the classification was accepted. Two researchers are specialists in sustainable development education (EDS) and in research of relevancy theory, and the third researcher is a specialist in research of online learning (MOOCs). The results of the qualitative case study are directional.

6. Research Results

In the following part, the results are analyzed according to the main research questions (see Section 5).

6.1. The Relevancy of the MOOC Course

The students thought that both the course and its theme were relevant (see Table 1 above). Students chose this course in particular because of the reasons of the principle of individual relevance. The three most popular reasons for taking part in this course were: (i) finding the theme of the course interesting; (ii) wanting to learn more about sustainable energy, and (iii) a general interest in production of energy. All in all, there were 80 participants in this research. According to the answers, there were 132 different "points" in accordance with the relevance theory, from which 61 answers belonged to these first three categories mentioned above.

The fourth most popular reason, according to the students, was general interest in the natural sciences; a large part of the other answers can also be counted to belong under individual relevance. All in all, individual relevance could be seen in 117 answers out of a possible 132.

In five of the answers, the student wanted to make the world a better place, five students thought that the theme of the course was generally important, and one student thought that people should know more about sustainable energy. These three answers all represent societal relevance. In total, the societal relevance in taking part in the course could be seen only in 11 out of 132 answers.

Vocational relevance was even less popular than societal relevance. The vocational viewpoint had been taken into consideration in only four answers.

6.2. The Opportunities and Challenges of the MOOC

According to the survey, the course participants reported that this MOOC provided them with a good learning experience in the three following areas (Table 2): (i) Course design (70 answers altogether); (ii) Providing a new way of learning (37 answers); and (iii) Personal benefit (19 answers). The course materials were well-prepared and easy to use (course design). Twenty-four answers claimed that the topic of the course was quite interesting for them. Thirty learners deemed that the lectures were clear and well organized and that they were also great. Seventeen answers commended the good quality of videos and quiz system for their clarity and reusability. Firstly, this course was a new way of learning for the participants. Thirty-seven answers mentioned that the characteristics of the MOOC, such as being available anywhere and anytime, free access, and online learning, and bringing out a flexible, new way of learning. Thirdly, the course participants got personal benefit from this course study. Some learners claimed that they had learned lots of new things, others felt it interesting to see what kind of research is done in Finland. Some teacher trainees thought that this MOOC would encourage kids towards studying natural sciences. Not only had the students' knowledge of energy increased, some Finnish learners reported that their English had been improved.

There are some challenges that this MOOC has to face, concerning: (i) course design; (ii) interaction; and (iii) learning support. At first, the design of the course needs to be improved. The survey showed that learners needed clearer instructions to leading study, and they wanted more practical examples to help them understand the learning content. Some learners thought that the reading materials were too long for them to read. Others thought that there should be more different forms of assignments and that they should be more varied. As an online course, open to the world, some learners suggested that the lecturers should speak better English in their lectures. Lack of interaction between teachers and students, and between students, was another problem in this xMOOC. Eighteen answers mentioned that there was not enough interaction among students and that the teachers did not give enough feedback. Learners also reported that they needed some technical help and learning support to assist their online study.

7. Discussion

7.1. The Relevancy of The Course

The adolescents experienced the course as individually relevant. Personal interest belongs to the front and upper corners in the left-hand side in the model of relevance theory [25] and it represents individual, present and intrinsic relevance. The desire to learn new things belongs to the front and upper corners on the right-hand side, so it belongs also to the individual and intrinsic relevance, but instead of present, belongs to the future. In addition to individual relevance, also societal and vocational relevance had an effect on the students' decisions whether or not taking part in the course, even though in noticeably lesser proportions. The societal viewpoint is most likely going to strengthen over time, when the awareness of the world strengthens through globalization. This will possibly also have an effect on the students' decisions about which courses to choose, and this might be an interesting subject of research in the future.

The answers that represent vocational relevance were those in which the responder wants to work with sustainable energy in the future or the responder wants to become a better teacher. From the basis of these results, it would be wise to ponder whether or not the students are able to think about their working lives in the future, or whether personal interests are just simply so much more important that the vocational viewpoint cannot be fitted into a small description about why the student has especially chosen this course? In the further revision of this course it would be wise to take this viewpoint better into consideration.

7.2. The Opportunities and Challenges of The MOOC

MOOCs, especially xMOOCs, are characterized as delivering high quality content from the world's best universities for free to anyone anywhere with a computer and an internet connection, and supporting choice-based learning [18,42]. Students in primary and secondary schools, have the opportunities to take MOOCs in topics not taught in their schools and to explore different disciplines in helping to weigh their academic and career choices [20]. In our MOOC practice, most of the learners chose this course because of their interest in the natural sciences and sustainable energy/sustainable development. This MOOC provided them with choice-based learning and expanded their learning opportunities.

MOOCs were respected to give rise to innovation on the existing education system. Although current critiques of MOOCs in the mainstream media are general and mostly focused on the failed "revolution in education" [12], our survey showed that MOOC did bring new learning strategies, including learning online, global learning, learning with media, self-paced learning, etc., to the learners and made a change on the individual level.

Ossiannilsson et al. [43] did a system literature review in order to identify factors affecting the quality of MOOCs. They concluded that the present research study identifies learning design and learning environment as key factors affecting experience and quality [43]. This research highlights some elements that affect the design of the MOOC, including the relevance of content to the learners, the design of instruction and guidance, the length and complexity level of the reading materials, the forms of assignments, etc. This will be helpful in the designing of online courses in the future.

How to support learners participating in a MOOC is an important issue. With the massive amount of participants taking part in a MOOC, it is not possible to provide tailored individual support [44]. Our findings showed that learners need support both in technical skills and learning strategies. In cMOOCs, the common method was to encourage participants to create their own PLE (Personal Learning Environment) consisting of tools and peers to support their learning [44], but in xMOOCs, it is still a problem that needs to be explored. Interaction between teachers and students is another key issue in the more individually focused, didactic MOOCs. Although e-assessment and peer review have been introduced to support learning, communication with other learners and getting feedback from teachers and tutors remain vital challenges for the developers of MOOCs.

7.3. Conclusions

The aim of the course was to give the students' more information about sustainable energy and its production through the help of the newest research and technology innovations, and to give an understanding of energy production in the future as a multidimensional entity. The MOOC course was personally relevant for the students on the basis of this case study. It gave adolescents a new holistic approach to learning about sustainable energy on the basis of the newest research. The theme of the course was also thought to be relevant. In particular, energy production was considered as one of the most useful topics. If we want to increase the societal and vocational relevance of the topic [4], then they should be more visible in the planning and carrying out of a course.

The characteristics of the MOOC, such as being available anywhere and anytime, free access, and online learning, bring a great opportunity to supporting learning about sustainable energy on the basis of the newest research [9], especially at school level, around the world, and thus promoting Education for Sustainable Development (ESD). Next time it would be useful to think about whether or not an xMOOC-shaped course is the best option. An online course that consists of videos, articles and multiple choice questions does not seem to support the students' interaction and learning enough; the students requested this for future courses. The xMOOC shape would seem to be better for independent studying of the theme. In the future, the cMOOC-shaped online course, which supports communal learning, could be used and studied. This would make it possible to include useful reflections and discussions pointed out in this study.

Acknowledgments: We would like to thank Lauri Vihma and Sakari Tolppanen for helping us to design the research questionnaires for this study.

Author Contributions: Maija Aksela as a principal investigator led the design, implementation and writing of this paper. Xiaomeng Wu and Julia Halonen as the co-principal investigators participated also to the analysis of data and writing of this paper.

Conflicts of Interest: The authors declare no conflict of interest.

References

1. Unesco. A Report: Education for People and Planet. Available online: http://gem-report-2016.unesco.org/en/home/ (accessed on 4 October 2016).

2. Juntunen, M.K.; Aksela, M.K. Education for Sustainable Development in Chemistry—Challenges, Possibilities and Pedagogical Models in Finland and Elsewhere. Available online: http://pubs.rsc.org/en/content/articlepdf/2014/rp/c4rp00128a (accessed on 4 October 2016).

3. Kaikai, M.; Baker, E. Engineering for Sustainable Energy Education within Suburban, Urban and Developing Secondary Schools. *J. Educ. Sustain. Dev.* **2016**, *10*, 88–100. [CrossRef]

4. Chu, S.; Majumdar, A. Opportunities and challenges for a sustainable energy future. *Nature* **2012**, *488*, 294–303. [CrossRef] [PubMed]

5. Keramitsoglou, K.M. Exploring adolescents' knowledge, perceptions and attitudes towards Renewable Energy Sources: A colour choice approach. *Ren. Sustain. Ener. Rev.* **2016**, *59*, 1159–1169. [CrossRef]

6. Tolppanen, S.; Aksela, M. Important Social and Academic Interactions in Supporting Gifted Youth in Non-Formal Education. *LUMAT* **2013**, *1*, 279–298.

7. Vesterinen, V.-M.; Tolppanen, S.; Aksela, M. Toward Citizenship Science Education: What Students Do to Make The World a Better Place? Available online: http://dx.doi.org/10.1080/09500693.2015.1125035 (accessed on 4 October 2016).

8. Tolppanen, S.; Tirri, K. How an Enrichment Summer Program Is Meeting the Expectations of Gifted Science Students: A Case Study from Finland. *Int. J. Talent Dev. Creat.* **2014**, *2*, 103–115.

9. Zhan, Z.; Fong, P.S.W.; Mei, H.; Chang, X.H.; Liang, T.; Ma, Z.C. Sustainability Education in Massive Open Online Courses: A Content Analysis Approach. *Sustainability* **2015**, *7*, 2274–2300. [CrossRef]

10. McAuley, A.; Stewart, B.; Siemens, G.; Cormier, D. The MOOC Model for Digital Practice. Available online: http://www.elearnspace.org/Articles/MOOC_Final.pdf (accessed on 4 October 2016).

11. Liyanagunawardena, T.; Adams, A.; Williams, S. MOOCs: A systematic study of the published literature 2008–2012. *Int. Rev. Res. Open Dis. Learn.* **2013**, *14*, 202–227.

12. Kovanović, V.; Joksimović, S.; Gašević, D.; Siemens, G.; Hatala, M. What public media reveals about MOOCs: A systematic analysis of news reports. *Br. J. Educ. Techn.* **2015**, *46*, 510–527.

13. Koxvold, I. MOOCs: Opportunities for Their Use in Compulsory-age Education. Available online: https://www.gov.uk/government/publications/moocs-opportunities-for-their-use-in-compulsory-age-education (accessed on 4 October 2016).

14. Lane, L. Three kind of MOOCs. Available online: http://lisahistory.net/wordpress/2012/08/three-kinds-of-moocs/ (accessed on 26 August 2016).

15. Bali, M. MOOC Pedagogy: Gleaning Good Practice from Existing MOOCs. Available online: http://jolt.merlot.org/vol10no1/bali_0314.pdf (accessed on 4 October 2016).

16. OpenupEd. Definition Massive Open Online Courses (MOOCs). Available online: http://www.openuped.eu/images/docs/Definition_Massive_Open_Online_Courses.pdf (accessed on 4 October 2016).

17. Jansen, D.; Schuwer, R. Institutional MOOC Strategies in Europe. Available online: https://www.surfspace.nl/media/bijlagen/artikel-1763-22974efd1d43f52aa98e0ba04f14c9f3.pdf (accessed on 4 October 2016).

18. Bates, T. Why the fuss about MOOCs? Political, Social and Economic Drivers. Available online: http://www.tonybates.ca/?s=Why+the+fuss+about+MOOCs (accessed on 4 October 2016).

19. Khalil, M.; Ebner, M. A STEM MOOC for school children—What does learning analytics tell us? In *2015 International Conference on Interactive Collaborative Learning (ICL)*; IEEE (The Institute of Electrical and Electronics Engineers): New York, NY, USA; pp. 1217–1221.

20. Schmid, L.; Manturuk, K.; Simpkins, I.; Goldwasser, M.; Whitfield, K.E. Fulfilling the promise: Do MOOCs reach the educationally underserved? *Educ. Media Int.* **2015**, *52*, 116–128. [CrossRef]

21. Chen, J.C.C. Opportunities and challenges of MOOCs: perspectives from Asia. Available online: http://library.ifla.org/157/7/098-chen-es.pdf (accessed on 4 October 2016).
22. Kurhila, J.; Vihavainen, A. A Purposeful MOOC to Alleviate Insufficient CS Education in Finnish Schools. *ACM Trans. Comp. Educ.* **2015**, *15*. [CrossRef]
23. Parr, C. MOOC completion rates "below 7%". Available online: https://www.timeshighereducation.co.uk/news/mooc-completion-rates-below-7/2003710.article (accessed on 4 October 2016).
24. Terras, M.M.; Ramsay, J. Massive open online courses (MOOCs): Insights and challenges from a psychological perspective. *Br. J. Educ. Tech.* **2015**, *46*, 472–487. [CrossRef]
25. Stuckey, M.; Hofstein, A.; Mamlok-Naaman, R.; Eilks, I. The meaning of 'relevance' in science education and its implications for the science curriculum. *Stud. Sci. Educ.* **2013**, *49*, 1–34. [CrossRef]
26. DeBoer, G.E. Scientific literacy: Another look at its historical and contemporary meanings and its relationship to science education reform. *J. Res. Sci. Teach.* **2000**, *37*, 582–601. [CrossRef]
27. Childs, P.E. Relevance, relevance, relevance. *Physical Sciences Magazine*, May 2006; 14.
28. Ramsden, J.M. Mission impossible? Can anything be done about attitudes to science? *Int. J. Sci. Educ.* **1998**, *20*, 125–137. [CrossRef]
29. De Haan, G. The BLK '21' programme in Germany: A 'Gestaltungskompetenz'—based model for education for sustainable development. *Env. Educ. Res.* **2006**, *12*, 19–32. [CrossRef]
30. Hofstein, A.; Kesner, M. Industrial chemistry and school chemistry: Making chemistry studies more relevant. *Int. J. Sci. Educ.* **2006**, *28*, 1017–1039. [CrossRef]
31. Gilbert, J.K. On the nature of 'context' in chemical education. *Int. J. Sci. Educ.* **2006**, *28*, 957–976. [CrossRef]
32. King, D. New perspectives on context-based chemistry education: Using a dialectical sociocultural approach to view teaching and learning. *Stud. Sci. Educ.* **2012**, *48*, 51–87. [CrossRef]
33. Lyons, T. Different countries, same science classes: Students' experiences of school science in their own words. *Int. J. Sci. Educ.* **2006**, *28*, 591–613. [CrossRef]
34. Mandler, D.; Mamlok-Naaman, R.; Blonder, R.; Yayon, M.; Hofstein, A. Highschool chemistry teaching through environmentally oriented curricula. *Chem. Educ. Res. Pract.* **2012**, *13*, 80–92. [CrossRef]
35. Keller, J.M. Motivational design of instruction. In *Instructional Design Theories: An Overview of Their Current Status*; Reigeluth, C.M., Ed.; Lawrence Erlbaum Associates: Hillsdale, NJ, USA, 1983; pp. 386–434.
36. Simon, S.; Amos, R. Decision making and use of evidence in a socio-scientific problem on air quality. In *Socio-scientific issues in The Classroom: Teaching, Learning and Research*; Sadler, T.D., Ed.; Springer: Dordrecht, The Netherlands, 2011; pp. 167–192.
37. Sjøberg, S.; Schreiner, C. *The ROSE Project: An Overview And Key Findings*; University of Oslo: Oslo, Norway, 2010.
38. Van Aalsvoort, J. Activity theory as a tool to address the problem of chemistry's lack of relevance in secondary school chemistry education. *Int. J. Sci. Educ.* **2004**, *26*, 1635–1651. [CrossRef]
39. Newton, D.P. Relevance and science education. *Educ. Phil. Theory* **1988**, *20*, 7–12. [CrossRef]
40. Eisenhardt, K.M. Building theories from case study research. *Acad. Manag. Rev.* **1989**, *14*, 532–550.
41. Huberman, A.M.; Miles, M.B. Data management and analysis methods. In *Handbook of Qualitative Research*; Denzin, N.K., Lincoln, Y.S., Eds.; Sage: Thousand Oaks, CA, USA, 1994; pp. 428–444.
42. Creelman, A.; Ehlers, U.; Ossiannilsson, E. Perspectives on MOOC Quality—An Account of the EFQUEL MOOC Quality Project. Available online: http://papers.efquel.org/index.php/innoqual/article/view/163 (accessed on 4 October 2016).
43. Ossiannilsson, E.; Altinay, F.; Altinay, Z. Analysis of MOOCs practices from the perspective of learner experiences and quality culture. *Educ. Media Int.* **2015**, *52*, 272–283. [CrossRef]
44. Gráinne, C. Designing effective MOOCs. *Educ. Media Int.* **2015**, *52*, 239–252.

MDPI AG

St. Alban-Anlage 66

4052 Basel, Switzerland

Tel. +41 61 683 77 34

Fax +41 61 302 89 18

http://www.mdpi.com

Education Sciences Editorial Office

E-mail: education@mdpi.com

http://www.mdpi.com/journal/education